THE
NATURAL
HISTORY
OF THE
USSR

THE NATURAL HISTORY OF THE USSR

Algirdas Knystautas

FOREWORD
Vladimir Flint

McGraw-Hill Book Company
New York St Louis San Francisco
Toronto Hamburg Mexico

Dedicated to Professor V E Flint and Dr A A Ivashchenko who have done so much for nature conservation.

This book was designed and produced by Swallow Editions Limited, Swallow House, 11–21 Northdown Street, London N1 9BN

First published in England in 1987 by Century Hutchinson Limited, First US publication in 1987 by McGraw-Hill Book Company.

1 2 3 4 5 6 7 8 9   8 7

ISBN 0-07-035409-X

Library of Congress Cataloguing-in-Publication Data:

Knystautas, A. (Algirdas), 1956–
    The natural history of the USSR
    1.   Natural history — Soviet Union.   I. Title
QH161.K55 1987   508.47   86–27731
ISBN 0–07–035409–X

Editor: Jonathan Elphick
Consultant Editor: Michael Wilson
Translation: John S Scott
Cartographer: M L Design
Index: Helen Baz

Filmset in 'Monophoto' Palatino by Keyspools Limited, Mono Lodge, Bridge Street, Golborne, Warrington WA3 3QA
Colour origination in Hong Kong by Imago Publishing
Printed and bound in Italy by Amilcare Pizzi s.p.a., Milan

HALF TITLE *Young Slow Worms* (Anguis fragilis) *photographed in August in the Lithuanian Soviet Socialist Republic.*

TITLE PAGE *Mixed forest near Kostroma, north-east of Moscow.* (L. Veisman)

AUTHOR'S ACKNOWLEDGMENTS

Many people helped in the preparation of this book. First, I would like to thank my good friend in England, Elizabeth Tindle, whose help, understanding, patience and friendship can hardly be overestimated. I also owe special thanks to the Lithuanian Society of Photographic Art and its Chairman A Sutkus and to Jeffery Boswall and Michael Wilson in England.

For their provision of photographs, information, advice, criticism and other valuable assistance, I sincerely thank the following: Yu Artyukhin, S Balandin, R. R. Budrys, V Hippenreiter, F Jüssi, A Kärvet, V Korkishko, A Krechmar, V and N Kuchin, A Liutkus, V Morozov, E Nazarov, B Nechaev, I Olontsev, V Orlov, R Papikian, U Pilinkus, P Romanov, Yu Shibnev, M Shteinbakh, A Sorokin, Z Valius, Yu Vaskovsky, and L Veisman.

I would also like to record my everlasting gratitude to my close friends and colleagues, including my photographic team, with all of whom I share my greatest love, that of nature. With them I have made many long and difficult — but also exciting and worthwhile — field trips to many different areas of the USSR. They are: Arunas Baltenas, Oleg Belyalov, Aurimas Blazys, Kestutis Kuchys and Henrikas Sakalauskas.

Last, but by no means least, I extend my sincere thanks to the editorial staff, particularly the Editor, Jonathan Elphick, and Mary Anne Sanders, who have worked so hard to make this the book I hoped it would be.

ALGIRDAS KNYSTAUTAS
Vilnius, USSR

Contents

Foreword

For forty years now I have been travelling around the Soviet Union and I have never ceased to wonder at the extraordinary diversity, contrasts and richness of her wildlife. It really is a huge country, and this is probably what first strikes anyone who encounters its vast expanse. No doubt it has a similar effect on the millions of migrating birds that pour into Soviet territory in several great streams in spring and disperse to their traditional nesting grounds. In fact, the distance between the Soviet Union's western borders and the shores of the Bering Sea washing it to the east is more than 7,000 miles (11,250 km), while the total land area exceeds $8\frac{1}{2}$ million sq miles (22 million sq km). When the inhabitants of Moscow and Leningrad are about to eat breakfast, their fellow countrymen on the Chukotka Peninsula are already getting ready for bed. When in the south they are beginning to harvest the wheat, in the north the ground is still snow-covered and there are blizzards blowing. Even in a high-speed jet airliner flying at more than 560 mph (900 km/hr), the journey from Moscow to Kamchatka takes no less than twelve hours. Sixty to seventy years ago the same journey would have taken at least six months.

Take a look at the map. Along the country's southern frontier stretch imposing mountain ranges: the majestic Caucasus, with its distinct horizontal belts, first of forest, then of alpine meadows, and finally glaciers; the sun-scorched and almost treeless Kopet-Dag; the massive and barely accessible Pamir Mountains with their snowy peaks, the highest in the Soviet Union; the lofty Tien Shan with their beautiful coniferous forests and welcoming green high-mountain pastures, giving way to sheer rocky crags and deep gorges; and the Altai and Sayan ranges, covered with dense dark conifer taiga and topped with bare land, resembling tundra. To the north of the Central Asian mountains lie vast deserts, the Kara-Kum, the Kyzyl-Kum, the Muyun-Kum and others, where sand dunes alternate with areas of *takyr*, isolated patches of clay desert where the vegetation is sparse and poor and the people with their herds of sheep and camels cling to remote wells fifty or more miles apart.

If we imagine we are travelling still further north through the wide belt of semi-desert, we come to the steppe. Man has long felt at home here and consequently much of the steppe is cultivated. Feather grass and other coarse wild grasses have been replaced by wheat, barley

and millet, and vast areas of arable land now stretch from one horizon to the other. But there are places where the original steppe has so far been preserved, untouched by tractor, where countless larks pour out a never-ending stream of song, where the watchful Great Bustard and the Demoiselle Crane still lay their eggs and raise their chicks, and where, above the ancient Scythian burial mounds, the fierce Steppe Eagles spy out their prey.

In early spring, the steppe explodes into a vivid and spreading patchwork of colour: the poppies and tulips are in flower, and on lower ground, the irises. Colonies of marmots, managing to look both sluggish and self-important at the same time, sit by their burrows, whistling to one another and keeping vigilant eyes on a passing eagle, their chief enemy.

The last remaining parts of the virgin lands are now reserves from which the wild animals of the steppe have begun to spread into cultivated land. Great Bustards and Demoiselle Cranes are already nesting in fair numbers on the rolling wheatfields. In depressions on the northern edge of the steppe the first groups of trees appear, growing shyly and uncertainly at first and then attaining full vigour, until the woodland encroaches on the steppe and the grassland and groves of aspen and birch begin to mingle, forming a wonderful mosaic. This is the forest steppe zone. Animal life here is just as mixed as the plant life: the typically woodland species, such as Roe Deer, Black Grouse and woodpeckers, live in close proximity to the true steppe-dwellers, like the souslika, jerboas and larks.

If we continue our imaginary journey northwards, we reach the forest. In the European part of the Soviet Union we come first to the broad-leaved forest zone, which gives way gradually to dark conifer taiga, but in the Asian part of the country taiga takes over abruptly from the broad-leaved forest, and predominates in the unexplored expanses of Siberia, flooding the mountain ridges and river valleys with an unending sea of conifers: larch, Siberian Stone Pine, fir and spruce.

To the uninitiated, it would seem that this was a veritable paradise for animals — after all, most places here are untrodden by man. However, this would be a false impression: animal life in the taiga is on the whole poor, and an encounter with an Elk, a Brown Bear or a Capercaillie would be a real stroke of luck. Birdsong too is rare here. The taiga is a largely silent world, and usually the only sound is that of the Chipmunks calling to one another in the ancient debris of a storm-wrecked forest or the melancholy cry of the Curlew ringing out over the impassable mossy bogs. The only exception is the Far-

LEFT *The Soviet Union is the world's largest country, embracing 12 time zones; as the autumn sun sets on the River Lena in Siberia, it is still morning on the Baltic Coast.*

Eastern taiga, where migrants from the south mingle with the inhabitants of the northern taiga. Animal and plant life here is strikingly rich and varied, but this is true only along the river valleys.

Let us now press on further north. Near the Arctic Circle, the taiga thins out. Increasingly, the mossy bog encroaches on the forest, confining it to the river valleys. And here already are the last of the trees, small and misshapen, constantly fighting the wind and frost from the Arctic Ocean. These solitary trees are a sad sight, like a thin line of sentries that the taiga, in its hasty retreat, has forgotten to relieve. Beyond them, open marshy expanses take over, with countless lakes and channels where the permafrost lies under a thin layer of moss and sedges. This is the realm of the tundra, where life is harsh. But just as we would be mistaken to assume that the hot deserts of Central Asia are without life, so we would be wrong to imagine the tundra as a dead, monotonous world. On the contrary, in spring, life simply bursts forth. You are unlikely anywhere on your travels to see so many birds as you do in the tundra. Innumerable waders, gulls, ducks, divers, geese and skuas appear like countless invading armies as the snow thaws, bringing life to the lake shores, marshy lowlands and gently sloping lichen-covered hills, and filling the air with their various calls, now melancholy, now sweetly exultant. In July, the dry hills and coastal cliffs are carpeted with a surprising variety of beautiful minia-ture flowers. The sun never sets and everywhere life flourishes, unafraid of man. But the tundra's short summer soon passes and the flowers fade, the birds fly away and their voices are heard no more. The tundra is deserted and then it would be no exaggeration to call it the bleakest, most lifeless and depressing place in the whole country.

But although the tundra reaches the shores of the Arctic Ocean, the land does not end there. Among the ice-floes, beyond the barrier of pack ice, lie the countless islands of Novaya Zemlya, Wrangel Island, the Novosibirsk Islands and Severnaya Zemlya. Here life is even harsher than on the mainland tundra. Plant growth is poor and consists mainly of lichens, dryads and low-spreading willows. Huge areas are covered with gravel where nothing grows. These places have aptly been called the polar wastes.

Only a few animal and bird species can live in the Arctic tundra and on the surrounding ice floes. Most of them are largely marine, like the polar bear, walruses and some seals. Huge colonies of guillemots and gulls breed on the steep cliffs. During the short summer a few species of waders fly there, as do ducks, skuas and the Lapland Bunting, which is found throughout the tundra. Few land mammals are likely

to be encountered, although there may be large numbers of lemmings and, in places, reindeer. The small number of species should come as no surprise — after all, this is the very frontier of life.

I have had the good fortune to see so much beauty in my travels throughout the Soviet Union. I find both joy and quiet melancholy in retracing the past years in my mind, recalling its stored treasures — my encounters with animals. I hope these few memories, chosen at random from many others, will give you an idea of some of the exciting sights and sounds that await the enquiring traveller.

… Northern Kazakhstan, the dry steppe, the sun hot and blindingly bright overhead. My colleague and I had pitched our tents on the shore of the brackish Lake Zharkul. In the daytime it was impossible to go anywhere without risking heatstroke. Besides, it would have been pointless, since almost all the animals were in hiding and remained completely silent. The only sound came from the thick overgrown reedbed at the edge of the lake, where the Great Reed Warblers kept up their ceaseless coarse and vapid chatter and the Bitterns boomed. We lay all day sheltering our heads in the shade of a blanket stretched between four poles and drinking glass after glass of tea.

At last, the sun gradually began to set. Then, all of a sudden, it started to get cold and we had to put on our clothes hastily over our naked bodies. It was time to set the traps for the small rodents that we were studying. With the traps in our rucksacks, we each set out in a different direction. I strode off along the slope of the valley in which the lake lies. To my left lay the open flat plain of the steppe, to my right a wall of reeds which thinned out in places, revealing a small expanse of water edged with a stretch of liquid mud in which I could see the tracks of Wolves which had visited the waterhole, and of Wild Boar which had been feeding on the young reed shoots. Having set the traps, I sat down for a short rest by one of these pools. The lake was perfectly still, its mirror-like surface undisturbed by wind. From beyond the barrier of reeds came the cackling of an invisible family of geese. Coots called in the thickets. Now and then a small flock of Teal flew over, circled round the lake and landed with a distinct slap on the water. An ancient primordial silence fell over the scene.

Then, suddenly, I was startled by a rustling and rattling from the dry reed stalks and the splashing of water: something was coming through the thicket towards the pool. Apart from me, there were no people there. I realized it must be an animal, and a big one at that. Another minute, and with a crash and a louder squelching noise, it emerged from the dense barrier of reeds — a huge male Wild Boar!

He stopped within ten paces of me, pricked up his large shaggy ears and noisily sniffed the air. I could even hear the sound of water dripping from his hide. The last rays of the sun caught his yellow tusks. I could see every hair on his body, and watched his small eyes blink as he seemed to gaze pensively at the glow of the sunset over the lake. Then, far more calmly than he had arrived, he disappeared behind the screen of reeds bordering the pool. And so he departed, unaware that for a minute he had been standing so close to his most serious enemy, man.

Another year, another place.... The tundra of the lower reaches of the River Indigirka, in the far north of East Siberia. The marshy lowlands were dotted with such a dense lacework pattern of lakes that it was impossible to tell which there was most of, water or dry land. The snow had only recently disappeared. The lakes were still deeply frozen, with ice-free water only at their edges. The tender young shoots of sedge and cotton sedge had still not appeared through the dried leaves of last year's grass. This made the tundra appear to be all of one colour, a sort of brownish yellow, lighter where there were lakes, and darker on the hummocks, on whose northern sides the wind-blown snow of winter still remained.

Despite the reluctant start to the brief Arctic summer, there were birds everywhere. On every hillock there was a group of brightly-coloured Ruffs, while on every lake swam Black-throated Divers, handsome in their breeding plumage, and clamorous Long-tailed Ducks. Meanwhile, the pirates of the tundra – the skuas – dashed about in twos and threes, while flocks of Red-necked or Grey Phalaropes flew busily from pool to pool. From all around could be heard the strange droning song of the Pectoral Sandpiper, the silvery tinkling song of Temminck's Stint and the plaintive whistling calls of the Lapland Bunting.

Extracting my feet with some difficulty from the deep carpet of wet moss, and picking my way between the small shallow lakes, I slowly approached a larger lake, gleaming white in the distance, which was still completely covered in ice, while all around the low-lying land was flooded with water from thawed snow and overgrown with yellow sedge. With my binoculars, I could make out some small white spots against the yellow background.

As I drew closer to the lake, I could see that those white spots were birds sitting on their nests. I realized they were probably gulls, but what species? Not until I was less than three hundred feet away did they start to fly off and circle around uneasily. Some of them flew towards me, uttering gentle, sad cries. Grey wings, pinkish breasts, velvety black rings around their necks – they must be the rare and elusive

Ross's Gulls! The birds swooped down on me, trying to chase me away from their nests, and I could clearly see their bright red feet and slender black bills. What wonderfully graceful and elegant birds they were!

Soon I was standing over the first nest, a shallow pit, thickly lined with stalks of sedge, and containing three olive-green eggs. Although it is now already eighty years since the Russian ornithologist, S. A. Buturlin, produced the first scientific report on the eggs and nests of this beautiful bird, my discovery could not but be exciting: few people have seen a living Ross's Gull, let alone the bonus of a nest with a clutch of eggs.

My next memory takes us from the extreme north of the Soviet Union to the extreme south.... Dawn, along the southern edge of the Kyzyl-Kum Desert, in the Uzbek SSR. Here, the silent ridges of sand resembled a yellowish sea that had suddenly frozen over. The strange, sparse shapes of the saxaul and calligonum bushes loomed out of the twilight, and between them areas of the purest fine sand. The sun had only just risen, and the bushes still retained the cool of the night, but the pre-dawn dew still sparkled on the surface of the sand. Faint tracks remained as the sole evidence of the night-time inhabitants of the desert – large black beetles, geckos and jerboas. In about an hour and a half, the sun would rise, the sand would dry out, and a slight breeze would start to blow, smoothing over the tracks and wiping out all traces of the hidden life of the desert. Then it would appear as though there was nothing all around except shifting sand, leafless grey bushes, and the relentless sun blazing overhead. But, for now, the morning chill still lay over the desert and I wandered happily from dune to dune, examining the confused series of tracks meandering across the sand.

The sun rose higher and higher, and the dark blue early morning sky gradually grew paler. I started to notice the first signs of the pervasive heat: objects began to lose their clear outlines, blurred by the rising streams of warmed air. There was not a living thing to be seen and it certainly was time to return to camp and the welcome shade and water.

Suddenly, I spotted some kind of movement far in the distance. I could make out neither an object nor the form of an animal but only an indefinable movement. In a moment I raised my binoculars excitedly to my eyes. And then, as if by magic, the blurred movement suddenly assumed a definite shape: it was a small herd of Goitred Gazelles, moving diagonally across my path and approaching nearer. They were running fairly quickly without stopping to graze as they often do, and after a few minutes they were already clearly visible to the naked eye.

They were handsome creatures, sandy brown in colour with darker flanks, white legs, contrasting black stripes on the muzzle and a black tail silhouetted clearly against the blindingly reflective white background. The rare gazelles looked unusually graceful, delicately proportioned and light-footed. They appeared healthy and well fed and their coats gleamed and shone in the sun as though wet. Their whole appearance suggested a special kind of animal strength. All seven gazelles were males, adorned with exceptionally elegant and exquisitely formed black lyre-shaped horns.

They passed me in single file, a mere 150 yards away, and were evidently on their way back from their watering hole, a small salt lake a few miles from our camp. They walked past calmly and steadily, not expecting to come across a human being, but at the same time ready for flight at any moment – life has taught them to be constantly on their guard. I watched the gazelles as they filed past, with a particular delight and excitement because they are among the wildest of all our animals and meeting them like that, close to, was a real stroke of luck. I was sad too as I watched them disappear because, who knows, would I ever have such an encounter again?

My final memory is of a very different world again.… The mountainous dark conifer taiga of Sikhote-Alin. The range of low mountains was overgrown with dense, gloomy, forbidding forests of fir and spruce. The ground was covered with green moss and a solid carpet of bracken, and there were many trunks and branches brought down by winter winds. Some were old and rotten, while others had fallen more recently. Occasionally, the high-pitched calls of a tit rang out, and from time to time the Mugimaki Flycatcher poured out its beautiful trilling song. Most of the time, however, the forest was uncannily silent, apart from the constant, even humming of millions of mosquitoes.

Our zoological team – the leader, two assistants and myself – were walking along one of the taiga's tracks. The tents, sleeping bags, food and other essential equipment for the expedition were loaded on our two horses. It was a long way to the abandoned geological settlement that was our destination – more than sixty miles. And the road was not easy, being barely visible in the dim light. The horses slipped frequently on the mossy debris and stumbled over tree roots, while their burden of packs scraped against the tree trunks and branches. Our way ahead was constantly blocked by fallen tree trunks, and we had to lead the horses round these obstacles. It was hot and intensely humid, making it difficult to breathe. Ignoring our insect repellent,

clouds of mosquitoes hovered round our faces, combining with our streaming sweat to produce a constant, unbearable itching. To make matters worse, there were myriads of gnats, which we grew tired of picking and brushing off our clothes every few minutes.

We sweated our way up to the top of the next ridge, then trudged down into the valley, across an icy cold, clear stream tumbling over a stony bed. Then came the long, slow haul up the mountain. Up, down, across, then again up, down, across … and so on, endlessly. At first we tried to find the shallowest water for each crossing, and then we abandoned all our precautions and walked straight into the stream, not looking where we put our feet and getting soaked nearly up to the waist. The monotony of the journey, the sheer fatigue and the thought of repeating the same thing all day long, and the same again from morning to evening the day after gave rise to feelings of indifference and apathy, until we no longer took any notice of the hordes of mosquitoes or the gnats, the sweat pouring down our faces or the sudden shock of our periodic plunges into the icy water. We simply carried on walking as though in a dream.

Suddenly, we were rudely awakened. From a grove of young spruce trees some fifty paces away to the left of us, we heard a sudden hoarse cough, a loud and terrifying growl, a crashing of branches, and then we saw a bear standing on all fours in a clearing in the trees. He was simply enormous, a figure of great power, with a broad chest, long hair bristling on his neck, a flat head, small eyes and round laid-back ears. He went on barking out short hoarse cries, clearly showing the white fangs gleaming deep inside his mouth, and scattering flecks of foam from his lips. Our entire party, humans and horses alike, stood rooted to the spot, watching the mighty animal. The bear was clearly in a fury and, although I had a heavy carbine in my hands, I really did not want him to go for us. After all, he was very large – and very close to us.

As a rule, wild bears, even large ones, do not attack humans when they meet them, preferring to leave the scene quietly, if possible without being seen. Usually, only a mother bear with cubs or an individual frightened while eating its prey may break this rule. What would happen now?

The answer came sooner than we had expected. Between us and the bear we noticed the leaning trunk of an old fir which remained standing after a storm only because it was propped up by its neighbours. Then, just as it seemed that the bear was about to attack us, out of the same fir tree shot three quite small and very agile bear cubs.

So the huge bear was a female — from her size I had judged her to be a male.

Finding themselves suddenly on the ground, the cubs rushed to their mother, who at once lost her aggressive mood and then, just as suddenly, turned and ran into a thicket of young spruce trees, from which she reappeared a minute later. The last we saw of her was her rounded rump, covered in long fur that shook with every step, and we just caught a glimpse of the three little rumps belonging to the cubs. The spruce branches swayed a little and then everything was still. For a long time we remained motionless and silent, for fear of breaking the spell of the scene we had just witnessed.

But why have I been telling you about all this that happened so many years ago? I should like the readers, by learning about the natural history of our country and looking at the beautiful photographs taken by my young friends, besides acquiring knowledge, to experience something of the real spirit of those places which they will reach mentally with the help of this splendid book. A knowledge of nature, delight in its perfection and its miracles — these can excite everyone, regardless of their country. Out of this is born the spiritual bond between people and nations.

PROFESSOR V. E. FLINT
Vice-President, All-Union Ornithological Society;
Director, Department of Animal Protection of the
All-Union Scientific Institute for Nature Reserves
and Nature Conservation

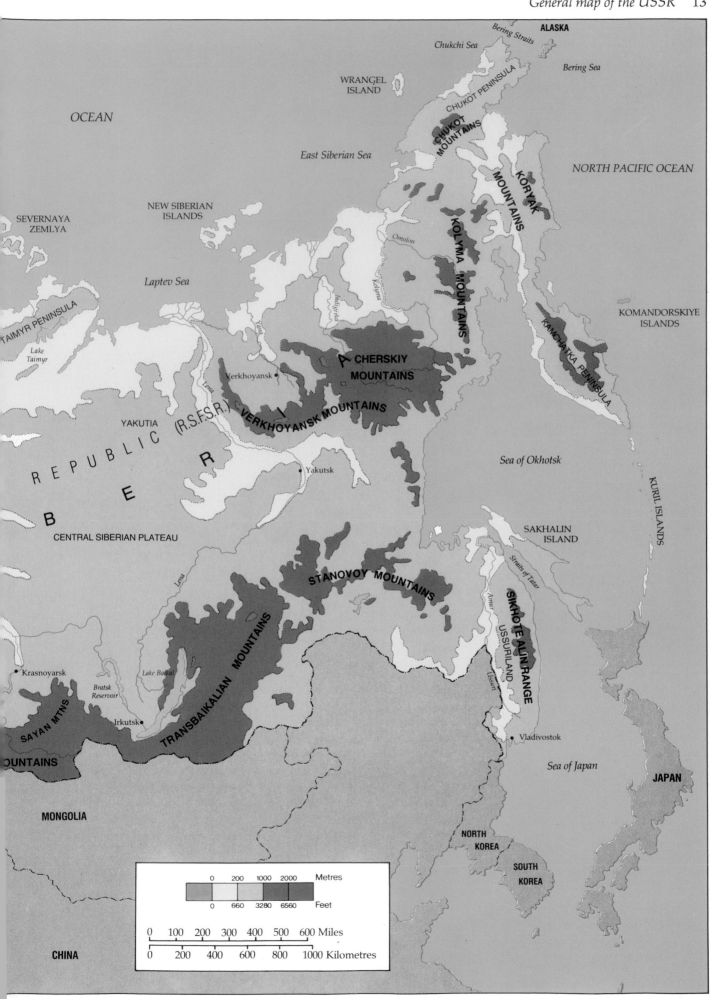

OCEAN

ALASKA

Chukchi Sea

Bering Straits

Bering Sea

WRANGEL
ISLAND

CHUKOT PENINSULA

East Siberian Sea

CHUKOT
MOUNTAINS

NORTH PACIFIC OCEAN

NEW SIBERIAN
ISLANDS

Omolon

KORYAK
MOUNTAINS

SEVERNAYA
ZEMLYA

Laptev Sea

KOLYMA MOUNTAINS

Kolyma

KOMANDORSKIYE
ISLANDS

TAIMYR PENINSULA

Indigirka

Yana

KAMCHATKA PENINSULA

*Lake
Taimyr*

CHERSKIY
MOUNTAINS

Verkhoyansk •

Lena

VERKHOYANSK MOUNTAINS

YAKUTIA

(R.S.F.S.R.)

Sea of Okhotsk

R E P U B L I C

S I B E R I A

Yakutsk •

B E R

KURIL ISLANDS

SAKHALIN
ISLAND

CENTRAL SIBERIAN PLATEAU

Straits of Tatar

STANOVOY MOUNTAINS

Lena

Amur

SIKHOTE ALIN RANGE

USSURILAND

Krasnoyarsk •

*Bratsk
Reservoir*

Lake Baikal

TRANSBAIKALIAN MOUNTAINS

Ussuri

SAYAN MTNS.

Irkutsk •

Vladivostok •

MOUNTAINS

Sea of Japan

JAPAN

MONGOLIA

NORTH
KOREA

SOUTH
KOREA

| | 0 | 200 | 1000 | 2000 | Metres |
| 0 | 660 | 3280 | 6560 | | Feet |

| 0 | 100 | 200 | 300 | 400 | 500 | 600 Miles |
| 0 | 200 | 400 | 600 | 800 | 1000 Kilometres |

CHINA

1 THE SHAPING OF A SUBCONTINENT

The evolution of life

During the immense span of the Pre-Cambrian era, life slowly emerged and began to colonize different environments. The original primitive, unicellular organisms probably first appeared in hot, chemically active pools and lakes near geysers, or in the warmer shallow continental shelf seas. Algae, not unlike many modern lime-secreting forms, developed as long as 3,800 million years ago. By about 700 million years ago, a dramatic proliferation of life forms had taken place, and their remains were preserved as the 'Ediacaran assemblage' of fossils (named after the Ediacara Hills in Australia, where the first examples were found). Various examples of this ancient fauna were identified later in the USSR, as well as in south-west Africa and the British Isles. They include algae, jellyfish, worms, primitive arthropods (the group to which insects, crabs and spiders belong) and various 'trace fossils' such as the tracks and burrows of animals.

During the Lower Palaeozoic Era (consisting of the Cambrian, Ordovician and Silurian periods), the areas of Russia which were beneath the sea – such as the Siberian Platform – were inhabited by a great variety of organisms, the ancestors of which are difficult to trace in the late Pre-Cambrian. These animals include the trilobites (segmented arthropods), the brachiopods (a group of shellfish very different from the molluscs in their biology, but rather like them in appearance), the graptolites (strange, delicate branched organisms rather like tiny fern fronds), the corals, and the molluscs. Towards the end of the Lower Palaeozoic, those areas of the USSR which were above sea level became clothed in a mantle of small mossy plants, rather like a miniature forest. Green plants began to flourish in fresh water, and the first primitive fishes swam in the lakes and rivers.

During the Upper Palaeozoic era (consisting of the Devonian, Carboniferous and Permian periods), there was a rapid evolution of life on the land areas of the USSR. Plants had by now acquired rigid stems and were able to stand up for themselves on land. By the Carboniferous period, they had evolved sufficiently to form the great tropical forests that eventually formed the USSR's great reserves of coal, in which their fossils are still found. Fishes also developed further, and in the Upper Devonian rocks of the USSR the first winged insect was discovered. Late in

LEFT *A geyser and associated hot sulphurous springs on Kunashir Island in the North Pacific Ocean; life probably started in similar environments.*

the Permian period, the insect fauna evolved further; fossils of this age of beetles and bugs have been found in various parts of the USSR.

During the late Upper Palaeozoic, amphibians began to flounder out of the swamps and gulp the air, and the mammal-like reptiles, or therapsids, are well represented in the fossil record of the USSR. At the end of the Permian period, many life forms vanished from the USSR, including the trilobites, rugose corals, many brachiopods and molluscs. The flora was little affected by this period of extinction, but over 70 per cent of the amphibians and over 90 per cent of the reptiles disappeared.

The USSR contains a wealth of fossils from the Mesozoic era (consisting of the Triassic, Jurassic and Cretaceous periods), found in shallow marine deposits. These include creatures such as bivalve molluscs, ammonites (also shelled molluscs, and distant relatives of the octopuses) and scleractinian corals. In these same marine waters lived various reptiles, including ichthyosaurs, plesiosaurs, crocodiles and turtles, while the great group of dinosaurs, ranging from chicken-sized animals to huge creatures such as the sauropods, became the ruling reptiles on land. Three main complexes of Mesozoic reptiles have been found in the USSR as fossils. Bony fishes became common in the seas and freshwaters.

During the Jurassic and Cretaceous periods, the reptiles evolved to fill more and more of the niches available to animals, and great flying reptiles, or pterosaurs, ruled the air. On land, the dinosaurs held their ground until the end of the Cretaceous period, when they all died out comparatively suddenly. Scientists have advanced a variety of theories to explain their extinction, ranging from a catastrophic change in the climate resulting from a huge meteor hitting the earth to a more gradual but equally disastrous climatic deterioration. None of the theories has yet established clearly why such a great group of animals disappeared so completely.

By the beginning of the Cainozoic era, during the early Tertiary period, the mammals had replaced the dinosaurs as the ruling land animals, and included monotremes (egg-laying mammals like the echidna), marsupials (pouched mammals like kangaroos) and primitive placentals (with a placenta for the nourishment of the young in the uterus, like foxes, deer and the rest of the USSR's present-day mammal fauna). By the end of the early Tertiary, the placentals were widespread. One characteristic placental of the period was *Indricotherium* (*Baluchitherium*). This gigantic hornless rhinoceros, whose fossils have been found in the USSR from Kazakhstan to Central Asia, was the largest land mammal that ever lived, standing about 18 ft (5.5 m) at the shoulders and weighing some 16 tons. It is one of a varied group of mammals that settled in the damp forests and bogs as well as in dry forest-steppes.

By the mid-Tertiary period, placentals were dominant on dry land. During the Miocene epoch, beginning about 26 million years ago, the climate became drier, many of the forest-dwellers died out, and hoofed mammals adapted themselves to live on the great expanses of steppe. Rhinoceroses were widespread, as were mastodons, giraffes, deer, pig-like mammals, various species of monkeys and numerous predators, including dog-like species. Tropical and subtropical vegetation gradually disappeared, and temperate zone plants took their place, similar to those that now grow beyond the Caucasus and in Japan and China. In the northern part of the USSR, tundra vegetation appeared, and almost all of Siberia was covered by dark coniferous taiga forest.

In the middle of the Pliocene epoch, about 4 million years ago, with the arrival of a glacial period, these mammals began to die out, unable to survive the grim advance of the ice sheets. Also during the mid-Pliocene, the first ancestors of human beings appeared.

The Quaternary period, beginning about 2 million years ago, is the shortest in the geological time scale, but in the northern hemisphere the most severe glaciations occurred at this time. During the Quaternary, our existing marine fauna and flora appeared. The vast steppes of the Pliocene were replaced by more varied landscapes resembling modern ones, and various groups of animals, including the

This woolly mammoth tusk was exposed by a river in the tundra of the Taimyr Peninsula; the giant elephant that owned it flourished during the last Ice Ages.

dwarf horse *Hipparion*, became extinct. Animals better able to adapt to the more complex conditions appeared, such as the Giant Elk, elephants, camels, rhinoceroses, wild goats, bears and wolves.

During the mid-Pleistocene, about a million years ago, a great series of glaciations began (see also pages 19, 32). Vast masses of ice, as much as $1\frac{1}{4}$ miles (2 km) high, slid down from the Scandinavian and Finnish mountains into the valleys, covering much of the land. The drastic change in climate had a profound effect on the animal and plant communities. To the south of the glaciers, the tundra was inhabited by mammals able to tolerate the cold, such as woolly mammoths, fleecy rhinoceroses, Musk Oxen, Reindeer, Red Deer, foxes and others. Such creatures evolved several methods of adapting to the cold – the evolution of a thick coat of hair, the accumulation of stores of fat, and a growth in size. Mammals that were not adapted to the bitter cold migrated south or died out.

The ethnic composition of the USSR

The Soviet Union is a multinational state, with some 130 different nationalities and ethnic groups living within its borders. Most of the population is of European stock – represented by northern, southern and transitional types. The indigenous peoples of eastern Siberia and the Far East belong to the northern branch of the Mongolian group. Among the peoples of Central Asia and Kazakhstan are groups of mixed Mongolian and European origin. Signs of European descent become rarer as one travels eastwards.

The most numerous of the ethnic groups in the USSR are the Russians, who form 52.12 per cent of the population. Their closest relatives are the natives of the Ukraine and Belorussia, although Ukrainians and Belorussians also live elsewhere. The Baltic coast is inhabited by Lithuanians and Latvians, who belong to an ancient Baltic-language group, and by Estonians, who are Finno-Ugrians, like the Finns and Lapps. Other Finno–Ugrians are found in the Volga region, and these include Karelians, Veps, Saams, Komis, Maritsis, Udmurtis and others. To the south of the Volga region and in the south Urals live the Turki-speaking Chuvash, Bashkirs and Tartars, and to the south-west of the Volga, the Kalmyks, who speak a Mongolian language. A Romance language is spoken by the Moldavians in the extreme south-west of the USSR.

The most varied region in its national composition is the Caucasus. Most of the peoples living there speak languages from the Iberian–Caucasus family, while the remainder speak Turkic languages. The Armenians speak a

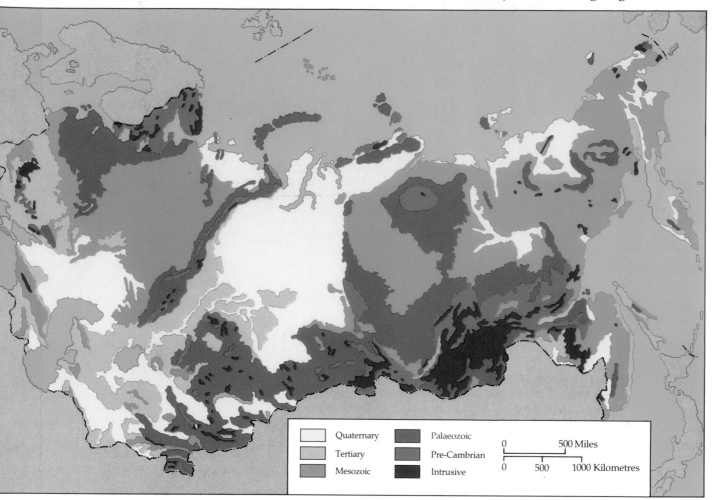

Quaternary		Palaeozoic
Tertiary		Pre-Cambrian
Mesozoic		Intrusive

0   500 Miles

0   500   1000 Kilometres

ERA	PERIOD	EPOCH	DURATION (years)		YEARS AGO	
Cainozoic	QUATERNARY	Holocene (Recent)	10,000 to date		10,000	
		Pleistocene	c.2m		c.2m	
	TERTIARY	Pliocene	5m		7m	
		Miocene	19m		26m	
		Oligocene	12m		30m	
		Eocene	16m		54m	
		Palaeocene	11m		65m	
Mesozoic	CRETACEOUS		71m		136m	
	JURASSIC		54m		190m	
	TRIASSIC		35m		225m	
Upper Palaeozoic	PERMIAN		55m		280m	
	CARBONIFEROUS	Pennsylvanian (USA)	65m	40m (USA)	345m	320m (USA)
		Mississippian (USA)		25m (USA)		345m (USA)
	DEVONIAN		60m		395m	
Lower Palaeozoic	SILURIAN		45m		440m	
	ORDOVICIAN		60m		500m	
	CAMBRIAN		100m		600m	
Pre-Cambrian	No worldwide system of naming subdivisions		Probably more than 4,000m		c.4,600m?	

ABOVE *The map indicates the age of the Soviet Union's major rock formations in terms of the geological periods and eras shown in the diagram on the left. Intrusive rocks are those that have been forced into existing rocks in a molten state and have solidified beneath the earth's surface.*

LEFT *The diagram shows how geological time is divided into different periods. The figures in the column on the extreme right show the approximate time when the era, period or epoch started. Few fossils of animals and plants have been dated back to before the Cambrian period, which began some 600 million years ago. (m = million.)*

language that is unique among the great Indo–European group of languages. The Osetins, Kurds and some other peoples of the Caucasus speak languages which belong to the Iranian group.

On the vast plain of Turan, to the east of the Aral Sea, and in the mountains of Central Asia and Kazakhstan live people of six nationalities, each of which has its own republic. They are the Uzbeks, Kazakhs, Tadzhiks, Kirgiz, Turkmens and Karakalpaks. Except for the Tadzhiks, who speak an Iranian language, all these peoples speak Turkic languages. Several other minor nationalities also live in this area of the Soviet Union.

The ethnic composition of Siberia and the Far East is even more varied. The region's indigenous inhabitants belong to various small ethnic groups whose total populations barely exceed one million.

Those living in the south of western Siberia (the Altais, Shorts and Khakas) speak Turkic languages, as do the Yakuts, who live in the Lena valley and further east. The remainder, living in the north and the Far East, belong to various ethnic groups. Throughout eastern Siberia and the Far East live peoples, such as the Evenkis, Nanaitsis, Ulchis and Udegeitsis, who speak Tungus languages. The peoples who are generally considered to be the ancient inhabitants of northern Asia are known collectively as Palaeoasiatics. They include the Chukchis, Koryaks, Itelmens, Yukagiris and Nikhvis. In the far north-east live the Inuits (Eskimoes) and Aleuts.

The smallest ethnic groups, such as the Tofalaris, Aleuts, Negidaltsis and Izhortsis, may have a population of less than a thousand. They are encouraged to maintain and develop their national cultures and traditions, but there may be restrictions if there is a conflict with nature conservation. For instance, various peoples of the north and Far East, who live by hunting and fishing, are allowed to do so only outside nature conservancy areas and they may be prohibited from taking more than a certain quota.

Population

The population of the USSR, estimated at over 268.8 million people in the 1982 census, is the third largest of any world state, after China and India. However, this impressive total, forming six per cent of the world's population, is spread over such a vast area that the average population density is no more than 28 people per sq mile (11 per sq km). This compares with an average figure of 1,122 per sq mile (433 per sq km) in Bangladesh, 593 per sq mile (229 per sq km) in the United Kingdom, and 60 per sq mile (23

per sq km) in the United States. Moreover, huge areas of the USSR have a much lower population density than the average, or are completely uninhabited.

The USSR has experienced one of the most rapid rates of urbanization in any of the world's developed countries. In less than 60 years, the proportion of the total population living in towns and cities has risen from 18 per cent to 64 per cent, as a result of migration from rural areas and the natural population growth in the towns themselves.

The largest nationalities in the USSR and their populations (1979 census)	
1 Russians	137,397,000
2 Ukrainians	42,347,000
3 Uzbeks	12,456,000
4 Belorussians	9,463,000
5 Kazakhs	6,556,000
6 Tartars	6,317,000
7 Azerbaidzhanians	5,477,000
8 Armenians	4,151,000
9 Georgians	3,571,000
10 Moldavians	2,968,000
11 Tadzhiks	2,898,000
12 Lithuanians	2,851,000
13 Turkmens	2,028,000
14 Germans	1,936,000
15 Kirgiz	1,906,000

The physical geography of the USSR

This brief review of the physical geography of the USSR is intended to give the reader an idea of the variety of natural conditions, provide some detail of the most typical landscapes and their distribution, and outline their characteristic vegetation (which is described in more detail on pages 30–40). The map on pages 12–13 shows the main physical features of the USSR.

Several methods exist for dividing the landscape into distinct zones according to their physical geography. This generally accepted modern scheme divides the USSR and neighbouring regions of Europe and Asia into 19 such zones. It includes the soil type, vegetation and other natural conditions of each zone.

The cliffs of Gerald Island in the Arctic wastes of the Chukchi Sea, in the extreme north-east of the USSR, in April.

1 THE ARCTIC ISLANDS

This zone includes the archipelagoes and individual islands of the Arctic Ocean. Some islands are flat (for example, the New Siberian Islands), while others (such as Novaya Zemlya and Wrangel Island) are mountainous. Typical landscapes are ice-locked shields, virtually lifeless Arctic wastes, and small areas of Arctic tundra.

2 FENNOSCANDIA

Much of this zone lies outside the USSR; within the USSR it embraces only the Kola Peninsula and Karelia. Its central feature is the Baltic shield. During the Quaternary ice ages, the whole area was ground down by glaciers. Hilly plains and low mountains, such as the Khibin Mountains, alternate with lake basins. The lakes are usually connected by short rivers. The climate is cold and damp, creating boggy soils. The dominant forest vegetation is of the northern taiga type, with dense stands of conifers. Pine (*Pinus*) trees grow on the rocky hills and ridges, while the lower ground is occupied by spruce (*Picea*) forest. In the north of the Kola Peninsula there is wooded tundra (tundra with scattered birch (*Betula*) trees) and tundra.

3 THE EAST-EUROPEAN (RUSSIAN) PLAIN

This is one of the largest zones in Eurasia. Much of it corresponds to the Russian part of the East European Platform; to the south it includes the Crimean steppes and the western and central areas north of the Caucasus. During the Quaternary ice ages, the northern plain was covered with ice from the continental glaciers. The rock fragments and other debris ground up by the moving ice were deposited as moraines, which give the landscape its characteristic relief of hills and large areas of low-lying land, often filled today by lakes or marshes. Outside the glaciated area, the wide river valleys are joined by canyons and gullies, forming a complex, highly ramifying network. The climate is moderately continental. In this zone, the effect of latitude on the landscape is particularly clear.

4 THE URAL MOUNTAINS

A system of mountain ranges extends in a more or less north–south direction for more than 1,240 miles (2,000 km). The individual peaks reach their greatest height in the north near the Arctic Circle, where there are some small glaciers. The clearly defined altitudinal zonation of the vegetation is superimposed on a background of zonation by latitude. The largest areas are clothed with mountain forest. In the north there are widespread areas of mountain tundra and bare summits.

5   THE UKRAINIAN CARPATHIANS AND THE TRANS-CARPATHIAN LOWLAND

These form a part of the Alpine–Carpathian zone, which lies mostly outside the USSR, in Romania and Czechoslovakia. The mountains are of medium height, with smooth summits. Their lower slopes are covered mainly by oak (*Quercus*) and beech (*Fagus*) forests, with a belt of mixed forest or pure conifer forest above. Sub-alpine meadows occupy much of the ground above 4,920 ft (1,500 m).

6   THE CRIMEAN–CAUCASUS MOUNTAINS

This area includes the mountains of Crimea, the Great Caucasus, the Talysh Mountains and the adjacent Lenkoran Lowland, the Rioni and Kolkhida basins, and the Kura and Kura–Araks Lowland. All these areas are subject to earthquakes. Large areas of the Crimean Mountains are clothed with forest. The south coast of the Crimea is distinctly Mediterranean in climate and character. On the lower slopes of the Great Caucasus, mixed conifer and broad-leaved forest are predominant, with sub-alpine and alpine meadows above. The jagged summits of the Caucasus Mountains are covered with glaciers and permanent snow, and their melt-waters feed the rivers far below them. The western part of the Great Caucasus is very wet, sometimes with up to 197 in (5,000 mm) of rain annually – the highest rainfall in the whole of the USSR. The eastern part has a drier, more continental climate, with hot summers and cold winters. In the Little Caucasus, mountain-steppe and mountain meadows predominate, but in the west of this region there are areas of mature forest, too. The summits of the Talysh Mountains are covered with meadow-steppe, but their slopes are clothed with broad-leaved woodland. The Lenkoran and Kolkhida lowlands lie within the wet and semi-wet sub-tropics, so broad-leaved forests and marshes are widespread. The Kura-Araks Lowland is an area of sub-tropical semi-desert.

7   THE ARMENIAN HIGHLAND AND KOPET-DAG

These areas form part of the near-Eastern Highland, and lie mainly outside the USSR, in Turkey and Iran. The Armenian Highland is on the north-eastern border of Armenia. Volcanic, mountain-steppe and mountain-meadow landscapes all occur there. The Kopet-Dag Mountains lie on the northern edge of the Iranian tableland. They consist of sub-tropical semi-desert and mountain-steppe landscapes, with drought-resistant plants and light juniper (*Juniperus*) forest. Lying on an unstable part of the earth's crust, both areas suffer earthquakes.

LEFT *The desert foothills of the Kopet-Dag Mountains in southern Turkmenistan, in the extreme south-west of the USSR, which are part of the near-Eastern Highland Zone. The mountains themselves rise to heights of more than 8,500 ft (2,700 m).*

8 THE CENTRAL ASIAN MOUNTAINS

This area includes the mountain systems of southeast and eastern Kazakhstan, Saur, Tarbagatai, Dzhungar Alatau, Tien Shan (except for its highest eastern and south-eastern parts) and Gissaro-Alai. In the foothills there are semi-deserts, while the lower and middle slopes are covered by mountain steppes, except in the Gissaro-Alai region. Here, the foothills experience sub-tropical conditions, and on the wetter outer slopes of the mountains, forests of nut trees, aspens, apple, spruce and juniper are able to flourish. In the high mountains of the Central Asian region there are sub-alpine and alpine meadows, meadow-steppes and many large glaciers.

9 THE HIGH-CATCHMENT ZONE OF TIEN SHAN AND PAMIR

This region includes the highest mountains in the USSR, and is part of the natural zone of the Central Asian Upland, most of which lies outside the USSR, in Afghanistan, Pakistan, India and China. The climate is markedly continental, especially in the valleys enclosed by the great mountains. Because of this area's high altitude, the climate is so harsh that even the high plateaus may be arid. The highest ground, across which the winds bring rain from the west, has thick ice with large glaciers in valleys such as Inylchek and Fedchenko. On the tablelands of the Tien Shan and eastern Pamir are cold wastes and semi-deserts and some stony mountain tundra. Much of the land is frozen to a great depth. In the wettest parts, there are steppes and high-mountain meadow-steppes.

10 THE CENTRAL ASIAN PLAIN

This is the desert and semi-desert region of the Turan Lowland, the Caspian Plain and the southern area north of Balkhash. Essentially, it corresponds to the underlying Turan Platform. It consists mainly of plains, with frequent sandy hillocks and ridges. The climate is markedly continental — dry with a very hot summer. The northern part of the zone lies in a belt of moderate climate, but the southern part is sub-tropical, with a relatively mild winter. There are sand and clay deserts and semi-deserts.

11 TURGAI AND CENTRAL KAZAKHSTAN

These areas have landscapes intermediate between the plains of Central Asia and Western Siberia. The western part of the zone occupies the Turgai Depression, with its flat plains. The middle and eastern parts are occupied by the Kazakh plains, from which rise many hills and ridges.

The high-mountain Lake Issyk-Kul lies between the Terskei and Kungei Alatau ranges, in the Tien Shan Mountains of Central Asia; it is 112 miles (180 km) long.

A caravan wends its way through the great Kara-Kum sand desert, in southwestern USSR; as in other sandy deserts, camels are the best method of transport.

12   THE WEST SIBERIAN PLAIN

This vast area of land lies on the West Siberian Platform. The surface is very flat and poorly drained; much of it is marshland. The northern part of this region has a thick layer of permafrost (permanently frozen ground). Throughout its extent there is tundra, wooded tundra, forest, and forest-steppe vegetation. To the south there are areas of steppe, pale soils (*solonchaks*) rich in soluble salts, and salt lakes, where salts are deposited by evaporation of the water, as there are no outlets for it.

13   THE CENTRAL SIBERIAN ZONE

Much of this region is situated in the Central Siberian Tableland, which has a relatively flat surface, deeply etched by river valleys. The climate is markedly continental, and there is permafrost throughout. The rivers carry a huge volume of water. The effect of latitude on the landscape is somewhat lessened by the effects of altitudinal belts and permafrost.

14   THE ALTAI–SAYAN MOUNTAIN ZONE

This includes the Altai, Sayan, Kuznetskii Alatau and Tuva Mountains. These dramatic ranges have been carved by glacial action into a typical alpine relief. The deep valleys between the towering mountains are characteristic features. To the west of this zone, where the climate is wetter, dense conifer forests grow, replaced on the higher slopes by open stands of Siberian Stone Pine (*Pinus sibirica*) and alpine meadows. In the valleys there are steppes and semi-desert, which are replaced on the mountain slopes by forests of larch (*Larix*) and pine (*Pinus*). Higher still, there are areas of mountain tundra and the bare summits. There are patches of permafrost and many glaciers.

15   THE LAKE BAIKAL ZONE

This is a mountainous region, with both flat-topped and conical summits, separated by long valleys. The climate is markedly continental, dry in the valleys, but wetter and colder in the mountains. Permafrost is widespread. Steppes occur in the valleys, sometimes with pine forest and meadows, while the mountain slopes are clothed with forests, mostly of larch (*Larix*) and Siberian Stone Pine (*Pinus sibirica*). The summits are bare.

16   THE DAURIAN ZONE

Most of this area lies in Mongolia and China, but a small part of it is in the USSR. It has vast hilly plains with flat-topped summits, none of them above 4,920 ft (1,500 m). The climate is markedly continental. There are patches of permafrost. In places, there are *solonchak* soils, which are pale-coloured and rich in soluble salts, and are often clothed with meadows.

A typical scene in the tundra in summer, near Lake Taimyr on the Taimyr Peninsula, in the Central Siberian Zone. The thick layer of permanent ice, or permafrost, impedes drainage and the vegetation holds water like a sponge.

ABOVE *The Ak-Kem River flows out of the Belukha glacier, in the Katun Range of the great Altai Mountain system, in southern Siberia.*

RIGHT *A dramatic example of a landscape carved out by glaciation, Mount Belukha is, at 14,783 ft (4506 m), the highest peak of the Altai Mountains in southern Siberia. There are almost 800 glaciers in an area of 225 sq miles (580 sq km).*

LEFT *There are many active volcanoes and frequent earthquakes in the North Pacific zone of the Soviet Far East, including the Kronoki Volcano on the peninsula of Kamchatka, seen here at rest (top picture) and during a recent eruption (bottom picture).*

ABOVE *The unique forests of the south Ussuri region, such as this one, of Korean Pine, on the coast of the Sea of Japan, contain a wealth of unique plants and animals.*

17 THE NORTH-EASTERN SIBERIAN ZONE

This is a mountainous area with a harsh, continental climate, especially in certain valleys. The coldest place in the USSR – indeed, in the whole world apart from Antarctica – is in this zone at Verkhoyansk (see page 27). Open stands of larch (*Larix*) forest predominate, with mountain tundra and bare summits; in the north of this region, the forest is absent.

18 THE NORTH PACIFIC ZONE

This includes the Chukot Peninsula, the Anadyr Tableland, the Anadyr Lowland, the Koryak Highlands, the Kamchatka Peninsula, and the Komandor and Kuril islands. There are many mountain ranges with sharp summits, and volcanic tablelands with volcanic cones and mountain ranges of medium height. This zone contains many active volcanoes, and earthquakes are frequent in Kamchatka and the Kuril Islands. In the northern and middle parts of the zone permafrost is widespread. The climate is maritime, with cool, overcast, rainy summers, and is subject to the influence of the trade winds. Tundra stretches far to the south in the Chukot Peninsula. Taiga is found only in the south of the zone. The southern Kuril Islands have broad-leaved and mixed forests, as well as copses of Kuril Bamboo (*Sasa kurilensis*). On the coastal plains there are mixed forests, meadows and marshes, while open stands of Erman's Birch (*Betula ermani*), dwarf pine (*Pinus*) and alder (*Alnus*) grow on the mountains. The summits are clothed in tundra or bare rock.

19 THE AMUR–SAKHALIN ZONE

This region includes the plains and mountains of the Amur region and the Pacific coast, the Sikhote–Alin Mountains, and the plains of the Ussuri region stretching westwards from them, as well as Sakhalin Island. Taiga landscapes predominate, with larch (*Larix*) and dark conifer forests, but marshland covers an appreciable area. Copses of dwarf pines (*Pinus*) grow on the summits. To the south of the zone, in the river valleys of the Ussuri region and on the lower slopes of the mountains, are the unique Far Eastern mixed broad-leaved and conifer forests and areas of tall grass. These are notable for the large number of plant species, including many endemic to the region and many relict species from the Tertiary period (which started about 65 million years ago) that were able to escape from the ice ages that subsequently affected much of the USSR.

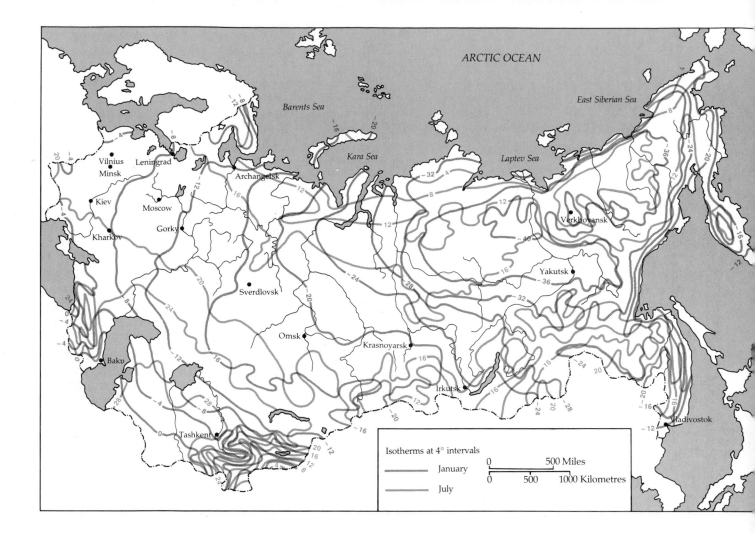

ARCTIC OCEAN

Barents Sea

Kara Sea

Laptev Sea

East Siberian Sea

Vilnius
Minsk
Leningrad
Archangelsk
Kiev
Moscow
Kharkov
Gorky
Sverdlovsk
Omsk
Krasnoyarsk
Irkutsk
Baku
Tashkent
Verkhoyansk
Yakutsk
Vladivostok

Isotherms at 4° intervals

January

July

0   500 Miles
0   500   1000 Kilometres

Climate and climatic belts

Vast areas of the USSR have a harsh, cold climate. Depending on latitude, the annual amount of solar radiation received over most of the country varies quite considerably. The islands in the Arctic Ocean probably receive less, and the Central Asian valleys more. Throughout the country there is a clear division of the year into a cold season and a warm one.

The Arctic and sub-Arctic climatic belts defined by the Arctic Ocean, the Arctic islands, and the northern continental margin have a particularly severe climate because of the alternation of long polar days and nights, the predominance of snow and ice, and the domination of the Arctic air masses. In summer there are often temperature inversions, low clouds, mists, rain, snow, or sleet. In the western Soviet Arctic, where the temperatures remain above freezing point for five months, the summer is warmer; but in the eastern Arctic the temperature stays above freezing point for only 2½ to 3 months of the year. Most of the cyclones occur in winter, with frequent blizzards and gales. The minimum temperature over the Arctic Ocean rarely drops as low as −58°F (−50°C), but the wind is usually strong and the relative humidity of the air is high.

Much of Soviet territory is in the temperate zone, but the country is so vast that there is a great variety of climates. The northwestern European part of the USSR has

The map of the USSR shows the isotherms — the lines joining places having the same mean temperature — for the months of January and July.

a climate varying from maritime to continental, with unstable weather and frequent cyclones bringing in air from the Atlantic. At the same time the Arctic air arrives from the relatively warm Barents and Norwegian Seas, so the winter is comparatively warm, and features alternating periods of hard frost and thaw. Rain or snow totalling 24 to 27 in (600 to 700 mm) each year falls mainly in the summer. Because of the clouds and frequent rain, the soil does not heat up enough to evaporate all the water, and there is excess soil water in most regions.

The north-east European part of the USSR has a continental climate, with a long, cold winter and very few thaws. Snow generally lies for 150 to 200 days but the total annual rainfall of about 20 in (500 mm) occurs mainly in summer.

The central area of the European part of the country, including the southern taiga and the zone of mixed or broad-leaved forests, has a relatively uniform climate. The winters are fairly cold with frequent thaws, the summers warm with short cold snaps. Rain, from 12 to 27 in (300 to 700 mm) annually, falls mainly in the summer.

Southern areas of the European part of the country have a warm and comparatively dry summer. The relative humidity of the air in daytime does not usually exceed 35 to 45 per cent. The annual rainfall is from 10 to 18 in (250 to 450 mm), but the snow does not fall every year.

Western Siberia has a continental climate, influenced chiefly by air masses from the Arctic basin. In summer the Arctic air interacts with the warm continental air to create clouds and rain. Very occasionally in western Siberia, damp Atlantic or dry Central Asian air masses may move in. Most of the cyclones produced by the meeting of the two air-masses travel through the north of western Siberia, with high wind, clouds, and plentiful snowfalls. From November to March, temperatures usually remain below −22°F (−30°C). The summer lasts for three months, with a mean July temperature of 68 to 72°F (20 to 22°C). Surprisingly, for an area with such a severe winter climate, summer temperatures can reach 104°F (40°C). As a whole, western Siberia has great contrasts of climate because of the vast distances from north to south.

The most continental climate in the whole country is that of eastern Siberia. The annual difference of air temperature between summer and winter in this vast region amounts to a remarkable 108 to 117°F (60 to 65°C); rainfall and cloud cover are slight. Throughout the year cold Arctic air is dominant as well as the continental air of temperate latitudes. Most of the cyclones occur in the summer − and in the north. In summer the air warms up appreciably. The mean July temperature of 66°F (19°C) at the town of Yakutsk makes it warmer than Moscow, but the winter frosts are extreme. The 'pole of cold' of the Northern Hemisphere − indeed, the coldest place on earth except for parts of Antarctica − is in the region of Verkhoyansk, in the centre of eastern Siberia. Here, the January temperature falls to −90.4°F (−68°C). Winter here lasts a dreary seven months, although the snow cover is not deep. Lake Baikal, in the south-west of this region, has a moderating effect on the climate around it.

The Far East region is in the trade-wind zone, with a maritime climate. The winter is cold with little snow and mainly clear and sunny weather. Winter rainfall or snowfall is only 10 to 15 per cent of the year's total. The summer trade wind from the Pacific Ocean brings ample rain and mist, most noticeable in the south of the Far Eastern USSR, in the regions of the Amur and Ussuri rivers. The annual rainfall on the coast is 20 to 35 in (500 to 900 mm), whereas inland it only measures between 12 to 16 in (300 to 400 mm).

The plains of Central Asia and Kazakhstan have an arid, markedly continental climate and receive more solar radiation than anywhere else in the USSR. The summer temperature is very high, 81 to 90°F (27 to 32C). The

Lake Ak-Kem in the Katun Range of the Altai Mountains, in southern Siberia. The complex air circulation in the great southern mountain systems of the USSR results in a corresponding complexity in climate.

summer is very long, with anti-cyclones and little rain. The winters are very cold for such latitudes because of the unchecked access of cold air from Siberia. The annual rainfall of the region is 8 to 12 in (200 to 300 mm), mostly in spring. Snow cover is either brief or non-existent.

The sub-tropical belt includes southwestern Central Asia, the Trans-Caucasus, and the south coast of the Crimea. Over most of this territory the climate is arid, with a long, hot summer, low relative humidity and few clouds. The mean July temperature is about 81°F (27°C), and the annual rainfall only 4 to 8 in (100 to 200 mm) − although in the Lenkoran Lowland, with its semi-moist sub-tropical climate, there was a single downpour in 1966 amounting to an astonishing 17 in (441 mm) of rain! The western area beyond the Caucasus is also rainy and sub-tropical, with 39 in (1000 mm) annual rainfall, rising in the mountains to 126 in (3,200 mm). In some years the high mountains of the Caucasus have as much as 197 in (5000 mm) of rainfall.

Although the climates of the southern mountains of the USSR have many features in common, they also have important differences, chiefly as a result of the complex air circulation over the various mountain masses. The climates of the Pamir and Tien Shan ranges are divided into horizontal belts, but tend to share a general aridity. This is also true of the Caucasus, except for its western peaks, where the rainfall is much higher, as described above. As one climbs the mountains, the climate becomes colder and wetter. The great contrasts of mountain climates over very short distances result in abrupt variations in landscape.

2 VEGETATION AND ANIMAL DISTRIBUTION

Soil types

Before taking a look at the great variety of natural vegetation in the USSR, we should consider briefly the different types of soil and how they are formed. Soils can be classified on the basis of the distinct layers, or horizons, which they contain, together with an examination of the soil structure and texture. Together, the various horizons make up what soil scientists call a 'soil profile'. This can be revealed by digging down several feet to expose a 'cliff' of the soil. The uppermost layer is the O horizon, consisting of leaf-mould or other organic debris. This is followed by the A horizon, a mixture of mineral and organic matter from which soluble salts and very fine particles called colloids are removed by being leached out by rainfall, for example. Finally, there is the B horizon at the bottom, which is enriched by the salts or organic matter washed down from above. Each of these three main layers is subdivided in great detail.

The USSR has a huge variety of soils, and the world is indebted to her soil scientists for their pioneering research in classifying and studying them. Climate, soil and vegetation share a complex interrelationship. Soil type changes with latitude chiefly as a result of changes in climate; the soil is also affected by the nature of the vegetation that grows on it. The distribution of the vegetation itself depends largely on climate, as we shall see later in this chapter. On a mountainside, the soil type changes from the foothills to the summit for the same reasons. On the plains, soils are divided into two main groups: leached soils and unleached soils.

Leached soils

These are formed under tundra, forest or meadow vegetation in conditions where the inflow of water is greater than its evaporation from the surface. Water-soluble salts are removed from the soil, giving it an acid reaction. The main types of leached soil are gleys and podzols.

Tundra gley soils have a layer of peat near the surface, and lower down a blue-grey or mottled grey and brown horizon, a result of the reduction and oxidation of iron salts caused by the poor drainage of these waterlogged, usually permanently frozen soils.

LEFT *Here, in the Repetek Biosphere Nature Reserve, in the southeastern Kara-Kum desert, the shifting sand is stabilized by a variety of tough bushes and other drought-resistant plants.*

Podzols are poor, sandy soils formed beneath conifer forests or mixed conifer/broad-leaved forests. They have very distinct profiles, and the A horizon typically contains an ash-coloured acid layer (the word podzol is Russian for 'ash-soil').

The podzols are of three main types. Frozen-taiga soils are linked to a cold, highly continental climate, as in the eastern Siberian open-conifer forest. From a depth of $3\frac{1}{2}$ to 4 ft (1 to 1.2 m) downwards, the ground is permanently frozen. Grey forest soils are widespread in the zone of deciduous forests. Finally, brown forest soils are formed in broad-leaved forests, as well as in the southern conifer forests of the Carpathians, Crimea, Caucasus, southern Urals and Altai.

There are a number of other series of leached soils in addition to these.

Unleached soils

Unleached soils develop where evaporation exceeds the inflow of water. Simple salts are not washed out of the soil, but accumulate at certain depths. The soil reaction is neutral to alkaline. These include Arctic island soils, usually thin and neutral; chernozems (meaning 'black earth' in Russian), formed beneath the steppe and forest-steppe vegetation of the East European Plain, West Siberia and northern Kazakhstan; chestnut-coloured soils, formed beneath the vegetation of dry steppes; and many other types.

A wealth of plants

Approximately 90,000 to 100,000 species of plants grow in the USSR. This includes some 35,000 to 40,000 species of higher plants, including conifers, broad-leaved trees, shrubs and flowers, horsetails, clubmosses and ferns. The regions richest in these species are Central Asia (7,000 species), Caucasus (6,000), Crimea (2,000), Far East (2,000). The sparsest floras are those of the Arctic islands of Siberia, where there are only 100 to 150 species. The USSR has no fewer than 15,000 species of lower plants — some 10,000 species of algae and 5,000 species of lichens — plus about 35,000 species of fungi.

Forests have enormous importance for the USSR. Their area, as estimated on 1 January 1978, was 3,058,151 sq miles (7,920,000 sq km) occupying 35.6 per cent of the area of the country. The total reserves of timber amount to almost 3 million million cu ft (84,000 million cu m), about 80 per cent of it conifer wood. The most widespread

conifers are various species of larch (*Larix*), occupying about 1,023,000 sq miles (2,650,000 sq km) and of pine (*Pinus*), occupying 444,000 sq miles (1,150,000 sq km); Siberian Stone Pine (*Pinus sibirica*), occupying 154,450 sq miles (400,000 sq km); and various species of spruce (*Picea*), occupying 297,320 sq miles (770,000 sq km). The forests are not distributed evenly throughout the various union republics making up the USSR. Most of them are in the Russian Soviet Federal Socialist Republic (RSFSR). Some 400 species of medicinal plants grow in the USSR. The seas, too, are rich in plant life; reserves of algae and other water plants total an estimated 21,652,500 tons (22,000,000 tonnes).

Plant distribution

The vegetation of the USSR is very rich and varied, particularly in the south of the country and in the mountains of the Caucasus and Central Asia. Although it contains such a variety of different plant communities, the whole of the USSR's vast territory lies within the Holarctic floristic kingdom, the northernmost of all the earth's plant kingdoms. The distribution of vegetation in the various natural vegetation zones is determined by many factors, chiefly temperature and rainfall.

The great extent of the USSR from west to east has resulted in the distribution of the vegetation zones by latitude more distinctly than anywhere else on earth

ABOVE *Taiga (coniferous forest) in the River Muya basin, eastern Siberia; almost 80 per cent of the USSR's forestry resources are in Siberia and the Soviet Far East.*
RIGHT *Mixed forest in Lithuania; the mixed forests of European Russia are similar to those in other parts of Europe, unlike those of the Soviet Far East.*

although some, such as the European and Far Eastern zones, which are influenced by the oceans, run north–south or diagonally. Many local features, such as mountains or lakes, influence the development and appearance of the vegetation, so that the main zones are subdivided into subzones or provinces. Also, there are belts of different vegetation with increasing altitude within each major zone, and the influence of other factors, such as grazing animals and human land use, play their part in creating the rich natural tapestry.

Although the main reason for the clear zonation of plants is the vast area of the USSR, another very important factor is the relative flatness of much of the country: between its western frontiers and the River Yenesei the USSR has no mountains apart from the low Ural Range dividing Europe from Asia. This general flatness allows the climate to exert its full effect.

The types of vegetation characteristic of the different geographical zones will be described in more detail in later chapters. One problem facing botanists studying plant distribution is that some plants or entire plant communities

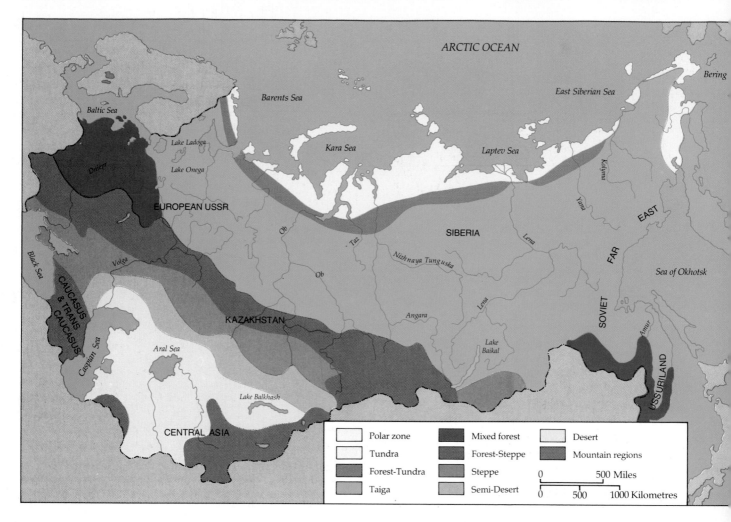

The map shows the distribution of the major vegetation zones.

Polar zone
Tundra
Forest-Tundra
Taiga
Mixed forest
Forest-Steppe
Steppe
Semi-Desert
Desert
Mountain regions

0   500 Miles

0   500   1000 Kilometres

are not typical of the zone being examined. Most often these are what are known as inclusions, or intra-zonal elements. An intra-zonal plant is one which nowhere has its own zone and is found only as an inclusion in another zone. The vegetation of areas of pale, salty *solonchak* soil or black alkaline *solonets* soil, and sphagnum-moss bogs are all intra-zonal elements.

Azonal plants are like intra-zonal ones, but they may find a place in every zone. Examples are water meadows, growing on the rich deposits of sediment that accumulate on the banks of rivers, which are present in every zone. Azonal plants may also be found on sandy soil, or in rocky, denuded areas.

Finally, there is extra-zonal vegetation, that is, vegetation which belongs to a certain zone, but also extends outside it, usually in islets, as with trees growing on the edges of the steppes bordering a forest. The existence of extra-zonal vegetation has intrigued botanists, who have provided a neat explanation for its distribution. If the islets of extra-zonal vegetation lie to the north of a particular zone, they are likely to be more suited climatically to conditions intermediate between the two areas, and might be expected to occur on the warmer, drier south-facing slopes in the north. Similarly, the extra-zonal plants in the islets to the south of a zone might be expected to occur on the cooler, wetter northern slopes, where the climate is intermediate between the two areas. This hypothesis is generally supported by the evidence from nature.

The effects of glaciation

Glaciation has had a profound effect on the evolution of the USSR's vegetation. During the various Quaternary ice ages, the great glaciers completely destroyed large areas of vegetation and, throughout the northern area of the country, created vast areas of frozen soil (permafrost) on which only the toughest vegetation could survive. More ancient plant communities were conserved for the most part in the south, and included the interesting groups of warmth-loving plants protected by the mountains of the Caucasus and Central Asia.

Natural vegetation zones

The vegetation of the USSR can be divided into eight different zones, as follows:

1 THE HIGH ARCTIC ZONE
The high Arctic zone includes those parts of the Arctic islands which are not covered by ice; on the Soviet mainland, it consists only of the northern margin of the Taimyr Peninsula. On the accumulated boulders and gravel, vegetation is generally absent or develops only very slowly, although the surface of the fine-grained

Larches, the most widespread conifers in the USSR, are tough trees; here, they manage to survive the harsh climate of the Katun Range in the Altai Mountains.

subsoil is from 20 to 30 per cent encrusted with lichens, mosses and algae. In cracks and depressions where snow accumulates, flowering plants manage to eke out an existence by huddling together, but mosses and lichens are far more successful, occupying about 10 to 15 per cent of the surface area.

2 THE TUNDRA ZONE

Arctic tundra occupies a more or less narrow strip of the north of the continent and some southern Arctic islands. The vegetation is treeless, mainly because of the cold, but there is a healthy surface layer of mosses and lichens. Arctic tundra may also contain a tier of shrubs and perennial grasses. A large area is occupied by hummocky marsh. In the most northerly Arctic tundra the vegetation is of the grass/shrub/moss or shrub/lichen type. Further south lies a strip of northern, or typical, tundras which contain plants that also grow in the taiga; these are known as hypo-Arctic species. In the southern, or shrub, tundras there is a well-developed tier of Dwarf Birch (*Betula nana*). In the southernmost strip of wooded tundra, or near-tundra, sparse forest with hypo-Arctic or taiga vegetation predominates, with Siberian Spruce (*Picea obovata*) and Daurian or Siberian larch (*Larix dahurica, L. sibirica*).

3 THE NORTH PACIFIC MOUNTAIN ZONE

The North Pacific tall-grass/small-leaved forest/low-mountain zone covers the Kamchatka Peninsula and the north Kuril and Komandor Islands, flourishing in the cold, wet climate. There are widespread open woods of Erman's Birch (*Betula ermani*), alternating with dense stands of tall grass. In the mountains, there grow such typical high-mountain shrubs as Japanese Stone Pine (*Pinus pumila*) and Kamchatka Alder (*Alnus kamtschatica*). The conifer forests are mainly of Yeddo Spruce (*Picea jezoensis*) and Kajander Larch (*Larix dahurica*), but these are restricted to the valley of the Kamchatka River and are surrounded on three sides by mountains.

4 THE TAIGA ZONE

The North-European–Siberian taiga zone stretches from the Baltic Sea to the Pacific coast. Throughout its huge length, there are great conifer forests which cover almost 40 per cent of the area of the USSR. The main trees are pines (*Pinus*), spruces (*Picea*), firs (*Abies*) and larches (*Larix*), with different species throughout the zone. Large areas, especially on the West Siberian Plain, are covered with a ground layer of raised sphagnum-moss bog. In the North European part of the country, and in West Siberia as far as the Sayan Mountains, the forests consist mainly of species of spruce and fir, together with Siberian Stone Pine (*Pinus sibirica*). East of the Yenesei River, larches predominate.

In the Far East, along the middle reaches of the Amur River, as well as in Sakhalin Island and the southernmost Kuril Islands, most of the land is covered by dark conifer forest, mainly of mountain types, usually containing Yeddo Spruce (*Picea jezoensis*) and two species of fir (*Abies*). In the mountains of the taiga zone, conifers cover the lower and middle belts of the mountain; above them grow shrubs such as Dwarf Birch (*Betula nana*) and Dwarf Siberian Stone Pine (*Pinus sibirica*). In the Far East these belts are occupied mainly by Erman's Birch (*Betula ermani*).

The composition and structure of the taiga forests varies greatly from north to south. In the northern taiga, the trees are sparse and the undergrowth is similar to that of the tundra, with a dense ground layer of mosses and lichens. In the middle taiga, the stands of trees are denser and shrubs are usually absent. Mosses are abundant, but lichens are common in the pine forests only. In the southern taiga, the trees are dense and the ground cover sparse. As well as yielding huge quantities of timber, the taiga is also the main area where country people harvest wild berries and edible fungi, which form an important contribution to the rural economy in many parts of the Soviet Union.

TOP LEFT *The bright yellow flowers of the Marsh Buttercup make a splash of colour in the damp taiga forest in May.*
TOP RIGHT *The great dark conifer forests cover almost 40 per cent of the USSR; this pine forest is in Lithuania.*
ABOVE *Cones of the Scots Pine; found throughout the western taiga of the USSR, this is one of the most widespread of all pines, growing as far south as Spain.*

TOP FAR LEFT *Little vegetation can survive on the dry rocky tundra of the high Arctic, photographed in July in the Byrrangi foothills of the Taimyr Peninsula.*
LEFT *There is a transition zone between tundra and taiga, seen here in the Kola Peninsula in north-west USSR.*

5 THE EUROPEAN BROAD-LEAVED FOREST ZONE

This stretches from the Carpathian Mountains, on the border with Romania and Czechoslovakia, to the western slopes of the southern Ural Mountains, and includes the Crimea and Caucasus in the south. The northern part of this zone is not particularly rich in tree species. The mountain summits are occupied by alpine meadows. In the southern section, including the Caucasus and the mountains of the Crimea, there is a richer variety of broad-leaved trees. Five species of oak (*Quercus*) predominate, but on the higher slopes there is a belt of beech (*Fagus*). Thanks to its abundant rainfall, the western Caucasus has very distinctive vegetation. In the lower belts of the mountains, and in the plains by the foothills, mixed broad-leaved forests flourish, with chestnut (*Castanea*), beech (*Fagus*) and several species of oak (*Quercus*), often with an undergrowth of evergreen trees and shrubs. Higher up are beech (*Fagus*) forests, and higher still a belt of dark conifer forest of spruce (*Picea*), fir (*Abies*) and some broad-leaved trees. The upper tree-line contains dwarf beech (*Fagus*) or birch (*Betula*) trees. In the sub-alpine belt, Caucasian Rhododendrons (*Rhododendron caucasicum*) flourish; in drier places, there are dwarf junipers (*Juniperus*). The alpine belt of the Caucasus contains low-grass alpine meadows, including a rich variety of plant species. The Crimean Mountains are dominated by oak (*Quercus*) forests, with European oak species alternating in places with beech (*Fagus*). On the southern slope of the Crimean Mountains are Mediterranean species of pine (*Pinus*) and juniper (*Juniperus*).

6 THE FAR-EASTERN BROAD-LEAVED FOREST ZONE

This is represented in the USSR only by its northernmost part. Most of it lies outside the country – in Korea, China and Japan. This zone, influenced by the trade wind climate, has an exotic and varied flora. No less than one third of the plants in the Far Eastern taiga are endemic to the region, including a huge variety of trees and shrubs. In the plains and on the lower slopes of the mountains, deciduous trees predominate, mainly Mongolian Oak (*Quercus mongolica*), various species of hornbeam (*Carpinus*), lime (*Tilia*) and maple (*Acer*). Above the broad-leaved belt is mixed conifer/broad-leaved forest, in which the main species are Korean Pine (*Pinus koraiensis*) and Khingan Fir (*Abies nephrolepis*). Among the broad-leaved and especially the mixed forests a number of climbing plants flourish, and in the undergrowth are many interesting and valuable plants, including 'Wild Pepper' (*Eleutherococcus senticosus*) and Ginseng (*Panax ginseng*). Higher still, there is a belt of dark conifer forest, with Yeddo Spruce (*Picea jezoensis*) and Khingan Fir (*Abies nephrolepis*), which are replaced on the summits by dwarf Erman's Birch (*Betula ermani*), large thickets of dwarf Japanese Stone Pine (*Pinus pumila*) and the rare, endemic *Microbiota decussata*, a coniferous shrub resembling juniper.

ABOVE *Swampy taiga forest to the south of Irkutsk, near Lake Baikal in south-central Siberia.*

FAR LEFT *Climbing plants, such as these actinidias, are common in the broadleaved and mixed forests of the Ussuri valley in the Soviet Far East.*

LEFT *Dense mixed forest thickly carpets the spurs of the mountains in the south of the Ussuri region.*

RIGHT *Giant lichens clothe the trees in the wet taiga forest of the Altai Nature Reserve in southern Siberia.*

ABOVE *Sheep's Fescue grass and sagebrush grow on the saline soil of the dry steppe south of the Sea of Azov.*
RIGHT *The 'Singing Mountain' sand dune near the River Ili in Kazakhstan: it is surrounded by the low mountains of the Great and Little Kalkhan Ranges.*
FAR RIGHT *A sparse forest of pistachio-type trees grows in the desert in the Badkhyz Nature Reserve, Turkmenia, in the extreme south of the Soviet Union.*

7 THE EURASIAN STEPPE ZONE

This lies entirely within the temperate zone, stretching from the lower reaches of the River Danube in Romania to the inner part of Dunbey in China. Within the USSR, it is best represented in the southern region, western Siberia and the north of Kazakhstan. The dominant vegetation consists of drought-resistant perennial grasses, mainly turf-forming species, such as feather grasses (*Stipa*), oat grasses (*Avena*) and sedges (*Carex*).

The composition and structure of the plant community changes from west to east. Thus, in the steppes near the Black Sea and in Kazakhstan, large feather grasses predominate, such as Lessing's Feather Grass (*Stipa lessingiana*) and Ukrainian Feather Grass (*Stipa ucrainica*). Everywhere in this area there is Sheep's Fescue (*Festuca ovina*). Because of the warm climate and relatively high humidity in the Black Sea and Kazakhstan steppes, plants such as Viviparous Bluegrass (*Poa bulbosa*), species of goose onion (*Gagea*) and tulips (*Tulipa*) appear in spring. They are

ephemeral, completing their life cycle and setting seed in a very short time. They make a brief blaze of colour as they flower in spring and then shrivel and die in the hot summer sun. Hair-like feather grasses predominate in the steppes near the Black Sea and in Kazakhstan. These grasses are similar to those of Central Asia that occur east of Lake Baikal and in some areas of the Yenesei region.

In the Central Asian steppes, which have a a cold dry spring, there are practically no ephemeral plants, but in wetter years there are large numbers of plants that survive by long-term vegetative reproduction, especially worm-woods, or sagebrushes (*Artemisia*).

In the steppe region, the dominant species and the ecology of the plant and animal communities change considerably from north to south. The drought resistance of the plants increases, as does the number of ephemeral species. This zone is therefore divided into four belts of latitude. In the meadow-type steppe, there are species that are typical of meadows generally. In the dry, herbage/turf-

grass steppe, steppe herbage is dominant. In the arid turf-grass steppe, the proportion of steppe herbage diminishes. Finally, there is a belt of desert/shrub/turf-grass steppe.

In the Trans-Baikal region, meadow steppes predominate, and here, besides hair-like feather grass (*Stipa baicalica*), there are often many species of the daisy family (Compositae), such as the Siberian Tansy (*Tanacetum sibiricum*).

8 THE SAHARA-GOBI DESERT ZONE

The portion of this zone lying within the USSR stretches from the western Caspian region to the Chinese border. This zone is dominated by semi-shrubs, shrubs and tree-like species, such as saltbushes (*Atriplex*), saxauls (*Arthrophytum*), and 'acacias' (*Eremosparton*). Much of it lies in the temperate area, but most of the south is in the sub-tropics. Within the desert zone there are three latitudinal belts. In the northern belt of steppe-desert, which along its northern edge merges into steppe, semi-shrub species, such as

wormwoods, or sagebrushes (*Artemisia*), Russian Thistle (*Salsola kali*), turf-forming grasses and needle grasses (*Stipa*), predominate. The central belt of true desert lacks turf-forming grasses, while the southern belt contains various species of ephemeral plants.

The vegetation of the mountain systems within the desert zone is very varied. The mountains concerned are those of the southern and eastern Trans-Caucasus, Kazakhstan and Central Asia. It is here that more than half of the total number of higher plant species of the USSR are found. A general feature of all these mountains is that they have few trees, sometimes none at all. Also, the vegetation is adapted to resisting drought.

In the Dzhungar Alatau Range, in the north and central Tien Shan, the lower and middle belts of the mountain are covered mainly with turf-forming grass and meadow steppes, which are close in their composition to those of northern Kazakhstan. The upper parts of the mid-mountain slopes bear forests of Schrenck's Spruce (*Picea schrenckiana*), while higher up are copses of prostrate junipers (*Juniperus*). Communities of ephemeral plants grow in the Gissaro-Alai, the western Pamir, the southern Tien Shan and the Kopet Dag foothills. On some of the lower slopes, there are open forests of trees of the cashew family (Anacardiaceae). In the mid-mountain belt are meadows and shrub thickets, open juniper (*Juniperus*) woods and, on stony slopes, communities of thorny, drought-resistant shrubs and the grass-like *Cousinia* species, members of the daisy family (Compositae). Proper forests, of Persian Walnut (*Juglans regi*), Montpelier Maple (*Acer monspessulanum*) and Crab Apple (*Malus pumila*) are uncommon, and found mainly on northern slopes. In the high-mountain belt are high-mountain steppes, meadows, and sparse stands of creeping junipers (*Juniperus*). The eastern Pamir is part of the Central Asian desert sub-zone. Very little vegetation manages to survive in this high-mountain desert.

Human influences and endangered plants

The natural vegetation cover of the USSR has been changed greatly by felling and other human activity over large areas of forest. In the European part of the country, conifers are already less common than broad-leaved trees, such as aspen (*Populus*) and birch (*Betula*). The vegetation of meadowland has been altered considerably by intensive cattle grazing, and vast areas of steppeland have been turned over to the growing of huge prairies of wheat and other cereals. People also use the plants for making hay, they pick their berries, use a whole range of herbs and

BELOW *Although a few areas of original steppe still remain, preserved for future generations in nature reserves, vast areas of the steppelands have been ploughed up and turned over to cereal cultivation.*

other medicinal plants and gather mushrooms. As a result, some species have become scarce or endangered, but the necessary steps for their conservation are currently being taken and about 30 per cent of Soviet plant species are currently protected in nature reserves and sanctuaries. A total of 444 species of plants with a limited distribution or small population is included in the Red Book of the USSR. Some of them are described in other chapters of this book. Lists of species which need active conservation have been drawn up by the Botanical Institute of the USSR's Academy of Sciences and by the All-Union Research

The peaks of the Talass Alatau Range of the western Tien Shan Mountains appear through a break in the clouds, soaring above the foothills, after a May thunderstorm.

Institute for Nature Reserves and Nature Conservation. By a special decree of its Council of Ministers, each republic must conserve rare plants on its territory. These include 50 species in Estonia, 117 in Lithuania and 40 in Byelorussia, for example. Conservation is particularly urgent in areas rich in relict species, such as the Talysh Mountains, some parts of the Far East, and the Caucasus.

LEFT *Reindeer (called Caribou in North America) range widely over the tundra in summer. They have broad hooves which act as snowshoes in winter.*
RIGHT *Musk Oxen at Wrangel Island Nature Reserve in the high Arctic. Once common in the Siberian tundra, they had become extinct about 3,000 years ago, but were reintroduced from North America after 1945.*

Animal life

As with the plants, the richness and variety of the USSR's animal life reflect the country's varied climate and other natural conditions, as well as its vast area. Despite this, the USSR's northern position means that there are fewer species than in more southerly countries. Even so, 130,000 animal species are known to live there. It might be expected that the USSR, which, including its seas, occupies some 8 per cent of the surface of the globe, should contain about 8 per cent of the total number of species. In fact, the USSR has 10 per cent of the world total of about 1.3 million animal species, or 25 per cent more than the expected 8 per cent. It contains many species with huge populations, including some of the largest stocks of fish and game animals in the world. Many groups of animals, especially among the invertebrates, are little known, and new species are discovered every year. The composition of the fauna of the USSR according to zoological groups is shown on pages 210–19.

Each of the natural zones of the USSR contains characteristic faunas; the following summary indicates their main features and describes how they came to live where they do today.

TUNDRA

The tundra faunas consist of few species, but they are distinctive. Many are endemic to the tundra, where they are found over vast areas; some of them have a circumpolar distribution, occurring right around the North Pole. The sparseness and distinctiveness of the tundra faunas can be explained by the long isolation of this tough, independent group of animals.

The most widespread endemic species range over practically the whole tundra zone. They include the Arctic Fox (*Alopex lagopus*) and Arctic Lemming (*Dicrostonyx torquatus*) among the mammals, and the Snowy Owl (*Nyctea scandiaca*) and Snow Bunting (*Plectrophenax nivalis*) among the birds. Apart from the Snow Bunting and several other species, there are few passerines (perching birds) in the tundra. There are many species of waders, geese and ducks, which breed in the large areas of water and marsh.

Tundra animals experience long, bitterly cold, windy winters, with little sunlight; a brief, relatively cool summer; lack of shelter; a thick layer of permafrost (permanent frost beneath the surface); and a shortage of food plants. All these conditions are unfavourable to life. But there are bonuses, too, including the period of constant sunlight in summer, the large number of evergreen plants, the rich crops of berries in the southern tundras, the general absence of human interference, and the small numbers of harmful micro-organisms.

The tundra landscape is divided into Arctic, northern and southern areas, each of which has a distinctive animal population. But there are even greater differences between the fauna from west to east, and the long belts of the tundra can be divided into several areas on an east-west basis.

The Scandinavian-Kola tundras are not truly Arctic and have only one endemic species, the Norway Lemming (*Lemmus lemmus*). It is interesting that other lemming species, in particular the Arctic Collared Lemming (*Dicrostonyx torquatus*), widespread in the tundra, are absent from the Scandinavian-Kola region (see page 88).

The European–Siberian part of the tundra extends from the White Sea to the mouth of the River Lena, and is the home of the Siberian Lemming (*Lemmus obensis*). The endemic Red-breasted Goose (*Rufibrenta ruficollis*) nests here: this is one of the world's rarest wildfowl.

The east Siberian part of the tundra, from the mouth of the River Lena to Chukotka, has more endemics than the preceding two regions. These include breeding colonies of the rare Ross's Gull (*Rhodostethia rosea*) and the little-known Spoon-billed Sandpiper (*Eurynorhynchus pygmeus*). Many other species of waders breed here. There is a striking similarity between the east Siberian tundra and similar areas of Alaska and Canada.

As far as we know, the present fauna of the tundra came together during the ice ages. Not all of the animals evolved at that time; clearly defined endemic tundra species must have originated much earlier, possibly in the middle of the Tertiary period, about 30 million years ago. Also, various newcomers were able to move in after the glaciers withdrew. Typical members of the tundra fauna also occur today in widely separated areas of high-mountain tundra further south; they were stranded there after the retreat of the ice from the surrounding plains, unable to adapt to the warmer conditions.

TAIGA

The taiga belt has richer faunas than the tundra, but, considering its enormous area, there is not a great variety of species and they are remarkably uniform throughout their range. All over the taiga, from north-east Europe to the Pacific coast, live the Elk (*Alces alces*), Red Squirrel (*Sciurus vulgaris*), Siberian Chipmunk (*Eutamias sibiricus*), Arctic Hare (*Lepus timidus*), Lynx (*Felis lynx*), Red Fox (*Vulpes vulpes*), Siberian Weasel (*Mustela sibirica*), Stoat, or Ermine (*Mustela erminea*), Sable (*Martes zibellinus*), Wolverine (*Gulo gulo*) and Brown Bear (*Ursus arctos*). Only three of these mammals — the Elk, Wolverine and Sable — are endemic to the taiga habitat, and the first two are widely distributed throughout the taiga, from Scandinavia to

The Sparrowhawk is a common bird of prey in the taiga of the European part of the USSR, preferring more open areas of forest; this one was photographed in Lithuania in June.

Alaska and Canada. The rest of the mammals are also found in other natural zones.

A number of taiga birds also range over great areas of the Soviet taiga, in particular the Hazel Grouse (*Tetrastes bonasia*) and Capercaillie (*Tetrao urogallus*), various species of owls and woodpeckers, and many species of passerines (perching birds). Unlike those of the tundra, the taiga's bird faunas contain large proportions of passerines. More of the birds than the mammals are endemic to the taiga zone, including the Hazel Grouse, the Capercaillie, the Black-billed Capercaillie (*Tetrao parvirostris*) of eastern Siberia, the Great Grey Owl (*Strix nebulosa*), Hawk Owl (*Surnia ulula*) and Tengmalm's or Boreal Owl (*Aegolius funereus*), the Black Woodpecker (*Dryocopus martius*), Northern Three-toed Woodpecker (*Picoides tridactylus*), Siberian Jay (*Perisoreus infaustus*) and Nutcracker (*Nucifraga caryocatactes*). The three owls range throughout the world's taiga zone, from Scandinavia to North America.

The main features of the taiga compared with other types of forest are its distinctly continental climate with very cold winters, and the slim, tough needles and well protected seeds of its conifer trees, which certain animals are able to eat.

Most of the taiga birds are year-round residents. Truly migratory birds are rare, although many of them fly long distances north or south in search of food. A characteristic feature of the taiga, as well as of the tundra, is that vast areas seem at times to be completely deserted, with neither bird song in summer, nor animal tracks on the snow in winter — let alone any sight of the wildlife.

Insect life in the taiga is far richer than in the tundra; this Brimstone Butterfly is one of the first butterflies to appear in the forests in spring.

Although there is little difference in faunas over the entire 4,000-mile span of the Soviet taiga, and some animals extend right round the world's coniferous forest belt through Alaska and Canada, there is a distinct vertical tiering of species; for example, different animals feed at different levels. Conifer seeds, especially those of the Siberian Stone Pine (*Pinus sibirica*) form the main diet of a number of typical taiga animals, such as the crossbills (*Loxia*), woodpeckers (*Dryocopus, Picoides*), the Red Squirrel (*Sciurus vulgaris*), the Siberian Flying Squirrel (*Pteromys volans*) and Siberian Chipmunk (*Eutamias sibirica*). In years when the trees bear a particularly good harvest of cones, bears eat large quantities of conifer seeds. Other important foods in the taiga are berries and fungi, and, for some animals, such as the capercaillies (*Tetrao*), pine needles.

Although the fauna of the Eurasian taiga is remarkably uniform over its whole vast area, there are some differences between its eastern and western parts. It can be divided into two main faunal zones: the European-Ob, including the area west of the Yenisei; and the East Siberian taiga, east of the Yenisei. These two enormous territories show clear differences in the tree species that grow in their forests, in the marshiness of their soils, and in their climates. In eastern Siberia, with its extreme continental

climate, the very hard winters with little snow contrast with the more temperate snowy winters of western Siberia and northern Europe. Some animals, such as Musk Deer (*Moschus moschiferus*), Black-billed Capercaillie (*Tetrao parvirostris*) and the Common Treecreeper (*Certhia familiaris*), do not penetrate westwards beyond the Yenisei River – except in the area south of Krasnoyarsk, where the Yensisei boundary is broken by the large mountain ranges of Altai and Sayan, which have been colonized by many east Siberian species of animals.

The faunas of Kamchatka and Sakhalin have several distinctive features. Most of the Kamchatka Peninsula, more than 600 miles (1,000 km) long, is covered with taiga. In spite of the abundance of food there, many animals are absent from Kamchatka. The peninsula has no Elks, Musk Deer, Chipmunks, Lynxes, Siberian Weasels or other species so characteristic of the continental taiga. The main obstacle to the penetration of these animals into Kamchatka is the tundra covering the narrow neck of land joining the peninsula to the mainland. Species from open landscapes, for which the tundra presented no obstacle, are found in Kamchatka. They include the Snow Sheep, or Siberian Bighorn (*Ovis nivicola*), the Long-tailed Siberian Souslik, or Arctic Ground Squirrel (*Spermophilus undulatus*) and the Black-capped, or Kamchatka, Marmot (*Marmota camtschatica*). The Brown Bears (*Ursus arctos*) of Kamchatka are the largest in Eurasia.

The fauna of Sakhalin Island includes a number of species that have evolved there in isolation, but not as many as on Kamchatka. The Elk (*Alces alces*) is absent from Sakhalin, as are the Roe Deer (*Capreolus capreolus*), Eurasian Badger (*Meles meles*) and Siberian Weasel (*Mustela sibirica*). Compensating for this, there are more typical taiga species than in Kamchatka, including the Lynx (*Felis lynx*), Musk Deer (*Moschus moschiferus*), Siberian Chipmunk (*Eutamias sibirica*) and Siberian Flying Squirrel (*Pteromys volans*). This may be partly because the Strait of Tatar separating Sakhalin from the mainland is only 5 miles (8 km) wide at its narrowest point and freezes over in winter, enabling the animals to cross it relatively easily.

Studies of the ecology of taiga animal species has revealed that they are linked closely not specifically to the taiga, but rather to the general area of temperate-zone forest. This suggests that the taiga faunas are relatively young, and evolved in recent geological times, mainly from south-eastern newcomers. The youth of the taiga vegetation, too, is indicated on the one hand by the poverty of tree species, and on the other by the poor adjustment of its conifers to the harsh climate. Spruces

(*Picea*), firs (*Abies*) and pines (*Pinus*) are all evergreen; only the larches (*Larix*) lose their leaves.

During the late Tertiary period, about 2 million years ago, the taiga region seems to have enjoyed a warm-temperate climate, and was covered with broad-leaved forest. As a result of the Quaternary glaciations, all the warmth-loving animals must have become extinct or moved southwards. To the west and east there was nowhere but the sea to retreat to, and in the centre of this vast region they came up against obstacles in the form of mountain ranges, which for many species were insurmountable. Only a small number of species were able to remain to form today's taiga fauna.

Many biologists believe that the main nucleus of the taiga fauna evolved in eastern Siberia. The ancestors of this nucleus included both species which had survived the glaciations and could adapt to the new conditions and those which came from the mountains of Central Asia, particularly those of Tibet, and from North America.

MIXED FORESTS

Neither the landscapes nor the faunas of the mixed forests are unique; mixed-forest faunas contain elements of both the taiga and broad-leaved forest faunas, with few really characteristic animal species. On the one hand, the typical taiga animals, such as the Elk (*Alces alces*), Siberian Flying Squirrel (*Pteromys volans*), Arctic Hare (*Lepus timidus*) and Capercaillie (*Tetrao urogallus*), are widespread; on the other hand, so are most of the species typical of the western European broad-leaved forests.

Apart from the two groups of animals mentioned, there are immigrants to the western European forests from the steppes, such as the Common Hamster (*Cricetus cricetus*), European Hare (*Lepus europaeus*) and Grey Partridge (*Perdix perdix*). This is chiefly due to human activity, especially the felling of forests.

The fauna of the broad-leaved forests are much older than those of the taiga. Their nucleus evidently formed before the Quaternary glaciations, and continued to evolve in those parts of western Europe which were covered by the great ice sheets.

Apart from the belt of mixed forest in the European USSR, there are large areas of mixed forest in the south of the Far East, which extend outside the USSR. The fauna of the Amur and Ussuri river regions contains a fascinating mixture of animals, some from the harsh Siberian taiga and others from the lush sub-tropical region to the south. In winter the winds bring biting frosts from Siberia, but in summer, when warm winds blow in from the Pacific Ocean,

TOP *The lush mixed forest of Ussuriland contains a wealth of animals and plants that were able to invade the region from south-east Asia, unhampered by natural barriers, such as mountains or glaciers.*

ABOVE *One of the exotic southern members of the Soviet Far Eastern fauna is the Crested (or Greater Pied) Kingfisher, which nests on Kunashir Island just north of Japan. Its main range is from the Himalayas to Japan.*

this area is extremely damp and the vegetation grows luxuriantly, and includes many species of lianas. The forests that clothe the river valleys resound to the songs of exotic birds, and large, brightly coloured butterflies and moths float through the air. Such areas are in striking contrast to the dark conifer forests of spruce (*Picea*), fir (*Abies*) and larch (*Larix*) that grow on the great north–south Sikhote–Alin Range of mountains, whose eastern flanks plunge down to the Sea of Japan. These forests provide a home for typical members of the Siberian taiga fauna.

The reasons for the existence of such a wealth of animal species and subspecies in the Ussuri and Amur regions are connected with their unique climate and vegetation, and their geological history. From the Tertiary period onward, over a period of many millions of years, a unique local fauna evolved within the area since it escaped the ice. Throughout this time, many immigrants arrived from the forests of east Asia and Indo-Malaya. Thus the present-day Ussuri fauna is a complex mixture of survivors from pre-glacial times.

There is very little similarity between the broad-leaved forests of Europe and those of the Far East. The Ussuri and Amur fauna is generally very different from the faunas of the rest of the USSR, and has much more in common with those of China and Indo-Malaya. Because of its great interest and richness, it is discussed in detail in Chapter 7 (pages 116–134).

THE MOUNTAINS OF SOVIET CENTRAL ASIA AND THE CAUCASUS

Although the Central Asian mountain faunas are fairly distinct from those of the adjoining deserts, they do not form a neat, single unit. The high-mountain zones of the Pamir, Gissaro-Alai and Tien Shan contain outposts of the mountain fauna of the main part of Central Asia, including the Snow Leopard (*Panthera uncia*), the Argalis, or Argali (*Ovis ammon*), which is the world's largest wild sheep, and the Himalayan Snowcock (*Tetraogallus himalayensis*).

Below the eternal snow of the high mountain zone are the alpine meadows of low, lush grass, which remain fresh until the end of summer, when the sub-alpine meadows beneath have partly dried out. Here live many species of marmots (*Marmota*), the High-mountain Vole (*Alticola macrotis*), the Alpine Chough (*Pyrrhocorax graculus*) and Red-billed Chough (*P. pyrrhocorax*), several species of Snowcocks (*Tetraogallus*) and the Shore Lark, or Horned Lark (*Eremophila alpestris*).

Below the sub-alpine meadows is a belt of light juniper (*Juniperus*) forest. Alone among the animals, the White-

ABOVE *The Mountain Souslik is a small ground squirrel found only in the foothills of Mt Elbrus in the Caucasus. They live at altitudes of between about 4,000 and 10,000 ft (1,200 and 3,000 m).*

ABOVE *The Grey Marmot is a stocky ground squirrel found in the mountains of Kazakhstan and southern Siberia. Many other species of marmots live in the mountains.*

Dagestan Mountain Goats, photographed in June at the Severo Osetin Nature Reserve in the Great Caucasus; they often climb the cliffs to find a quiet resting-place.

winged Grosbeak (*Mycerobas carnipes*) is closely dependent on the junipers, its diet consisting solely of their berries. Below the juniper belt is a belt of Schrenck's Spruce (*Picea schrenckiana*) forest, occupied by creatures that are not primarily of Central Asian origin. In the spruce forests of the northern Tien Shan, for example, there are species from the taiga, such as the Hawk Owl (*Surnia ulula*), the Northern Three-toed Woodpecker (*Picoides tridactylus*), the Red Crossbill (*Loxia curvirostra*) and the Nutcracker (*Nuciraga caryocatactes*). In the Dzhungar Alatau range of the northern Tien Shan, even the Arctic Hare (*Lepus timidus*), an animal of the tundra and taiga, can be seen.

By contrast, the lower slopes of the southern Soviet Central Asian mountains contain many immigrants from the south. Birds such as the Himalayan Streaked Laughing Thrush (*Garrulax lineatus*) and Asian Paradise Flycatcher (*Terpsiphone paradisi*) live among the dense thickets of wild roses (*Rosa*), honeysuckle (*Lonicera*) and hawthorn (*Crataegus*) and the stands of walnut trees (*Juglans*). In the forests to the south-west lives the Forest Dormouse (*Dryomys nitedula*).

Both the semi-desert foothills and the dry steppes carpeting the lower slopes of the mountains, beneath about 4,800 ft (1,500 m), contain many desert animals.

The fauna of the eastern Pamir, although sparse, includes some species typical of the Central Asian tableland, especially of Tibet. Species such as the Bar-headed Goose (*Anser indicus*), the Tibetan Snowcock (*Tetraogallus tibetanus*), the Tibetan Sandgrouse (*Syrrhaptes tibetanus*) and the Brown-headed Gull (*Larus brunnicephalus*) live alongside typical Central Asian mountain animals, such as the Long-tailed Marmot (*Marmota caudata*), the High-mountain Vole (*Alticola macrotis*) and the Argalis (*Ovis ammon*). On the whole, however, the high eastern Pamir is an extremely harsh environment of bare rocks and snow, and few animals are seen.

The western Pamir is deeply dissected by narrow river gorges, as are the Gissaro-Alai Mountains to the north. It contains a number of tropical immigrants from the south, such as the Asian Paradise Flycatcher (*Terpsiphone paradisi*) and the Himalayan Streaked Laughing Thrush (*Garrulax lineatus*). Along the mountain torrents lives the beautiful White-capped Redstart, or Water Redstart (*Chaimarrornis leucocephalus*), from the Himalayan fauna.

A completely different fauna inhabits the desert tableland of Kopet-Dag, which lies beneath the level of permanent snow. Trees and shrubs grow only in the deep moist ravines. There are no marmots, Snow Leopards or most of the other species typical of the high mountains of Central Asia. On the other hand, there are the mountain Goat (*Capra aegagrus*), the Caspian Snowcock (*Tetraogallus caspius*) and the Caucasian Agama Lizard (*Agama caucasica*),

ABOVE *The handsome Great Rosefinch lives in the alpine belt of the mountains of the Caucasus and Central Asia.*

ABOVE *The magnificent Steppe Eagle is a typical bird of the steppeland, which has sadly become rarer.*

ABOVE *The European Nightjar is found in all habitats except the tundra, catching insects by night.*

all species of the Trans-Caucasus fauna. There are also some animals characteristic of the Gissaro-Alai foothills, such as the See-see Partridge (*Ammoperdix griseogularis*).

The fauna of the Caucasus region is extremely distinctive. This is understandable when one bears in mind the complex geological history of this isthmus between the Black Sea and the Caspian Sea. On its northern side, the steppe rises right up to the foothills. The fauna of the high mountain forests of the Great Caucasus has much in common with the faunas of the western and central Transcaucasus. The endemic creatures of the high mountains and forests of the Caucasus include two species of mountain goats, the West Caucasian Tur (*Capra caucasica*) and East Caucasian, or Dagestan, Tur (*Capra cylindricornis*), the Long-clawed Mole (*Prometheomys schaposchnikowi*) and the Caucasian Snowcock (*Tetraogallus caucasicus*). The distribution of the Caucasian Black Grouse (*Tetrao mlokosiewiczi*) extends a short distance outside the region, to north-east Turkey and part of northern Iran.

Discovering how the rich endemic fauna of the Caucasus evolved is a complex problem that awaits a solution by scientists. Some geologists think that many millions of years ago, long before the recent glaciations, the Great Caucasus Range was an island surrounded by sea. If we assume that the endemic animals of the Caucasus region, whose nucleus is the Great Caucasus Range, began to be isolated during this island period in the remote past, their confinement to the locality becomes easier to understand.

The main section of this book (pages 66–209) features a chapter on each of the major geographical zones of the USSR, and gives detailed information on some of their most typical and interesting animal inhabitants.

STEPPES AND DESERTS

The animal life of the steppes has a variety of origins. In general, it is transitional between the fauna of the broad-leaved forests of Europe and those of the Central Asian plains. This is not surprising, because the steppes lie between these two great natural regions. Nevertheless, there is a clear endemic nucleus of purely steppe animals, which includes various species of sousliks, or ground squirrels (*Citellus*), the Bobak Marmot (*Marmota bobac*), the Greater Fat-tailed Jerboa (*Allactaga jaculus*), the Common Hamster (*Cricetus cricetus*) and a few other mammals. Typical steppe birds include the Steppe Eagle (*Aquila rapax*), the Demoiselle Crane (*Anthropoides virgo*), the increasingly rare Great Bustard (*Otis tarda*) and Little Bustard (*Tetrax tetrax*) and the Sociable Lapwing, or Sociable Plover (*Chettusia gregaria*).

Included in the Red Book of the USSR, the Bukhara Deer, a race of the Red Deer (called Wapiti in North America) is now found only in thickets along desert river valleys.

Being 'cold-blooded', few reptiles can live in the mountains, except in hot, arid areas, such as the Kopet-Dag Range, Turkmenia, home to this Little Caspian Gecko.

Thanks to the abundance of food, animal life in the virgin steppe is rich in numbers if not in variety of species. The Saiga Antelope (*Saiga tatarica*), for example, may form large herds, and its total population numbers over a million (see also page 167). Like other hoofed mammals of open country with nowhere to hide from enemies, it has evolved excellent sight and an ability to run very fast to escape danger. Rodents, by contrast, hide underground. Most of the steppe rodents dig only shallow burrows, but some, such as the Bobak Marmot (*Marmota bobac*), tunnel much deeper. The abundant population of birds of prey depends mainly on the presence of large numbers of rodents.

The Mongolian and Trans-Baikal steppes are isolated by mountain ranges, and contain a mainly Mongolian fauna.

The Central Asian deserts belong to one of three main groups: gravelly, clayey or sandy. The gravelly deserts, with salty *solonchak* soils, are particularly inhospitable places, and few animals live there. Clayey deserts also contain few species; their main vegetation consists of scattered wormwood, or sagebrush, bushes (*Artemisia*). In early spring, however, when plentiful rain falls in the southern half of Central Asia, the clay desert is covered with short, thick grass that teems with animal life. The clay deserts' most typical animals are the Small Five-toed Jerboa (*Allactaga elater*), the Chinese Striped Hamster (*Cricetulus barabensis*), various species of sousliks (*Citellus*), the Greater Sand Plover (*Charadrius leschenaultii*) and the Steppe Agama lizard (*Agama sanguinolenta*). The sandy deserts have considerably richer and more distinctive faunas than the other types, even in their most extreme form, the sand-dune deserts, with endless vistas of crescent-shaped barkhan dunes.

3 CONSERVATION

State ownership of the land, including its surface, rivers, lakes, mountains, forests and coastal waters, is the basis of the conservation of nature in the USSR, but the aims and tasks of nature conservation have changed with the times.

There was considerable understanding of the need for conservation of game, forestry and other resources long before any legal document on the subject existed. The first laws limiting the hunting of game animals and birds appeared in Kiev in the eleventh century.

During the seventeenth century, 67 hunting laws were enacted, protecting the lands where the valuable fur-bearing Sable lived, along the rivers of northern Europe. In 1683, when forestry began to be organized, the felling of trees was forbidden in the sable grounds of Siberia. During the rule of Tsar Peter the Great (1682–1725), forest conservation was introduced, both to reduce flooding and to protect individual species of trees.

ABOVE *The Sable, a member of the weasel family with one of the most valuable pelts of any mammal, is now protected from severe overhunting by strict conservation measures.*

At the beginning of the twentieth century, Russian scientists began to formulate their ideas on the conservation of nature. In 1909 the Russian Geographical Society set up a nature conservancy committee. Thanks to its activities, the first law concerning nature reserves was enacted in 1916.

LEFT *A young Siberian Crane; saving this rare bird is the most famous success story of Soviet conservation, and a superb example of international co-operation.*

In the first five years after the 1917 Revolution, more than 200 decrees and regulations for the conservation of nature came into force, most of them on Lenin's initiative. In 1921 came the creation of the State Committee for the Conservation of Nature, followed in 1924 by the All-Russian Society for the Conservation of Nature.

The next stage of development came between 1957 and 1963, when individual legislation on nature conservation was instituted in the constituent republics of the USSR. For the first time it was decreed that the conservation of nature was a most important task of the State, and the first conservationist approach was made to the proper use of natural plant and animal communities in all their variety and complexity.

After the new Soviet constitution came into force in 1977, the Government drafted a series of laws which attempted to improve the system of nature conservation. At present a complex system for monitoring natural resources is being worked out and introduced. Monitoring stations keep a watchful eye on various types of background pollution. The purpose of their work is to establish the reaction of natural communities to general, background pollution, identify its effects and make appropriate recommendations for decisions at State and international levels. The USSR takes part in many international programmes for nature conservation and has signed bilateral treaties with the USA, Japan, and many other countries in the field of environmental protection.

Air pollution legislation

Separate parts of the environment are protected, bearing in mind the interaction of all its elements. Air pollution is regulated by the USSR's law 'On the Protection of Atmospheric Air'. Effective cleaning devices must be installed at factories which release pollutants into the atmosphere. A great deal of research is being done towards designing new and more effective types of cleaning devices, and new methods and equipment for pollution control are being introduced constantly. Apart from its obvious benefits for wildlife, improvement in air quality creates new possibilities for planting trees and creating parks in towns and for developing suburban green areas.

Water pollution legislation

Water pollution is dealt with by basic State water legislation and by individual laws in the various republics. All water has to be protected from pollution, unintentional

TOP *There is considerable concern among conservationists in the USSR about the pollution of Lake Baikal, which contains some 960 species of animals and 400 species of plants that are found nowhere else in the world.*

ABOVE *The diminutive Caspian Seal is found only in the Caspian Sea, the world's largest inland sea; as with its relative the Baikal Seal, protection from hunting has helped this attractive mammal to survive.*

damming or exhaustion, whether it is a source of supply for the population, an energy source, a means of transport, or a home for wild plants and animals. Lakes and rivers are also important for recreation and tourism. New industrial developments must incorporate cleaning devices before being allowed to start work, and equipment is also being installed on farms to prevent fertilizers and industrial pollutants being washed into rivers.

Special attention is given to protecting major seas and lakes, such as the Caspian Sea, Black Sea, Sea of Azov, Baltic Sea, Lake Baikal and Lake Balkhash, to maintain both their purity and the total volume of water they hold. Despite this, there is considerable concern over the pollution of some lakes, especially Lake Baikal (see page 57). Because their water is used for essential irrigation, great problems have occurred with the maintenance of the water levels of the Aral Sea and Lake Balkhash. The water level of the Sea of Azov is steadily falling and its salinity is increasing. A number of measures are planned to correct this disturbing situation and to re-establish the fish stocks. Underground water also belongs to the State, and a variety of legislation has been passed with the aim of controlling its pollution and exploitation.

Forest conservation

The management of forests, all of which are State-owned, is another extremely important aspect of nature conservation. The USSR contains vast areas of forest, but its problems of forest conservation are acute. Besides serving as a source of immense amounts of timber, the forest brings other benefits, such as water conservation, and the protection of the soil and cultivated land, not to mention its vital role as a home for wild plants and animals.

Forest conservation is supported by State legislation as well as by the individual forestry codes of the various republics. Forests are regulated to keep the trees at their best, both in variety of species and productivity. Legislation may forbid felling for reasons of soil protection, water conservation or protection of cultivated land. Methods of timber haulage that harm the soil or growing saplings are forbidden. In accordance with its situation, functions, and economic significance, a forest may be classified in one of three groups. Depending on its group, and its management, a decision is made whether to take a particular area of land out of production for a particular purpose. Woodland of the first group has high conservation value and includes woods in nature reserves, national parks, reservoir catchments, shelter belts, and woods near hospitals or in green belts. Forestry in these areas is planned above all with the aim of saving or re-establishing the natural forest environment.

Apart from forests, other types of vegetation have by law to be conserved, not only isolated pockets of rare and endangered species, but also whole communities of vegetation, which may in future serve as a source of new crops or medicinal plants.

Animal protection

The protection of animals is now regulated by the 1980 law 'For the Protection and Rational Exploitation of the Animal World'. This important legislation regulates the protection and use for economic purposes of wild animals living on the land or under it, in the water, or in the air, permanently or temporarily in the USSR or along the whole of its continental shelf.

Wild animals regarded as rare or endangered, and those which are widely hunted for their meat or fur, or exploited for other economic purposes, receive special protection. Similar protection is given to animals useful for the biological control of farm or other pests.

The legislation requires that the rules for hunting and

ABOVE *Many plants, as well as animals, enjoy full protection in Soviet nature reserves; this Alpine Squill, found in the USSR only in the Caucasus, was photographed at the Lagodekh Nature Reserve.*

ABOVE *The European Beaver is one of the animals to have benefited most from the strict control of hunting and other conservation measures, including protection of its habitat and re-stocking of nature reserves.*

fishing be strictly observed; that help be given to improve the animals' conditions of existence and to ensure healthy breeding levels to maintain populations; and that the exploitation of stocks of hunted animals be regulated. It is forbidden to exterminate animals by any method if they do not harm the economy or the people's health, but conservation does not exclude the control of harmful animals. These include mice, rats and other rodents, any animals which carry diseases dangerous to cattle, and some predators, such as the wolverine (*Gulo gulo*).

LEFT *The Caucasus Biosphere Nature Reserve looks at its best in May, when the rhododendron bushes adorn the mountain slopes with their magnificent flowers.*
RIGHT *In recent years, the dashing Peregrine Falcon has become much rarer over most of the USSR, as it has throughout its vast world range, due mainly to pollution with pesticides; fortunately it is still quite common in the Soviet tundra.*

Firm measures for the protection of animals, and for the suppression of poaching and regulation of hunting, have produced excellent results in re-establishing the populations of a number of valuable animals, including the Elk (*Alces alces*), Beaver (*Castor fiber*), Saiga Antelope (*Saiga tatarica*), and Sable (*Martes zibellina*). The European Bison (*Bison bonasus*) is no longer threatened with imminent extinction. The conservation of rare and endangered animals is discussed in detail below.

Specially protected land

Land which is specially protected plays an important part in the USSR's programme of nature conservation. Unfortunately, its progress has sometimes been hampered by lack of overall co-ordination, because the various nature reserves and national parks are under the control of different ministries or departments. In July 1985 the Supreme Soviet made a special study of nature conservation and pointed out the need to co-ordinate work between the various conservation bodies and set up a joint leadership. This unification has not yet been achieved but it is likely that it will be in the near future.

The main type of special conservation area in the USSR is the nature reserve or *zapovednik*, which is the most rigorously protected type. The country's network of these reserves has been planned scientifically with the overall aims of national nature conservation in mind. The USSR has created a firm foundation for the State nature reserves by forbidding any economic activity in them. Unorganized visits are forbidden to non-specialists, including tourists. The country's nature reserves serve as 'barometers',

indicating the general health of natural populations. As far as possible, they are maintained in their natural condition, unchanged by man. They are needed for the maintenance of genetic resources, for protecting unique landscapes or the habitats of plants and animals, and for the study of the processes in a completely natural community.

International conservation programmes

The fruits of this research are shared with conservationists in other parts of the world. The USSR plays an active role in many international conservation programmes, including those of specialist agencies of the United Nations, international government organizations and professional non-government organizations, such as the International union for the Conservation of Nature (IUCN), based in Geneva, and the associated World Wildlife Fund, the International Council for Bird Preservation (ICBP), and the International Waterfowl Research Bureau (IWRB). The USSR hosts many important international conferences and congresses on nature conservation, and is a signatory to numerous conventions and treaties for the protection of wildlife. UNESCO's system of biosphere reserves, now created in many countries, has the same purpose as those which have existed for 65 years in the USSR — the protection of the genetic diversity of plants and animals and of ecosystems in all their variety, and the furtherance of scientific research into natural processes. Another important development was the publication in 1966 of the first Red Data Book of the IUCN, listing and describing the status of rate or endangered animals throughout the world; 1978 saw the publication of the first Soviet Red Data Book (see pages 60 and 220 for further details).

ABOVE *Desert nature reserves, such as the 862 sq mile (223,300 ha) of this one, in Ustyurt, Kazakhstan, established as recently as 1985, protect a wide variety of rare and endangered plants, reptiles, birds and mammals.*

In 1979, the Soviet government upgraded the laboratory of the same name into the All-Union Research Institute for Nature Reserves and the Conservation of Nature (see also page 60). Work on nature conservation is also undertaken by many other organizations, including research institutes of the USSR Academy of Sciences and various universities or other institutes of higher education. Intensive investigation is continuing, not only into the biology and ecology. of a whole range of animal and plant communities, but also into the legal aspects of nature conservation and the associated economic and social problems. Attention is increasingly being turned towards educating the public about the need for conservation, and there have been many recent successes in this area. However, much still remains to be done. It is sadly still true that there is little appreciation of the urgency of conservation in many parts of the country, especially in remote, inaccessible areas where many important nature reserves are located. Poaching still continues, and conservationists have to be constantly vigilant in their attempts at thwarting illegal hunting, a task in which they are fully supported by the law enforcement authorities.

Long-term planning

Because of the increasing population, fewer and fewer areas remain untouched by man, despite the vast size of the USSR. Even the most rudimentary development, such as the construction of a few workers' houses in the forest, can damage at least part of a community of animals and plants. Major disruptions, such as the carving out of a great highway or the building of a huge dam, may threaten the entire community. Excessive exploitation of individual species of plants and animals, or destruction of their habitat, leads to their disappearance from the area. Each species serves as a vital part of the whole complex community. Like any other system, a natural community remains stable only when all its parts are interlinked and functioning interdependently. The removal of only one, seemingly unimportant species may affect the stability of the whole community and disturb a harmony that may have taken many thousands of years to evolve.

Monitoring pollution

Just as in other countries, there has been much concern in the USSR over the use of chemical methods of controlling pests, diseases and weeds. Comparative investigations undertaken in the forests of the Voronezh Nature Reserve, in central Russia, about 300 miles (500 km) south of Moscow, where chemical pesticides and weedkillers were never used, and in neighbouring commercially managed forests yielded interesting results. Comparing similar plantations, there were three times as many birds in those of the nature reserves as in those of the commercially managed forests. The populations of useful insects showed a similar trend. My own studies in Lithuania, from 1979 to 1981, showed how various changes in the bird populations of pine forests were caused by air pollution; the air contained oxides of sulphur and nitrogen discharged in the smoke from factory chimneys. The bird population altered,

TOP *Air pollution has damaged the delicate living community of the Lithuanian pine forests, like the one seen in this photograph, as evidenced by the author's study of the changes in the bird population from 1979–81.*

ABOVE *Animals such as this woodland* Poligonia *butterfly serve as living monitors of pollution.*

the birds' fertility fell, and there were changes in the natural interrelationships between the species, as well as in the competition between them — especially among birds that nest in tree-holes.

The USSR is currently setting up a nationwide system for monitoring environmental pollution, designed to detect the smallest changes in natural communities against a background of overall low-level pollution. It is a sad but inescapable fact that there is nowhere on this planet that is completely free from pollution. The ease with which pollution spreads is dramatically demonstrated by the traces of DDT found in Antarctic animals. Investigations are continuing in Soviet nature reserves which will help scientists foresee the effects on major habitats and communities of pollution, whether it remains at the same level or increases. The forecasts that emerge are passed on to a great variety of decision makers at both national and international levels.

There is growing concern about the state of Lake Baikal, the world's deepest lake, which contains about 960 species of animals and 400 of plants that occur nowhere else. Many scientists believe that the lake is excessively polluted and, judging by recent pronouncements made by the Soviet government, a series of even more stringent measures than those already in force will soon be put into effect in an attempt to reduce the pollution. Levels of pollution from various industries sited near the lake are currently being checked, and, in cases of infringement of the law, various sanctions are applied, ranging from fines to closure of the offending works.

The natural world is indivisible; it is a single, giant ecosystem, subject to natural laws of development and stability, and no amount of ingenuity on the part of scientists and technologists can alter this basic fact of life. Human activity is now so intense that there is a real danger of disturbing the stability of the entire system, on which every one of us, rich or poor, depends. It is no exaggeration to say that humanity is — perhaps sooner than we think — faced with the task of self-preservation. The USSR is co-operating with other countries in a concerted attempt to understand more of what is happening and what can be done to improve the situation.

Nature reserves in the USSR

At the time of writing, there are 147 nature reserves in the USSR, occupying a total area of 59,805 sq miles (154,883 sq km). For the largest country in the world, which covers a staggering area of 8,648,500 sq miles (22,402,200 sq km),

ABOVE *The 1,017 sq mile (2,635 sq km) Caucasus Biosphere Nature Reserve was established in 1924 in the western Caucasus. It protects a great variety of endemic species.*

ABOVE *One of the 1,500 species of plants found in the Caucasus Biosphere Reserve is the bellflower* Campanula bibirschteniana, *found only in the Caucasus.*

or one-sixth of the earth's land surface, this may not seem particularly impressive; the nature reserves occupy only 0.52 per cent of the USSR. However, these are not the only protected areas; there are also seven national parks, seven nature-reserve/hunting-management units and numerous other conservation areas. Although these do not receive as high a degree of protection as the nature reserves, they form a vital refuge for wildlife in many parts of the USSR, and add to the total of land receiving at least some degree of protection. This total is due to increase annually because of the planned creation of new nature reserves and national parks.

Nature reserves have played an important part in counting and monitoring the populations of especially valuable animals, such as the Beaver (*Castor fiber*), Sable (*Martes zibellina*) and Elk (*Alces alces*). Many species of rare or endangered wild animals have been saved from extinction by being protected in nature reserves, including the Goral (*Nemorhaedus goral*), a mountain goat; the Sika

Another view of the desert plateau of Ustyurt, west Kazakhstan, declared a state nature reserve in 1985. A number of other new reserves are planned, including one in the Betpak Dala semi-desert and one at Lake Balkhash.

Deer (*Cervus nippon*); the Bukhara Red Deer (*Cervus elaphus bactrianus*), the middle-eastern race of the Red Deer; the Asian Wild Ass, or Kulan (*Equus hemionus*); the Goitred Gazelle (*Gazella subgutturosa*) and the Siberian race of the Tiger (*Panthera tigris altaica*). The nature reserves also serve as refuges for a whole host of rare plants. If necessary, the eggs or young of animals and seeds or seedlings of plants may be taken by authorized workers for re-establishment of the species elsewhere.

Surrounding each nature reserve is an area of semi-protected land, which serves as a buffer zone between the nature reserve and the surrounding country. Existing economic activity is allowed to continue in the buffer zone, provided that it does not harm the reserve.

Nature reserve management

The task of managing a nature reserve is complex, because we do not know enough about the way natural ecosystems develop. Any human intervention in the natural life of a reserve will, to some extent, disturb the structures, functioning and development of the natural ecosystems and of their individual communities of animals and plants, threatening the reserve's very basis of existence. Many conservationists believe that it is wise to avoid any interference with natural processes in a reserve, if possible. Such interference should be resorted to only when all the likely effects can be accurately forecast and when the situation that needs to be changed can clearly be remedied or reversed.

There is plenty of evidence from Soviet nature reserves that very strict enforcement of a well-planned, non-interventionist conservation programme can re-establish a damaged ecosystem. This policy can have beneficial side-effects, too, such as a reduction in the numbers of various pests. For example, after tree felling was prohibited in the Voronezh Nature Reserve in central Russia, some 300 miles (500 km) south of Moscow, the spread of pine canker disease diminished. Similarly, in the Khoper Nature Reserve, another forest-steppe reserve about 150 miles (240 km) to the east, the cessation of felling was followed by a reduction in the numbers of caterpillars of the oak tortrix moth, which had up to then eaten 100 per cent of the first leaves.

Education and research

Nature reserve staff devote a great deal of time to the education of local people in the basics of nature conservation and ecology. They also appear frequently on Soviet radio or television and give many public lectures. Just like their Western counterparts, some nature reserves have set up study centres or museums where the public can learn more about the plant and animal life of the reserve. There may even be a 'mini-zoo', where animals are kept and bred in captivity. In some nature reserves there is a lecture room where visitors can watch films or listen to talks on nature conservation. It may be possible to visit certain reserves at particular times of the year, but the route generally lies through the outer protected area or along the boundaries of the nature reserve.

The varied scientific research carried out on Soviet nature reserves includes work connected with forestry, palaeontology, botany, zoology, ecology, game manage-

ment and soil science. Valuable work has been done in counting and assessing the changing populations of animals and plants in the reserves. Much of the work involves long-term observation and investigation. The scientific results are published in various periodicals, monographs and other special publications.

Increasingly, scientists and naturalists from other countries — from famous professionals, such as Sir Peter Scott and Gerald Durrell, to organized parties of amateur birdwatchers — have been able to visit Soviet nature reserves. There is growing co-operation between conservationists in the West and their Soviet counterparts, in which they take part in joint research programmes and share their knowledge and expertise.

National parks

National parks are relatively new to the USSR. The first one was created in 1972 in Estonia, and others soon followed, also in the Baltic region, in Latvia and Lithuania. More recently, national parks have been established in other parts of the USSR, including ones in Kazakhstan and Kirghizia and near Moscow.

The legislation governing the parks is more complex than that relating to the nature reserves. The parks contain areas in which economic activity is not banned completely. Usually, they also contain a nature reserve area, representing the best example of the original natural environment and its wildlife, where economic activity and visits by tourists are forbidden. In the *zakaznik*, or sanctuary zone, tourists are allowed but economic activity is strictly limited. Finally, there are areas of more intensive economic activity, where the reasonable and controlled exploitation of nature, including fishing, is allowed, and where people live. The nature reserve areas of a park is thus protected by the large buffer zone of the sanctuary surrounding it.

Much valuable conservation work and scientific research is done in the national parks. Tourists can visit all the USSR's national parks, apart from the reserve areas at their core, without paying any admission charges.

Sanctuaries

Sanctuaries (*zakazniki*) are another type of nature conservation area. A sanctuary consists of land partly withdrawn from economic activity because it contains outstanding landscape, rare plants or a breeding colony of endangered birds, for example. Controlled hunting is allowed on some sanctuaries. Many of the sanctuaries — or parts of them, at least — are fully protected only at certain seasons, especially those that contain breeding colonies of birds. During the nesting season, there is a ban on all economic activity on the land and on visits by anyone but authorized people. When the birds have finished breeding, farmers may be permitted to graze cattle and visitors re-admitted.

There are differences in status and in the details of their administration between sanctuaries in the different republics making up the USSR. For example, there is a sanctuary at Lake Alakol, in the south-east of the Kazakh Soviet Socialist Republic in south-central USSR, which contains a nesting colony of the rare Relict Gull (*Larus relictus*). Two wardens, aided by modern transport, protect the birds and their habitat. In Lithuania, by contrast, there are almost 200 sanctuaries, yet this Baltic republic's administration does not allow for any permanent on-site conservation staff. Instead, there are inspectors of nature conservation in each one of the republic's 44 district. These district inspectors are provided with jeeps and other means of transport and spend most of their time on active duty out in the field. Inspectors of hunting and fishing play an important part in checking the effectiveness of the conservation measures. Together with the inspectors of nature conservation, they make regular circuits of the areas under their control, and also 'swoops' on specific localities where they suspect the presence of poachers.

Rare and endangered species: the Red Books

Nature conservation measures at many sites include the protection and maintenance or growth of populations of rare or endangered plants and animals. Most of these species are listed in the Red Data Book of the IUCN (see also page 55), and the Soviet government and scientists recognize their moral obligation to the world to do all they can to protect species that are rare or threatened with extinction. These are also covered in more detail in the Soviet Red Book, first published in 1978. In 1985 a new edition of the USSR's Red Book appeared, with many changes and additions. It is published in two volumes, one for plants and the other for animals. The plant volume contains entries on 444 different species. The animal volume contains 204 species of insects, 9 of fishes, 9 of amphibians, 37 of reptiles, 80 of birds and 94 of mammals. Species listed in the Red Data Book of the IUCN which occur in the Soviet Union are automatically included in the Red Book of the USSR. Red Books are also published for each separate republic of the USSR.

A Siberian Crane chick examines its reflection one day after hatching at the International Crane Foundation, USA.

Among the rarest mammals and birds of the USSR are two subspecies of the Leopard, the Amur Leopard (*Panthera pardus orientalis*) and the Anatolian Leopard (*P.p. tullianus*); the Siberian race of the Tiger (*Panthera tigris altaica*), the world's largest living wild cat; the Caracal Lynx (*Felis caracal*); two species of mountain goats, the Goral (*Naemorhedus goral*) and the Markhor (*Capra falconeri*), the world's largest wild goat; the Desert Dormouse (*Selevinia betpakdalensis*); the Oriental White Stork (*Ciconia boyciana*); a duck called the Chinese Merganser (*Mergus squamatus*); the Manchurian Crane (*Grus japonensis*) and the Siberian, or Great White, Crane (*Grus leucogeranus*); the Little Curlew (*Numenius minutus*) and Slender-billed Curlew (*Numenius tenuirostris*); the Spotted Greenshank (*Tringa guttifer*); the Relict Gull (*Larus relictus*); the Tibetan Sandgrouse (*Syrrhaptes tibetanus*); the Reed, or Yangtze, Parrotbill (*Paradoxornis heudei*); and Hodgson's Bushchat (*Saxicola insignis*).

Nature reserves form vital sanctuaries for many of these species and their habitats, and some are taken into captivity, where there is a good chance of building up healthy breeding stocks for later resettlement in the wild. Various scientific institutions in the USSR are concerned with the conservation of rare plants and animals, notably the All-Union Scientific Institute for Nature Reserves and Nature Conservation, whose Department of Animal Protection is under the directorship of the eminent scientist and pioneering conservationist Professor Vladimir Flint. It was at Professor Flint's suggestion that captive breeding stations were created.

The USSR maintains a sensible balance between conservation and controlled hunting of species such as this Elk (called Moose in North America), the world's largest deer.

Captive breeding programmes

To date, captive breeding programmes have been set up for birds of prey, including the Lammergeier, or Bearded Vulture (*Gypaetus barbatus*) and Peregrine Falcon (*Falco peregrinus*), cranes, waterfowl, the Great Bustard (*Otis tarda*) and, among mammals, the Goitred Gazelle (*Gazella subgutturosa*). The work involved in captive breeding is slow and painstaking and needs a great deal of effort, sometimes for limited results. International co-operation was required to save the Siberian Crane (*Grus leucogeranus*). This is the

USSR's rarest species of crane, and one of the world's rarest birds, with a population estimated at less than 2,000 birds. 'Operation Siberian Crane' was a programme initiated jointly by Professor Flint and Dr George Archibald, the Director of the International Crane Foundation, based in Baraboo, Wisconsin, USA. This unique international rescue operation to maintain a viable population of

Red-breasted Geese in July on the Garbita River in the Taimyr Peninsula. Breeding only in three areas in Siberia, this rare goose is totally protected in the USSR.

cranes was aimed mainly at providing safe wintering sites. Siberian Cranes nest only in two relatively small areas of Siberian tundra, in Yakutia and along the lower reaches of the River Ob, both of which are relatively safe from disturbance, thanks to the efforts of conservationists in educating the local people to help protect the birds. It is a different matter when the cranes make their annual southward migration in autumn to wetlands in Iran, India and China. The great birds may be killed by hunters on their long journey, and when they arrive, they may find their wintering quarters have been drained and developed, or lie stagnant and polluted, especially in India.

To try and persuade the cranes to use a safer wintering area, the scientists decided to create an artificial breeding population in a nature reserve in the European part of the USSR. The Oka Nature Reserve, about 300 miles (480 km) south-west of Moscow, was chosen, because of its considerable area of marshland and large staff of specialists. Since only one chick usually survives from the clutch of two eggs in a crane's nest in the wild, taking one egg from each of the nests in the Yakutia breeding area involved virtually no sacrifice of the population there. The precious eggs were flown by helicopter and aircraft to Moscow, and from there via London and Chicago to the International Crane Foundation at Baraboo. The chicks hatched out and

laid their first eggs when they reached sexual maturity at six years old. In 1985, almost ten years after the experiment began, these eggs were flown to the Oka Reserve and placed in the nests of Common Cranes (*Grus grus*), which make ideal foster parents for their larger and much rarer relatives.

Recently, 12 young Oriental White Storks (*Ciconia boyciana*), another rare species, which are found only in the Soviet Far East, have been sent from the USSR to Walsrode for breeding in captivity.

Regional aspects of conservation in the USSR

The vastness of the Soviet Union, the fact that it straddles several geographical and biological belts, and various other factors unconnected with this zonation, including human influences, mean that it contains a remarkable variety of landscapes and associated animal and plant communities. In turn, this presents a variety of problems to Soviet conservationists, who need to use a wide range of methods and a great deal of imagination in their attempts at solving them. Apart from the general task of nature conservation throughout the USSR, there are specific needs linked to regional or more local conditions.

TUNDRA

The harsh climates of the tundra and wooded tundra create some of the toughest environments on earth for living things. The very short growing season combines with the bitter cold, strong winds and driving snow, and the thick layer of permanently frozen ground, or permafrost, to make life extremely hazardous. The generally slow growth and maturation of tundra animals may make it difficult to establish reasonable stocks of animals and plants. Damaged areas of tundra take a long time to recover; the frozen, marshy soils are easily deformed by the giant caterpillar tracks or tyres of heavy vehicles. It is especially difficult to protect frozen ground from damage by heat sources, such as hot waste water from industrial installations. Surface pipelines cut across the migration routes of Reindeer. Conservationists working in these harsh northern lands are concerned particularly with protecting the fragile surface layers from damage, preventing fires, saving the Reindeers' pastureland from overgrazing, maintaining natural migration routes, and restricting or banning tree-felling in the wooded tundra areas and near the northern limits of the great dark coniferous forests of the taiga. There are several tundra nature reserves (see page 89).

FORESTS

In the forest zones, nature conservation is intimately linked with forestry activities. Special problems arise with the excessive use of chemical insecticides against forest pests, and conservation programmes are aimed at preventing the deaths of birds and useful insects and the poisoning of the soil. Large areas of marsh within a forest, unproductive in terms of forestry, have been reclaimed by drainage. But continuous drainage has long been considered a narrow approach, because it may dry out the soil too much, breaking up the constant flow of nutrients to the rivers in the water from the marshes, as well as destroying habitats for wildlife, valuable berry-bearing bushes and hunting areas. There are many nature reserves in the taiga and in

Marshland, under threat from drainage in many areas, is protected here at the Lahemaa National Park in the pine forest belt of Estonia, the northernmost of the USSR's three Baltic republics. This was the first national park to be created in the USSR, in 1972; other ones include those in the Baltic republics of Latvia and Lithuania.

the broadleaved and mixed forest zones (see pages 111–13 and 134–7).

STEPPES

In the steppe and wooded steppe zones, special efforts are being made to combat erosion by wind or water, dust storms and excessive soil salinity, and to establish and

ABOVE *Spring brings colour to the Repetek Biosphere Nature reserve in the Kara-Kum desert in Turkmenia.*
ABOVE RIGHT *A Desert Acacia bush at Repetek.*

maintain plantations which protect the grassland from the wind. Forest edges and forests with a distinct tiered arrangement of plants need special conservation, as do the relatively small areas of virgin steppe, with their unique vegetation, that still remain between the vast cultivated areas. Fortunately, most such land is protected in nature reserves (see pages 174–5 and page 191).

DESERTS
In the semi-deserts and deserts of the temperate and subtropical belts, a vital task is to prevent too much of the soil from blowing away in the wind, especially with stabilized sandy soils. Trees are planted to act as shelter belts against the wind, and also plants with extensive, vigorous root systems, to bind the light, sandy soil. Excessive salination of the soil must be prevented and overgrazing by cattle is forbidden. Pastureland and arable land in deserts are especially vulnerable because of the shortage of water. There are several major desert nature reserves (see pages 191–2).

MOUNTAINS
In mountain regions, with their vegetation arranged in altitudinal belts, a major task of conservation is to maintain the soil-protecting role of plants, since their removal from a steep slope inevitably causes soil erosion and landslides. It is important to prevent overgrazing, too, especially by sheep. Nature conservation in mountains also involves the prevention of avalanches and mud-flows, protecting not only human lives but whole communities of plants and animals. Caves, areas of extinct or active volcanoes, unique formations of weathered rocks and so on present unusual challenges for conservationists. Various mountain reserves help to preserve these splendid natural habitats and their exciting flora and fauna (see pages 162–5).

The State administration of conservation

Executive and management roles in nature conservation are played by members of the central government's Council of Ministers, the Councils of Ministers in each republic, executive committees of councils of peoples' deputies, and by other bodies specially empowered under

LEFT *Rarely seen, let alone photographed, the Ibisbill is a scarce, highly specialized mountain wader that is restricted to high-mountain rivers with shingle banks in Central Asia and the Himalayas. There are more pictures of this exciting bird, and a full description, on pages 154–5.*

BELOW *A view of the 1640 ft (500 m) deep Aksu Canyon in the Aksu-Dzhabagly Nature Reserve, established in 1927 in the Talass Alatau Range of the western Tien Shan Mountains.*

Soviet legislation. These are the USSR State Committee of Agricultural Industry (Agroprom); the USSR Ministry of Land Improvement and Water Economy; the USSR State Forestry Committee; the USSR State Fishery Committee; the USSR State Committee for Meteorology and Control of the Natural Environment; the USSR Ministry for Energy and Electrification; the USSR Ministry of Health; the USSR Ministry of Geology; the USSR State Plan Committee; and the USSR State Committee for Science and Technology. Each of these bodies has specific duties towards the conservation and controlled use of nature.

There are also State Committees for Nature Conservation in the republics of Ukraine, Belorussia, Azerbaidzhan, Lithuania, Moldavia and Georgia, and a Ministry for Nature Conservation and Forestry in the republic of Estonia. The co-operation of trade unions, scientific institutions and societies for nature conservation in the various republics plays an important role in the co-ordination of nature conservation. Societies that play a part in this connection include the USSR Geographical Society, the USSR Theriological Society (for the study of mammals) and the USSR Ornithological Society. The basis of nature conservation is taught both in schools and in universities and other institutes of higher education.

4 THE ICY NORTH

An introduction to the region

The Arctic coastline stretches for thousands of miles along Soviet territory. The cold grey waters of the Arctic Ocean wash its beaches and rocky cliffs, and the harsh cries from the great crowded seabird colonies resound in the short summer of the bleak but beautiful landscape. Inland, the treeless tundra stretches as far as the eye can see, occupying an enormous area of the Soviet Union. Here in the far north, one is surrounded by countless examples of nature's struggle for existence among tough conditions.

The traveller to these desolate regions is left with many powerful impressions: the carpet of tiny, bright flowers covering the tundra in summer; the sea immobilized by ice; the mighty Polar Bears, kings of this glittering world; the herds of Reindeer swimming across the rivers; and the haunting cries of the rare Siberian White Cranes echoing across the lonely landscape. The north includes all this — and more. Here it is possible really to see and understand the remarkable resilience of nature, still completely untouched by human influence in some places, and also to reflect on the transience of life during the short summer.

ABOVE *The coast of the Chukchi Peninsula, viewed from the Bering Sea: a scene that epitomizes the uncompromising harshness and bleakness of the high Arctic — and this picture was taken in July!*
LEFT *Polar Bears wander immense distances over the Arctic coasts and ice floes; this female and her cub were photographed in the Wrangel Island Nature Reserve in June.*

The northern seas, bays and inlets are inhospitable places. The black rocks of the island cliffs plunge sheer into the ice-cold, lead-grey waters. Despite this apparently uninviting aspect, these areas may contain flourishing animal communities, although they are rich only in number of individuals, not in diversity of species, as there are few distinct niches for different species to exploit.

The populations of some of the inhabitants may reach astonishing levels. The islands are famous for their vast seabird colonies; everywhere, Arctic Foxes hunt; from afar, one can hear the roars of the Walruses echoing from their breeding grounds; while masses of fish, molluscs, starfish and sea urchins live in the fertile coastal waters. The sparse but tenacious covering of plants manages to survive the harsh conditions by a range of ingenious adaptations.

Further south, in the vast flat spaces of the tundra, the lakes and rivers are uncountable. The unique beauty of the tundra vegetation is unforgettable, with its unusual combinations of soft, subtle colours. Here there are hills and plains, marshes and dry, stony places: the tundra, of which there are various quite distinct types, is anything but monotonous when one really studies it. During the brief summer, the tundra becomes alive with a variety of bird life. I shall return to this fascinating world later.

The Arctic deserts

The north of the USSR can be divided into two great geographical belts, the Arctic and the sub-Arctic. In the high Arctic latitudes, few living things manage to survive in the polar deserts that occupy much of these regions. Such areas in the USSR are Novaya Zemlya ('New Land'), Zemlya Frantsa Iosifa ('Franz Josef Land') and Severnaya Zemlya ('Northern Land'). These three island groups are covered with ice and snow almost the whole year round. The frozen seas contain huge brilliant white icebergs, and often the only living things to be seen are the equally white Ivory Gulls (*Pagophila eburnea*) wheeling overhead.

The warmest months here are July and August, when the mean temperature rises to 40 to 41°F (4 to 5°C); for most of the rest of the year, the temperature remains well below freezing. The frozen soil thaws only slightly during this brief summer, remaining permanently frozen as a rock-hard layer of permafrost ranging from a few inches to hundreds of feet below the surface. Vast areas are covered with gravelly screes. In these cold desert conditions, there is very little water available for plant growth. Erosion by water is virtually non-existent, so the thin Arctic soils are usually neutral or only slightly acid.

Arctic plants

Vegetation in the Arctic is extremely sparse. Various species of algae, lichens and mosses live there, and a few flowering plants, of which the most familiar is the Arctic Poppy (*Papaver radicatum*), manage to survive, too. To the south of the Arctic belt grow stunted willows (*Salix*) and the delicate little flowers of Mountain Avens (*Dryas octopetala*). The plants' productivity is low – only 2 tons per acre (5 tonnes per hectare) of dry material each year. An interesting observation is that the mass of living vegetation above ground is greater than that of the underground roots. The opposite is true in the tundra and in the deserts at other latitudes. This may be because the plants in the Arctic can obtain very little food from the frozen soil, and must rely mainly on that manufactured in their leaves by the process of photosynthesis.

Animals of the Arctic

As with the plants, there are very few different species of animals in the extreme north, although there may be huge numbers of individuals. Compared with more temperate regions, with their teeming communities, the Arctic contains few invertebrates. On the islands of Novaya Zemlya in the western Arctic USSR, for example, there are only 250 species of invertebrates, while from the Bering Sea to the Chukchi Sea, in the extreme north-eastern USSR, biologists have estimated there to be about 1,500 species of marine invertebrates.

BELOW *A flock of Black-legged Kittiwakes takes a rest on an ice floe in the East Siberian Sea. These dapper northern gulls nest in huge noisy colonies along the Arctic coast of the USSR, spending the winter months far out on the Arctic Ocean.*

If we include those that live on the Soviet Arctic coastline, there are 11 species of land mammals. These include the Polar Bear (*Thalarctos maritimus*), the Arctic Fox (*Alopex lagopus*) and various species of Lemming (*Lemmus*). During the short summer, Reindeer (*Rangifer tarandus*) may venture into the Arctic wastes from their home on the tundra in search of food.

The world of marine mammals is much richer, totalling 23 species. Nine of these are pinnipedes (seals, sea-lions, fur seals and walruses) and 14 are cetaceans (whales, dolphins and porpoises).

The Arctic coast of the USSR teems with life in summer, especially at the great seabird colonies, such as this one at Cape Waring, on Wrangel Island. The birds jostle one another for space on breeding ledges only inches wide.

Compared with the wealth of bird-life in other regions of the USSR, there are few bird species in the high Arctic; no more than 50 species nest there. But what they lack in variety they make up for in sheer numbers, for along the rocky coasts and islands are some of the biggest seabird colonies in the world.

TEEMING SEABIRD COLONIES

Vast numbers of seabirds arrive in the spring from southerly oceans to breed on the massive cliffs, with their ledges and overhangs. When the young are fledged, they return south before severe weather sets in.

Many species of auk fly in from the open sea. These include the Razorbill (*Alca torda*), the diminutive Little Auk, or Dovekie (*Alle alle*), no longer than a starling, the Guillemot or Common Murre (*Uria aalge*), Brünnich's Guillemot or Thick-billed Murre (*U. lomvia*), the Black Guillemot (*Cepphus grylle*), and the Atlantic Puffin (*Fratercula arctica*). These auks are more typical of the western coasts of the Soviet Arctic. Black-legged Kittiwakes (*Rissa tridactyla*), delicate ocean-going gulls, breed in many places along the Arctic coast of the USSR as far east as the Chukotka Peninsula and Kamchatka.

On the North Pacific coast the seabird colonies contain different species. There are various auklets, including the Crested Auklet (*Aethia cristatella*), the Whiskered Auklet (*A. pygmaea*), the Least Auklet (*A. pusilla*) and the larger Parakeet Auklet (*Cyclorrhynchus psittacula*) and Rhinoceros Auklet (*Cerorhinca monocerata*), and two species of puffin, the Horned Puffin (*Fratercula corniculata*) and the Tufted Puffin (*Lunda cirrhata*).

What is it that compels these seabirds to nest in such dense, deafeningly noisy colonies? As the Russian proverb has it, 'Every stick has two ends'. Although there might seem to be disadvantages in nesting so close that the birds are literally almost standing on each other's feet, the colony can collectively conserve heat and resist the onslaughts of predators better than if they were in scattered groups.

Nevertheless, they need some ingenious adaptations to their precarious existence. Guillemots, for example, lay their single eggs directly onto the bare rock of ledges only a few inches wide. How is it that they are not all knocked off into the icy waters far below in the commotion when the birds jostle for a landing place? The secret is in the unusual pear shape of the eggs. This ensures that they do not roll straight forwards as would a more normally shaped egg, but instead simply spin around their own axis. Even so, it is hardly surprising that quite a few of the eggs are lost every year.

The safest place to nest is in the middle of the bustling colony, away from predators and the worst of the winds and as warm as it is possible to be in the harsh climate. This is where the earliest arrivals and the most experienced old birds settle, leaving the edges of the colony to the inexperienced young birds.

Colonial seabirds feed mainly on small sea fishes, of which there are usually huge stocks in the fertile northern waters. Occasionally, however, these supplies dwindle, and a change in behaviour helps the birds avoid losing their young through starvation. Kittiwakes, for example, may not nest at all. Most often, however, in such lean seasons, they lay only one egg instead of the usual three of the food-rich years.

The first-time visitor to a seabird colony is often unprepared for the birds' remarkable tameness, a result of their isolation from man that makes them particularly vulnerable. Guillemots even allow themselves to be stroked by visiting ornithologists.

Once you have become acclimatized to the cacophony of harsh calls that fill the air, it is possible to distinguish the individual voices of the different species. As you leave the breeding cliffs, these merge once again into a chorus that is like no other sound on earth.

There is a strict vertical distribution of the various species in a typical colony. As we have seen, guillemots occupy the narrowest rock ledges on the steepest overhangs. Razorbills, on the other hand, seek out narrow, elongated crevices in the cliff face to lay their eggs, while kittiwakes build their neat cup-shaped nests of grass, mud, moss and seaweed on the most inaccessible sites, on small vertical shelves of rock. Puffins choose more gently sloping sites, usually at the top of the cliffs, with a covering of grass and soft soil. They dig this out with their sharp claws to form a long burrow, at the end of which they lay a single egg. This is a necessary protection against predators, which would otherwise eat the eggs and chicks in such a relatively accessible site.

The 'tower block' arrangement just described is typical of a seabird colony in the Barents Sea, in the western Arctic. In the Far East, the pattern changes with the different species. Most of the seabirds that breed on the North Pacific coast nest in cracks in rocks or in burrows which they dig themselves.

The seabirds share their colonies with various interlopers which are there for two very different reasons. First there are birds, notably Eider Ducks (*Somateria mollissima*), some other ducks and sandpipers, that seek a safe refuge from predators.

The second group of outsiders joins the colony for more mercenary reasons, feeding at the expense of its seabird inhabitants. They do this in two different ways. The first method, of direct predation on adults, chicks and eggs, is that favoured by the larger gulls. Most birds are defenceless faced with the Great Black-backed Gull (*Larus marinus*)

or the Glaucous Gull (*L. hyperboreus*), though seabird chicks may escape by diving if attacked on the water.

The second method is a form of piracy. This is adopted by the smaller gulls, such as the Common or Mew Gull (*L. canus*), and the three Russian species of skua, or jaeger – the Arctic Skua (*Stercorarius parasiticus*), Long-tailed Skua (*S. longicaudus*) and Pomarine Skua (*S. pomarinus*). All these species are very adept at stealing food from guillemots, puffins and other seabirds in flight, forcing them to drop it, and then swooping down to pick it up.

Although much reduced in numbers by hunting for their ivory, walruses can still be seen hauled out in large groups along the Arctic coasts of the USSR, and now receive total protection throughout their range in the Soviet Union.

WALRUSES

No less impressive than the bustling seabird colonies are those of the marine mammals, particularly the Walruses (*Odobenus rosmarus*). Sadly, these unmistakable creatures have become increasingly rare as a result of hunting, and are now fully protected throughout their range in the USSR. The Atlantic subspecies, *O. r. rosmarus*, is registered in the Red Data Book of the USSR as well as in that of the International Union for the Conservation of Nature (IUCN), although the Laptev Sea race, *O. r. laptevi*, is listed only in the Soviet Red Data Book. The Pacific race, *O. r. divergens*, is not regarded as endangered.

Walruses are the largest pinnipedes in the USSR, and, apart from the huge elephant seals of the Antarctic, the largest in the world. Males of the larger Pacific race can reach 10 to 13 ft (3 to 4 m) long and may weigh as much as $1\frac{3}{4}$ tons (1,800 kg). They live among ice floes, in the shallow waters off the coasts and around the islands and are usually encountered in family groups of five to 10 individuals, although larger groups of up to 100 unmated males also occur. They tend to remain where they are for much of the year, although they do wander south in winter to find patches of water that are not totally ice-bound.

It is usually only the males that develop the distinctive tusks, which are greatly enlarged incisor teeth. Made of pure ivory, they were greatly valued by hunters, and may grow up to 3 ft (1 m) long in the Pacific race. Like the antlers of deer, they are used primarily in contests between rival males vying for a female's attention, and can inflict serious wounds, despite the Walruses' thick, leathery skin. They also help the huge beasts to drag themselves up onto the ice by using the tusks as levers.

Female Walruses are only about half the size of a full-grown male. They give birth on the ice to a single pup in April or May. The mother feeds her offspring for about a year, and then defends it bravely against any danger, bellowing fearsomely.

Walruses feed mainly on bivalve molluscs, which they prise out of the sea-bed with their flexible snouts and a jet of water shot from the mouth. They may also eat shrimps, crabs, worms, octopuses, fish and even seal pups. Walruses can carry on feeding even when ice forms on the sea by breaking through it with their massive heads.

SEA LIONS AND FUR SEALS

In the Bering Sea, the Sea of Okhotsk and the Sea of Japan, there are large breeding colonies of Steller's Sea Lions (*Eumatopias jubatus*) and Pribilov Fur Seals (*Callorhinus ursinus*). Both these pinnipedes are unable to cope with the extremely cold conditions tolerated by the Walrus, and have not spread along the north coast of the Soviet Union for this reason.

Although not as large as Walruses, male Steller's Sea Lions can weigh over $\frac{3}{4}$ ton (800 kg) and reach more than 8 ft ($2\frac{1}{2}$ m) long. The females are only a quarter of their weight. The largest breeding colonies are on the island of Iona, on the Yamskiye Islands in the Sea of Okhotsk and along the coast of Kamchatka.

The sea lions spend the winter on the open ocean to the south, avoiding the ice, and return to the breeding grounds in spring. The first to arrive, in May, are the males. They soon go about establishing their territories, which usually involves noisy fights with rival males. A month later, the females appear. A successful male collects a harem of 15 to 20 females. The animals mate in June, but development of the fertilized egg is delayed until October, so that the single pups are not born until early June of the following year. This arrangement ensures that the young are born just before mating, when they will be surrounded by a protective harem of females.

Fortunately, these impressive animals are now fully protected and their hunting is totally forbidden.

Pribilov Fur Seals breed on the Pribilov Islands in the Bering Sea, on the Komandorskiye Islands off the east coast of Kamchatka and on Robben (Tyulenii) Island in the Okhotsk Sea. Males are about $6\frac{1}{2}$ ft (2 m) long and weigh about 600 lb (270 kg); females weigh only a quarter as much. They spend the winter as far south as Japan and California, returning to the rocky breeding beaches in spring. The males gather harems of 40 to 50 females. They have the same breeding cycle as the sea lions. And, like the sea lions, they feed on fish which they catch by diving; they are superb swimmers.

Fur seals have been a major quarry of hunters for 200 years for their valuable thick fur. Since 1911, however, hunting has been strictly limited as recommended by scientists, so the population remains at a healthy level.

POLAR BEARS

Of all the Arctic mammals, the Polar Bear (*Thalarctos maritimus*) is the undisputed monarch. Equally at home on the dazzling rafts of ice and swimming or diving beneath the waves, it spends most of its life wandering far and wide over the frozen Arctic Ocean. It ranges right along the coastline and islands of the USSR, as well as through Greenland, Canada and Alaska.

It is among the largest of the world's bears. A well-grown male may stand $3\frac{1}{2}$ ft (1 m) high at the shoulders, measure 10 ft (3 m) from the tip of his jet-black nose to the end of his stubby tail, and weigh more than half a ton (500 kg). The sharp claws are used both to give the animal a purchase on the slippery ice and to inflict death-dealing wounds on its prey – mainly seals, but also fish, carrion

Polar Bears are among the largest of bears; fully-grown males may measure almost 10 ft (3 m) long and weigh over half a ton (650 kg).

and, in summer, even such small fry as the eggs and chicks of seabirds. In the water, the broad feet act like paddles, and the thick oily fur provides a waterproof coat, as well as keeping out the bitter cold.

Polar Bears are solitary for much of the year, meeting up only to mate. They have an extended breeding season, which lasts from spring right through summer. Females excavate snug dens in the snow in which they hibernate during winter, and give birth to two (rarely one or three) cubs in the shelter of this lair in January or February. Males do not hibernate.

Polar Bears are becoming rarer, and are now fully protected by the USSR, being listed in the Soviet Red Data Book as well as in that of the IUCN.

The tundra

To the south of the bleak Arctic wastes lies the tundra. The southern limit of the tundra is the northern limit of the great forests of the taiga, but here, as with other botanical regions, there is a transition zone of wooded tundra between the two.

Like the Arctic wastes, the tundra is a region of extreme cold. Temperatures in the continental Siberian tundra may fall as low as $-58°F$ ($-50°C$) or more in winter, but the 'pole of cold' – the coldest place in the world apart from Antarctica – lies to the south in the forest near Verkhoyansk. Temperatures as low as $-90.4°F$ ($-68°C$) have been recorded there.

Because the tundra sprawls over such a vast area from east to west – it covers 15 per cent of the USSR – its climate is not uniform. The harshest conditions are found in the Siberian continental tundra. The tundra to the west,

This panoramic view of Wrangel Island was photographed in August from the island's highest point, the peak of Mt Soviet in the Central Mountains. Few living things can survive in these Arctic deserts, where the mean temperature is only 40°F (4°C) in the brief summer, and plummets to −4°F (−20°C) during the long winter.

especially in the Kola Peninsula, has a gentler climate, thanks to the warming effect of the Gulf Stream. So, too, does the tundra to the east of the Kolyma River — it is the North Pacific current that warms up the climate in this case.

Like the Arctic, the tundra is a cold desert; the annual rainfall is a mere 8 to 12 in (200 to 300 mm), with the maximum in late summer; in spring, it is insignificant. Downpours occur only rarely. One might expect the tundra to be permanently buried under a thick layer of snow, but it is not. The strong winds soon blow away the

relatively little snow that falls. The wind is often so strong that it can knock a man down. During the frequent blizzards, when the wind speed can reach 90 mph (145 km/hr), the fine snow fills the air, blotting out everything else.

During the brief summer, the days are very long, with constant sunshine 24 hours round in midsummer, because of the tilt of the earth's axis. Also, the sun remains low in the sky and its rays strike the tundra at a very shallow angle, providing much less warmth than in tropical regions, where the sun passes almost vertically overhead. Although the constant midsummer light means that the plants can make food all the time by photosynthesis, which requires sunlight energy, the vegetation is restricted by the lack of warmth. In the depths of winter, the sun does not appear at all, and the tundra is then a bitterly cold world of perpetual moonlight.

The extent to which the permafrost layer thaws in summer plays a large part in determining what plants can grow in the tundra. The depth of thawing depends not only on the latitude, but also on the properties of the soil. Some particularly well-thawed sandy soils may even support small thickets of shrubs and dwarf trees, like islands in the generally treeless tundra.

Where the permafrost is thick and thaws but little, swamps are formed. The iron-hard layer of permafrost prevents water from draining away, and the soil is cold and stagnant. Despite the abundance of water, plant roots can take up little moisture under these extreme conditions, and those that do manage to survive have developed adaptations to minimize this physiological drought. They have scale-like or needle-shaped leaves with thick, waxy outer layers, and other features just like those evolved by the cacti and succulents that live in the dry deserts.

Different types of tundra

Vast areas of the tundra are relatively swampy and covered with moss, lichens and dwarf shrubs. But very different types of tundra also exist. Mountain tundras are unlike those of the plains. The different soil types also influence the form of the tundra — some peaty subsoils, for instance, produce hummocky, sedge-covered tundra, while at the outcrops of bedrock there are stony, gravelly and other kinds of tundra.

One of the most interesting types is the spotted tundra which occurs widely on peaty subsoils. Seen from above, the geometrical regularity of the spots is striking: they are more or less uniform both in size and spacing. The vegetation grows in a distinct network enveloping the bare spots, which vary in size from 4 in (10 cm) to 10 ft (3 m), depending on their age. Scientists have come up with

The vast areas of swampy tundra, dissected with countless meandering rivers and containing many lakes, are the breeding grounds for huge numbers of waders, geese and other birds in the short northern summer. This view shows part of the Taimyr Nature Reserve in July.

various theories to account for the origin of this strange landscape. Some consider that they result from the alternate freezing and thawing of the permafrost; others that they are caused mainly by surface frost or wind; and another theory claims that they merely represent a transitional stage which is linked in some way with the breakdown of the peaty layer.

Plant life in the tundra

Mosses and lichens are the dominant plants over much of the tundra. On the islands of Novaya Zemlya alone, for example, there are more than 500 known species of lichen. Seed plants are much scarcer. There are few trees on the tundra and there are only about 500 species of flowering plants in the entire Arctic region. This is a measure of the harshness of the conditions in the north.

Arctic plants can be divided into several distinct groups, according to their origin, as follows:

1 Those endemic to the Arctic (that is, confined to this region and thought to have originated there)

2 Arctic alpines, found both in the Arctic and in high mountains far to the south
3 'Hypo-Arctic' species, typical both of the wooded tundra and of the coniferous forest (taiga) zone
4 Boreal species, typical of the coniferous forest zone, which have colonized the Arctic from their original homes
5 Arctic-steppe species, natives of the cold steppes which penetrated the Arctic in the distant past
6 Seaside halophytes, species typical of saline sea coasts that tolerate soils with high salt concentrations.

Within the tundra, there is a marked increase in the number of species from north to south. The tundra on the islands of Novaya Zemlya, for example, contains only about 250 plant species, while the Bolshezemelskaya tundra, only about 300 miles (480 km) to the south, has some 350 species of plants.

There are hardly any annual plants on the tundra; the very short summers rarely give them enough time to flower and set seed before they die. Almost all the plants are perennials, which can survive for many years. If a particularly cool summer prevents them from producing seeds one year, they can sit it out and wait for better conditions the following year.

There are many evergreen plants on the tundra. These include dwarf conifers, such as *Juniperus nana* and *Pinus pumila*, with their drought-resistant needles; shrubs, such as Cowberry (*Vaccinium vitis-idaea*), Black Bearberry (*Arctous alpina*) and *Rhododendron lapponicum*, with stiff, flat leaves; shrubs such as Labrador Tea (*Ledum palustre*) and Crowberry (*Empetrum nigrum*); and shrubs such as *Diapensia laponica* that grow in the form of squat, flat cushions.

Other shrubs are deciduous — these include various species of Dwarf Willow (*Salix*), Dwarf Birch (*Betula nana*) and Mountain Avens (*Dryas octopetala*).

Many of the tundra plants creep low over the ground, especially the dwarf willows, such as *Salix polaris* and *Salix reticulata*. Their almost horizontal branches, pressed tightly together, resist being damaged by the wind, and they are further strengthened by developing extra roots. Their method of growth also ensures that the air is warmer around the leaves.

RIGHT *Dwarf Willows are among the most typical and widespread plants in the tundra, forming a miniature forest whose creeping branches reach only knee-height.*

Eriophorum scheuzeri (*Cotton Sedge*)

Minuarta arctica (*Pink family*)

Dwarf shrub Ledum decumbens

Parrya nudicaulis

Papaver polare (*Arctic Poppy*)

Typical tundra plants: all are low-growing, aiding survival in the cold, windy climate. Though shallow, the roots spread widely, ensuring a firm anchorage. Many grow in rosette shapes or as cushions, allowing the greatest number of shoots in a small space and protecting the interiors of the plants from the bitter winds.

Like *Diapensia*, herbaceous tundra plants often grow as a dense cushion. Saxifrages (*Saxifraga*) and Whitlowgrasses (*Draba*) are typical examples. The cushion shape enables the plant to produce the maximum amount of shoots for a given volume. Parts of the plant within the cushion are completely protected from the wind and can carry out respiration much more efficiently. Cushion-forming plants are also found on the cold, windy slopes of many of the high mountain ranges.

Tundra plants, especially those living at high latitudes, are slow growing, a result of the short growing season and the generally harsh conditions. A dwarf willow, for example, grows only a fraction of an inch (1 to 5 mm) in a year, and a mature tree may be only a few inches high.

The roots of tundra plants remain in the uppermost layers of the soil, which are the first to warm up in summer. The permafrost layer prevents them from growing deep. To compensate for this, their shallow root systems spread widely beneath the surface to obtain as much nutrient as they can from the soil.

The thickened underground storage organs — tubers, rhizomes, bulbs and so on — found in plants of other regions are rarely developed in tundra plants. This is probably because of the very short growing season.

A remarkable feature of some tundra plants is the ability of their flowers or fruit to withstand the freezing temperatures of winter, reviving in the spring thaw in perfect condition. One of the best-known examples is the Scurvy-Grass *Cochlearia arctica*.

Special features of tundra animals

Relatively few animals live in the tundra, and most that do are only temporary inhabitants. The main difference between the plants and animals of the tundra is that, since the animals can move, most of them leave to spend the winter in kinder climates to the south, visiting the tundra only to breed during the short, fertile summer. This is particularly true of birds, the most mobile of all creatures, which may migrate for many thousands of miles.

As with the plants, the typical animals of the tundra have certain features in common. In general, northern animals are larger than their close relatives living further south. Wolves (*Canis lupus*) on the tundra, for example, are noticeably larger than those in the coniferous forest to the south. This is because the larger the animal, the smaller its surface area in relation to its volume, and the less heat it loses to the surrounding air.

Another feature of tundra animals is the scarcity of species combined with the abundance of individuals. For instance, for many hundreds of miles, you will hear the same species of sandpiper singing its courtship song in the clear air of spring.

The animals, like the plants, have mixed origins. Typical tundra species have undergone a long period of adaptation and are incapable of living under other conditions. Other, less well adapted species are recent invaders from regions immediately to the south of the tundra.

Insect life

Relatively few species of insect live in the tundra compared with the bewildering variety found in other, more hospitable regions. There are only about 100 species of beetle, for example — mainly rove beetles, ground beetles and predatory diving beetles. This compares with many beetle species on a single desert plant.

The vast areas of swampy ground provide ideal breeding grounds for mosquitoes, biting midges and gnats. These bloodsucking insects swarm in summer in their millions, making life intolerable both for human visitors and native mammals, such as Reindeer (*Rangifer tarandus*).

Amphibians and reptiles

Amphibians, being cold-blooded, are generally unable to survive the northern cold. A few species of frogs manage to eke out an existence, although the icy waters of the tundra lakes and rivers are generally too cold to allow their eggs to hatch or their tadpoles to develop quickly enough to survive for long.

Reptiles, too, are cold-blooded, and are poorly represented. The few snakes and lizards that live in the tundra seldom emerge from hiding. Reptiles need direct sunshine, both to rouse them from their lethargy and to hatch their eggs. Those living in the cold north deal with the latter problem by giving birth to live young, but even so they hang on only with difficulty.

Birds

Birds are the most conspicuous animals of the tundra in summer, but only a few very hardy species are able to survive there all year. The rest must migrate to warmer climates, sometimes for thousands of miles.

Various bird species are endemic to the Soviet tundra, and some of them are now so rare that they are included in the Red Data books. One of the most beautiful of these, which is restricted as a breeding species to the peninsulas of Taimyr (where most of the birds occur), Yamal and Gydan, is the Red-breasted Goose (*Rufibrenta ruficollis*). Its total world population in the wild is probably no more than 25,000 individuals, including about 10,000 young non-breeding birds.

Red-breasted Geese arrive at their breeding sites after the other species of geese, such as the Bean Goose and White-fronted Goose. This may be because the grass shoots which form their staple diet has not yet appeared above the frozen tundra. The earliest arrivals gather on the thawing rivers and lakes at the beginning of June. By the end of the month, when all the rivers are ice-free, almost all the geese have flown in. Typical nest sites are on cliffs in river valleys and on rocky islands. The birds breed in widely separated small colonies, each containing no more than six pairs.

It is a remarkable fact that the colonies are almost always close to those of birds of prey, usually Peregrine Falcons (*Falco peregrinus*), and sometimes Rough-legged Buzzards (*Buteo lagopus*). These powerful predators never harm the geese, although they are pefectly capable of killing them. It seems that the falcons do not hunt near their nests and thus do not regard the geese as prey. The geese benefit from the relationship by being protected from the ravages of the Arctic Fox (*Alopex lagopus*), which is the main predator of eggs and young birds on the tundra. The Peregrines guard their own nests fiercely and drive away not only foxes but also gulls and skuas, which have an insatiable appetite for eggs and chicks. In return, the geese may warn the falcons of impending danger by their loud alarm calls.

More dubious neighbours are colonies of Herring and Glaucous Gulls (*Larus argentatus* and *L. hyperboreus*). Ornithologists report that when a group of geese and gulls return to their colonies after being disturbed, the gulls do not take advantage of the situation to eat their neighbours' eggs and goslings. This may be because the geese return very quickly and manage to sit tightly on their nests before the gulls get a chance to attack. They even allow people to approach so close that they can stroke them. But this is not the whole story, for the gulls do not touch the goslings when they roam around the colony. Clearly, this whole fascinating subject needs a good deal more investigation.

The geese build their nests in hollows in the ground, usually in the shelter of a dwarf willow, dwarf birch or a clump of dead grass, though they may sometimes choose a site in a hollow or in a cliff crevice without any other cover.

The birds may lay from one to nine eggs, but the usual number is six or seven. In years with a normal spring, the

ABOVE *A Red-breasted Goose at its nest in the Taimyr Peninsula. This rare bird gains protection from predators by nesting within the territory of the Peregrine Falcon.*

ABOVE *Four species of eider duck breed on the Soviet tundra; this female King Eider is incubating her eggs on the Taimyr Peninsula in July.*

geese begin to lay soon after their arrival, in the second half of June. The males do not stay close to the sitting females, as do most other species of geese, but keep watch as much as 300 ft (100 m) away from the river bank or the water itself. They usually perform their sentry duty in small flocks, constantly alert to any danger.

The fluffy brown and yellow goslings hatch at the end of July and remain in the nest for the first few days, where they are kept warm by snuggling under their mother's breast feathers. Soon, she leads them to the nearest water, where they swim and dive with great enthusiasm and expertise, despite being only a few days old. Like the adults, the goslings eat grass. Sometimes, the mothers club together to keep a watchful eye on their adventurous offspring. At the first sign of danger, the gander self-sacrificingly draws attention to himself, while the mother leads the goslings away as quickly as possible.

The goslings begin to fly in the second half of August, sometimes not until early September. This coincides neatly with the end of their parents' wing-feather moult, so that the whole family can prepare to leave the breeding grounds together. There are also a number of bachelors, which tend to remain separate; these days, they rarely number more than 100 individuals.

In mid-September, the geese embark on their long southward migration. By the end of the month, after having spent about 100 days in their birthplace, the last Redbreasts have left the tundra. They often travel with large flocks of White-fronted and Lesser White-fronted Geese (*Anser albifrons* and *A. erythropus*).

Formerly, most of the Redbreasts wintered on the shores of the Caspian Sea, with a few in Iran, but since the 1940s they have altered their destination to Romania, near the Danube Delta, with smaller numbers in neighbouring Bulgaria and a few in north-eastern Greece.

Their tragic decline is probably due to a combination of factors. In their winter quarters, they seem to have been affected by agricultural changes, such as the switch in the Caspian to growing cotton on a huge scale instead of cereals, which form an important part of their winter diet. Drainage of marshlands in the same area must also have had a serious effect. Sadly, too, they are still shot outside the Soviet Union, despite protection in some countries. Finally, the reduction in numbers of the Peregrine Falcon has probably affected their ability to breed successfully.

The Siberian White Crane (*Grus leucogeranus*) is another beautiful endemic bird of the Soviet tundra, much rarer even than the Red-breasted Goose. It is registered in the Red Data Books of both the USSR and the IUCN.

ABOVE *A pair of Siberian Cranes; these rare birds do not reach sexual maturity until six years old, and face many dangers on their long migratory flights.*

ABOVE *A nest of the Siberian Crane; despite laying two eggs, the cranes never raise more than a single chick from each clutch in the wild, but the joint Soviet-American captive breeding programme has greatly improved the chances of survival for this magnificent bird.*

The Siberian Crane is an impressive bird, over $4\frac{1}{2}$ ft (1.37 m) high, with a wingspan of $6\frac{1}{2}$ to 8 ft (2 to 2.4 m). An adult can weigh as much as 18 lb (8 kg). It has pure white plumage, apart from the black wing tips, and a prominent patch of bare bright red skin on the front of its face. Its long, dagger-like bill and long legs are dull red.

Today, the cranes are restricted to two isolated areas of the tundra, one in part of the vast region called Yakutia, between the Yana and Alazeya rivers, and the other over

2,000 miles (3,200 km) to the west, along the lower reaches of the River Ob. The Yakutia population is probably more than the often quoted figure of several hundred nesting pairs. The total world population is probably about 2,000 birds. According to reports from ornithologists at their wintering grounds in China, most of them are non-breeding birds; Siberian Cranes do not reach sexual maturity until they are six years old.

The Yakutia cranes arrive at their nesting sites in the second half of May, when the tundra is still covered with snow and the first thawed patches are confined to the warmer hilltops. As soon as they arrive, they gather in small groups on high, dry areas. Soon, the males start to perform their dramatic courtship dances. The bird droops his wings, rustling the feathers noisily, and alternately raises and lowers his head, stretching out his neck and bill. All the time, he circles round his chosen female, uttering loud, shrill cries.

Favoured breeding sites are on damp, lowland grassy tundra in Yakutia and moss-covered moors and swamps in the Ob region. The cranes build large, rather untidy nests of dried grasses, reeds or sedges on mossy hummocks or on grassy islands in the lakes. As with most other cranes, the female lays two eggs. She incubates them while the male stands on guard near the nest, warning his mate instantly of any approaching danger. He is a bold defender, able to see off many predators, including the persistent Arctic Fox (*Alopex lagopus*), with his powerful, sharp bill.

In spring, the cranes eat lemmings, voles and insects, but during the nesting period they usually switch to a vegetarian diet. Little is known about the details of incubation and rearing of the chicks. Siberian Cranes are extremely wary birds, and will not allow humans to approach nearer than 1,000 to 1,300 ft (300 to 400 m) without taking flight.

The cranes leave their vast, remote breeding sites in the second half of September, flying south to winter mainly in China, and also in India in the case of the Ob birds. They create an unforgettable spectacle as they pass high overhead, giving their wild, bugle-like calls.

Once, the cranes were widely distributed across the Siberian tundra. Their decline this century has been variously attributed to hunting, disturbance caused during the Second World War and destruction of their habitat by various means. Whatever the reason, a concerted effort is being made to save this handsome bird by a programme of research in the wild and captive breeding. Furthermore, it is being conducted jointly by Soviet and American scientists — a splendid example of international co-operation in nature conservation. This work is described in more detail in Chapter 3, pages 61–2.

TUNDRA WADERS

Large numbers of waders, of a variety of species, breed in the tundra, mainly in the vast marshy areas. They form a constant background to the other birdlife. Several species of sandpiper are endemic to the Soviet Union; others breed also in the tundras of Scandinavia, the United States and Canada.

Three species of plover breed on the tundra: the Grey Plover, or Black-bellied Plover (*Pluvialis squatarola*), the Golden Plover (*Pluvialis apricaria*) and the Lesser Golden Plover (*P. dominica*).

The Grey Plover is the largest, at 11 in (28 cm) long, and is the most widespread of the three. It breeds right across the world's tundra belt, from the western USSR through

Like those of many other waders, the pear-shaped eggs of the Grey Plover (known as the Black-bellied Plover in North America), which breeds throughout the tundra, fit snugly together for efficient incubation, and are superbly camouflaged to conceal them from the attention of predators.

Siberia to North America, and migrates thousands of miles each year to spend the winter on the coasts of Europe, Africa, southern Asia, Australia and South America.

In its breeding plumage, it is one of the most handsome of all waders, its jet black face and underparts sharply separated from the delicately spotted silver-grey back and crown by a line of pure white. In winter, it loses the bold black and white pattern, but still has a distinctive feature in the black-feathered 'armpits' under its wings.

Its wary nature, too, makes it one of the most conspicuous of all tundra birds: it regularly uses ridges of higher ground as lookout sites. One of the most evocative sounds in the tundra is this bird's sad, melodious whistling call. Like other plovers, the Grey Plover runs quickly when feeding, stopping suddenly to snatch its prey, mostly insects and their larvae, from the ground, then running on again to find its next meal. It can also pick crustaceans and other little aquatic animals from the surface of the water and probe to the bottom of shallow pools.

The Grey Plover is a solitary nester, favouring damp, though not swampy, areas of tundra. The female builds her nest — a shallow hollow lined with moss or lichens — on an area of higher ground, which affords a good view of any advancing danger.

In mid-June, she lays four pale brown eggs, mottled with darker brown blotches. Like those of most waders, they are markedly pear-shaped. The female arranges them with their pointed ends facing inwards, so that they fit snugly beneath her. Wader eggs are large relative to the size of the bird, so this is a necessary adaptation if they are not to become exposed and run the risk of cooling down. The male helps his mate with the task of incubation, but near hatching time he spends most of this time keeping watch over the nest from a high vantage point. At the first sight of any danger, he gives his loud, plaintive alarm calls and runs rapidly away from the nest in an attempt to lure the predator away from it. His mate then joins him, running from the nest in silence in an effort to escape detection. The eggs are beautifully camouflaged against the background of lichens and stones and stand a good chance of being missed, even by a keen-eyed fox or skua.

After 23 days of incubation, the downy yellow, black and white chicks hatch and immediately run about in search of food. When they are completely independent, about a month later, during late August or early September, their parents begin their long southward migration. As with most tundra waders, adults which either failed to acquire a mate or were unsuccessful nesters leave much earlier. The young birds migrate after the breeding adults: flocks of them can still be seen on the tundra in mid-September.

The Spotted Redshank (*Tringa erythropus*) is a common wader, breeding on the tundra right across northern Europe and Siberia. It winters mainly in the Mediterranean, Africa and southern Asia. It is especially handsome in its slaty-black and white breeding plumage. This is moulted in autumn to a duller greyish winter plumage. The four greenish eggs, covered with dark brown blotches, are laid in late May and early June in a shallow nest scrape lined with fallen willow or birch leaves.

The large group of calidrine sandpipers has many representatives in the tundras of northern Eurasia and America. A total of 15 species breeds in the Soviet tundra. One of the smallest is the Little Stint (*Calidris minuta*), whose body is little bigger than a sparrow's and weighs a mere $\frac{3}{4}$ to 1 oz (22 to 27 g). It breeds on the Eurasian tundra, from Norway in the west to the lower reaches of the River Lena in north-central Siberia. Despite its diminutive size, it flies huge distances to spend the winter in Africa, southern Asia, Australia and Tasmania.

ABOVE *A Spotted Redshank, resplendent in its breeding plumage, with one of its chicks on the Taimyr Peninsula.*

ABOVE *A female Ruff with one of her brood of four chicks. Breeding males are dramatically different, adorned with the ruffs of feathers that give the species its name.*

Immediately after arriving at the breeding grounds, the stints choose their nesting sites and the males begin their mating display. They fly with exaggerated upbeats of their wings, uttering an alternately loud and soft trill, rather like the chirping of a cricket. The nest is a little scrape in the soil, often sheltered by an adjacent shrub. Both male and female take turns to incubate the four brownish-speckled pale olive eggs. The chicks hatch in the last days of June.

Like most sandpipers, Little Stints are busy little birds, running about impatiently and snatching food, mainly insects and their larvae, from the ground with their straight, shortish bills. They are almost indifferent to the presence of humans; it is possible to walk right up to a sitting bird on the nest. Even if it does leave the nest, it may do so to try and expel the intruders, coming very close and even pushing at their hands. This happened to the author several times when photographing this bold little wader on its breeding grounds.

Very similar to the little stint, but slightly larger, is the Red-necked Stint (*Calidris ruficollis*), which breeds in north-east Siberia and Alaska. The range of the two species overlaps, and the best way of separating them is by the Redneck's very different courtship flight. He usually keeps his wings at body level, rarely raising them higher, and the flight is distinctly undulating. Also, the 'song' is very different, being a prolonged 'yek … yek … yek'. Another distinction is the reddish-brown colour of the four eggs. The Red-necked Stint winters mainly in Australia and Tasmania, also in parts of South-East Asia.

The Spoon-billed Sandpiper (*Eurynorhynchus pygmaeus*), as its name implies, has an extraordinary feature distinguishing it from all the other sandpipers: in fact, its bill is shaped more like a little shovel than a spoon, with a broadened tip as much as $\frac{1}{2}$ in (1.25 cm) across. This unique bird, endemic to the Soviet Union, is listed in the Red Book of the USSR. Its breeding range is extremely limited; it nests only on the North Pacific coast, from the delta of the River Amguema to the Gulf of Anadyr. It migrates to South-east Asia for the winter.

The Spoon-billed Sandpiper is even more active than the other sandpipers. It feeds while describing a half-circle with its head and neck, running rapidly across the marshy tundra, and may suddenly turn round and run off in the opposite direction without taking its bill out of the water. Sometimes, it wades into a pool up to its belly in pursuit of its tiny prey.

Although the bill is unmistakable when seen at close range, it is surprisingly difficult to make out at a distance. Then the Spoon-billed Sandpiper can be easily mistaken for other small sandpipers, which it often accompanies on its long migration.

GULLS AND TERNS

A typical tundra gull is Ross's Gull (*Rhodostethia rosea*). This beautiful, delicately built gull has a very restricted breeding distribution and is registered in the Red Data Book of the USSR because of its rarity. Its ash-grey back and upper wing feathers are set off to perfection by the delicate pink bloom of its head and body, with a neat black neck collar which is moulted during winter. There is a red ring around each eye, matching the red legs, and the bill is black.

A Ross's Gull at its nest in the east Siberian tundra.

The breeding sites of Ross's Gull, which were not discovered until 1905, are on the lower reaches of the Indigirka and Kolyma Rivers and on the Taimyr Peninsula. It nests on damp, coastal, grassy and wooded tundra. The gulls usually arrive at the breeding sites at the end of May or beginning of June, settling in small colonies of about 2 to 50 pairs. They sometimes form mixed colonies with Arctic Terns (*Sterna paradisaea*). Their numbers seem to fluctuate from year to year, and they often change their nesting sites, vanishing from a favoured site one year and reappearing at a long-abandoned one the next.

The nest is sited on a hummock, usually on an island in a lake. It is built – and lined – with dead grass and leaves, and usually kept damp. In the first half of June, the female lays from one to four eggs, usually three. The chicks hatch in a little over three weeks. Both parents share the incubation of the eggs and rearing of the chicks. The young are fed on insects and their larvae, and this is the main diet of the adults, too, on the breeding grounds.

When the old birds have moulted and the young are fully fledged, they all fly off to the open sea, spending winter in the Arctic and North Pacific Oceans. They are equally at home in the air, on the ice and in the water, swimming on the surface and plunging underneath to feed on small fish and marine invertebrates.

Other typical gulls of the Soviet tundra are Sabine's Gull (*Xema sabini*), the Glaucous Gull (*Larus hyperboreus*) and the Herring Gull (*L. argentatus*).

Terns are slender relatives of the gulls, with narrow wings, a graceful buoyant flight, long sharp bills specialized for catching fish, and forked tails; they are sometimes called 'sea swallows'. The most typical species of the tundra is the Arctic Tern (*Sterna paradisaea*), which breeds right around the North Pole. This delicately built bird is remarkable for its epic annual migrations to and from its wintering haunts as far south as the Antarctic pack ice, a round trip of about 22,000 miles (36,000 km) each year. It is unlikely that any other bird travels so far or experiences so much daylight as the Arctic Tern.

BIRDS OF PREY IN THE TUNDRA

One of the most impressive birds still relatively common in the tundra is the Peregrine Falcon (*Falco peregrinus*). It is not by chance that I describe it in this section on the tundra, although it occurs in other habitats, too. For it is in the tundra in particular that it thrives, while in many other places it is scarce and over large areas it has practically disappeared. The Peregrine is listed in the Red Data Book of the USSR as well as in that of the IUCN. One of the main reasons for the catastrophic fall in the population of this splendid bird – both in the USSR and elsewhere – is the effect of pesticides on its ability to breed. In the tundra this problem does not arise and the Peregrine Falcon is still relatively common. The northernmost birds migrate south for the winter. As with many other birds of prey, the female is considerably larger than the male. In the tundra, the nests are usually built on the ground, sometimes on a low hillock, but usually on a steep riverside cliff. The Peregrine lays two to four reddish-brown eggs; incubation

ABOVE LEFT *The Rock Ptarmigan is one of two species of grouse in the tundra; this one is moulting from its mainly grey-brown summer plumage to its white winter plumage.*
ABOVE *A splendid Snowy Owl on Wrangel Island.*
RIGHT *Rarest of the tundra birds of prey, the magnificent Gyrfalcon is the largest of the world's falcons.*

takes about 28 to 35 days.

Peregrines live almost entirely on birds; in the tundra, their chief prey are waders, Willow Grouse (*Lagopus lagopus*) and Rock Ptarmigan (*L. mutus*). They are caught on the wing in a spectacular dive or 'stoop', during which the Peregrine soars high into the sky and then plummets down, wings folded, at speeds of up to 112 mph (180 km/hr). The falcon's talons often hit the prey with such force that its head is knocked clean off.

A much rarer sight on the tundra is the magnificent Gyrfalcon (*Falco gyrfalco*). A good deal larger than the Peregrine, it is very variable in colour, some birds being dark brown above with greyish, mottled underparts, while others have a ghostly, almost all-white plumage. This very rare species is also listed in the Red Data Book of the USSR. In winter, it may wander as far as south Europe.

Much more common is the Rough-legged Buzzard (*Buteo lagopus*), which, like the Gyrfalcon, breeds right around the North Pole. In the tundra, it nests on the ground. The number of eggs is closely related to the food available in a given year, in particular, the population of lemmings, which form its staple diet. Lemming numbers fluctuate widely from one season to the next. In an average year, the buzzards each lay three to four eggs, but in particularly favourable years, there may be as many as seven. When there are few lemmings, the birds may not breed at all.

One of the most beautiful owls in the world, the Snowy Owl (*Nyctea scandiaca*) is perhaps the most impressive of all the birds that breed on the tundra. Males, which are about 21 in (53 cm) long, are almost pure white, with a few dark brown spots and bars. As with other birds of prey, the females are considerably larger, up to 25 in (64 cm) long,

and have a wingspan of as much as 5 ft (1.5 m). They are much more heavily barred with brown.

The Snowy Owl's thick plumage and feathered feet and bill protect it from the bitter winds and freezing temperatures. It is another circumpolar bird, breeding on the Arctic coasts and islands and on the tundra of Arctic North America, Greenland, Iceland and Scandinavia as well as throughout Siberia. It is one of the few birds to remain on the tundra the whole year round, though sometimes many owls are forced to fly south or west in particularly hard winters, when the snow is especially deep and food is scarce. They regularly turn up in Britain, central Europe and Asia and in the northern United States, to the great delight of birdwatchers.

As with the Rough-legged Buzzard, which may also travel south in severe winters, the Snowy Owl population fluctuates considerably from one year to the next, depending mainly on the numbers of its chief prey, the lemmings. In years when these little rodents are plentiful, the owls may lay as many as 10 or even 14 eggs, but in lean years with few lemmings, the nests contain only three or four eggs, or sometimes none at all.

A few Snowy Owls have wandered south during the summer and bred in Finland in 1974 and on the island of Fetlar in the Shetlands, to the north-east of Scotland, between 1967 and 1975.

The nest is a shallow depression on a high and relatively dry part of the tundra, scraped out by both male and female and lined with grass, moss or feathers. The owls are early breeders; the female may start laying in early May, when snow still carpets the ground thickly. The female starts incubating the eggs as she lays them, and because there is a gap of two days or more between each one, the chicks

hatch out at different times. This staggered hatching may mean that the last owlet is breaking out of the eggshell when its oldest brother or sister is two weeks old.

The female does all the incubation, her barred plumage helping to camouflage her from predators, while the male watches over her from a nearby lookout mound or stone. He defends his territory boldly, diving at any intruder – foxes, skuas and humans alike – with loud barking cries. He also brings his mate food while she is incubating.

As well as Norway, Siberian and Arctic Collared Lemmings (*Lemmus lemmus*, *L. obensis* and *Dicrostonyx torquatus*) the Snowy Owl eats various species of voles and sousliks. During the breeding season, the adults eat birds, too, and feed them to their chicks: mainly the young of Willow Ptarmigan (*Lagopus lagopus*), sandpipers, gulls, and even birds as small as the Lapland Bunting, or Lapland Longspur (*Calcarius lapponicus*). Outside the breeding season, the owls' diet is even more diverse. Then they catch hares, pikas, weasels and other small predatory mammals and a wide variety of birds. Their hunting technique is to scan the area from a convenient ridge or boulder, then, when they have sighted their prey, to take wing and drop silently on it. Sometimes, they may hunt by hovering over one spot like a Kestrel (*Falco tinnunculus*).

PERCHING BIRDS

I shall complete this brief survey of the birdlife of the tundra by describing some of the passerines, or perching birds, that breed there. In many regions, such as forests and farmland, they form the main proportion of the overall bird fauna, but relatively few occur in the cold north.

Typical Soviet tundra species include the Lapland Bunting, or Lapland Longspur (*Calcarius lapponicus*) and the

Snow Bunting (*P. nivalis*). Both these species breed right around the North Pole, wintering far to the south.

The Lapland Bunting prefers the hummocky tundra of the plains. It arrives in early spring, usually in May, the males preceding the females. They soon form flocks, separating into pairs only when almost all the snow has melted. During this time, the black-headed males utter their loud, trilling songs incessantly, and they often fight over their territories. Soon the drabber females build their neat nests of grass, moss and plant roots on the ground in the shelter of a bank or hummock or beneath a small bush. Each female usually lays five spotted, greenish-white eggs, though there may be as few as four or as many as seven. She does most of the incubation, taking about 14 days.

Both male and female are kept busy satisfying their ever-hungry chicks, bringing food to them throughout the long Arctic day, apart from a brief two or three-hour period when they take a well-earned rest. Although the adults are, like other buntings, chiefly seed-eaters, they feed their young mainly on insects, which provide enough protein for a healthy start in life.

By contrast with the Lapland Buntings, the mostly white Snow Buntings prefer stony areas of tundra and nest among scree-slopes, on cliffs along river banks, or on rocky coasts. They return earlier than the other birds, when only a few patches of snow have thawed. First to arrive are the males, which soon establish their territories. The females appear later, usually in May.

Unlike most northern birds, Snow Buntings do not begin to breed for a while after their arrival on the tundra. They do not usually start nest-building until the beginning of June. Favourite sites are under stones and in cracks between rocks. Occasionally, they nest on slopes against grassy hummocks, in gaps in a stone wall or even in the wall of a building. The hen alone incubates her five or six pale blue eggs for about 14 days. After two weeks in the nest, the chicks are fledged, but remain close to their parents for a while longer. By September, the Snow Buntings are ready to leave the tundra.

The neatly streaked Red-throated Pipit (*Anthus cervinus*) nests in hummocky grass tundra and also in peat-bog tundra. An insect eater, it arrives from the beginning of May onwards. The five or six grey, buff, olive or pinkish eggs are laid in a nest on the ground, usually sheltered by plants or tucked against a hummock. The Red-throated Pipit winters in Africa and southern Asia.

Other typical perching birds of the tundra include the Pechora Pipit (*Anthus gustavi*) and Little Bunting (*Emberiza pusilla*). Both breed there, migrating south in winter.

Where there are plenty of bushes, different species, such as the Red-spotted Bluethroat (*Luscinia svecica svecica*) and Pallas's Reed Bunting (*Emberiza pallasi*) appear.

Tundra mammals

Few land mammals live in the far north, but those that do are wide-ranging and often common. It is difficult to imagine the tundra without the Arctic Fox (*Alopex lagopus*). A cunning, bold predator, it is a real danger to many of the tundra birds. This wily creature spends much of its life on the tundra and wooded tundra. In winter, however, it wanders far to the north over the polar ice, and southwards as far as the great coniferous forests of the taiga. It is widely distributed throughout the Arctic region, right around the North Pole, occurring not only in Siberia and Kamchatka, but also in northern European Russia, Scandinavia, Iceland, Greenland, Alaska and Canada. It is equally at home on flat or hilly tundra, and also frequents river valleys, lake shores and islands. It does have a preference

ABOVE *The Arctic Fox, found throughout the tundra, shows a remarkable tolerance to cold; its soft, thick fur turns pure white in winter; there is also a 'blue' form.*

during the breeding season, however, for areas with rocky ridges and cliffs, which provide good breeding sites and lookout points.

Although slightly smaller than the European Red Fox (*Vulpes vulpes*), it looks bigger because of its very soft, bushy fur, which is highly prized by trappers. It has the longest fur, for its size, of any Arctic animal. The fur of individuals living in the high Arctic turns white in winter, providing an effective camouflage against the snow, while that of some of those living to the south remains blue-grey all year round. These 'blue foxes' are particularly valued by furriers, and they are reared on a large scale in fur farms, forming an important rural industry in the Soviet Union.

In summer, the foxes are active throughout the 24 hours of the perpetual Arctic daylight, but in autumn and winter, they are mainly nocturnal. Females are on heat from February to March, and the cubs are born in April and May at the end of a long, branching burrow. The foxes also dig less complex burrows for temporary refuge and for shelter from the wind and snow. There are as many as seven or even ten cubs in a litter. As well as birds and their eggs and chicks, Arctic Foxes eat lemmings, voles and mice. They also eat carrion, especially in winter, and shellfish or floating offal on the coast.

BELOW *Reindeer spend summer in the tundra, as far north as the Arctic coast, and migrate southwards to winter in the taiga. Here, a small herd is seen crossing a river in the Taimyr Nature Reserve, on the tundra, in July.*

The one animal above all associated by most people with the tundra landscape is the Reindeer (*Rangifer tarandus*), known in North America as the Caribou. Although it winters in the taiga, it is primarily adapted for life in the great open spaces. It prefers hilly regions, plateaus and river valleys, and avoids flat, uniform areas of the tundra.

The females and young are highly gregarious, forming large herds which migrate seasonally in search of food and to avoid the plagues of mosquitoes and midges that can make their life a misery. They are on heat from September to November, when the normally solitary males join the herd, gathering a small group of females around him. The young are born in May or June; usually there is only one, but occasionally there are twins.

In summer, Reindeer feed on a variety of tundra plants, including grasses and sedges, but in winter they eat lichens, scraping away the snow with their large, flattened hooves to reach the precious food. Their broad hooves also act as snowshoes, enabling them to travel

across areas of deep snow without sinking in. Reindeer are the only deer in which both sexes have antlers, although those of the females are generally smaller.

Only one species of hare occurs on the tundra – the Arctic Hare (*Lepus timidus*), also known as the Blue Hare or Mountain Hare it is a widespread animal in the USSR living not only in the tundra but also in forests and steppes in most parts of the country, except Central Asia, Kazakhstan and the Caucasus. Unlike baby rabbits, which are born blind and hairless in the protection of a burrow, those of hares are born above ground, with their eyes open and a covering of hair. The population of the Arctic Hare fluctuates markedly from year to year, depending on the severity of winter and the availability of food.

Various species of rodent live in the tundra. The ground squirrels of Western Siberia, such as the Long-tailed Souslik (*Spermophilus undulatus*), are close relatives of the squirrels that dig extensive underground burrows and hibernate for the winter.

The most typical tundra rodents, however, are the lemmings, which are closely related to voles. There are four main species in the USSR – the Norway Lemming (*Lemmus lemmus*), the Siberian Lemming (*L. obensis*), the Amur Lemming (*L. amurensis*) and the Arctic Collared, or Hoofed Lemming (*Dicrostonyx torquatus*).

The Norway Lemming is primarily a Scandinavian species that is found only in the tundra, wooded tundra and forest of the Kola Peninsula in the extreme north-east

Arctic Collared Lemmings; these attractive little rodents make their famous mass migrations when their numbers reach such a level that their food supply runs out.

USSR. The Siberian Lemming is widely distributed throughout the northern USSR, from the south coast of the White Sea in the West to Chukotka in the east, though it is absent from the Kola Peninsula, presumably because of competition from the Norway Lemming. It prefers low-lying areas of tundra with dwarf birch and willow. It often lives in large colonies. The Amur Lemming is rare, found only in scattered areas of eastern Siberia and the Far East. The details of this little animal's life are largely a mystery to biologists. The Arctic Collared Lemming is as wide-spread as the Siberian Lemming, and it is more flexible in its choice of habitat, which includes stony or swampy tundra, though it avoids lichen tundra.

Lemmings live in large colonies, and are active throughout the whole 24 hours of the northern summer, constantly searching for food to sustain their feverish activity. They eat various grasses and, less frequently, sprigs of willow and berries.

Their burrows are relatively simple, with one or two exits and a nest chamber. They take advantage of natural hollows in the tundra soil when excavating their homes. In winter, they build large nests of dead vegetation deep beneath the thick blanket of snow.

The females give birth throughout the year, but mostly in summer. They usually each produce five or six litters, each containing, on average, five or six young.

Lemming populations fluctuate widely from year to year. In a poor year, when food is scarce, the population is kept in check. In a good year, however, when the tundra grasses are particularly prolific, the landscape may literally swarm with the little animals, and then they embark on their famous mass movements in search of food. Many of them die *en route*, especially when attempting to cross ice floes, large rivers and lakes, or mountains, although they do not deliberately commit suicide, as legend would have us believe.

The Arctic Lemming is less fertile than the Siberian Lemming. The females give birth only two or three times a year and it is not forced to make mass movements as often as its relative.

Other rodents that live in the tundra include the Grey-sided Field Vole (*Clethrionomys rufocanus*), the Lemming-type Mountain Vole (*Alticola lemminus*) and Middendorff's Field Vole (*Microtus middendorffi*).

On pages 210–11 there is a table showing the distribution of some of the most typical birds and mammals of the tundra, Arctic coasts and islands of the USSR. This does not include the cetacean mammals – the whales, dolphins and porpoises – that range throughout the northern oceans.

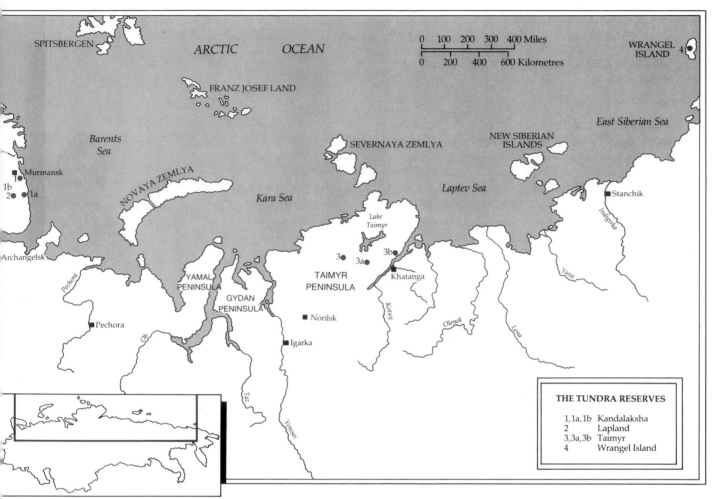

Conservation in the Far North

The map shows the nature reserves established in the Arctic and sub-Arctic regions of the USSR, including the country's largest reserve, on the Taimyr Peninsula, which protects more than 5,000 sq miles (13,000 sq km) of tundra.

Conservation of the northern wilderness is becoming desperately urgent. It is a complex task because nature in the Arctic is extremely fragile and any recovery from damage is extremely slow. This is graphically illustrated by the tracks cross-country vehicles make in the tundra, which show up like strips of ploughed land for many decades. Further examples of the vulnerability of the tundra to human influences are given, on page 62.

Conservationists have recently made many studies of the northern regions in an attempt to understand more about them and how best they can be saved for future generations. This task is all the more urgent because it has come late in the day. Several large areas of tundra of various types have been declared nature reserves. Here I will describe briefly the few reserves which have been established in the Arctic and sub-Arctic belts.

One of these, in Kandalaksha, was established as long ago as 1939. Its area has been increased repeatedly over the years. New sections have been added to it, including the island of Velikiy in eastern Murman and the Ainovy Islands in Varangerfiord. The originally separate nature reserve of 'Sem Ostrovov' (Seven Islands) has been combined with the Kandalaksha Reserve. The present area of the reserve, including all its various branches, is about 220 square miles (571 sq km). It contains 550 species of

plants, 210 of birds and 33 of mammals. Since 1975 the reserve has formed part of the Kandalaksha Bay area of the White Sea that has been declared a wetland of international importance, and which occupies a total area of 800 square miles (2080 sq km).

In 1930 the Lapland Reserve was created in the western part of the Kola Peninsula, some 75 to 100 miles (120 to 160 km) north of the Arctic Circle, with an area of 62 square miles (161 sq km).

In 1975 the large reserve of Wrangel Island was created, with an area of 3072 sq miles (7,956 sq km). Wrangel Island is unique. It still has a breeding colony of Snow Geese (*Anser caerulescens*), also rare breeding sandpipers, many Polar Bears and Walruses, and 300 species of plants.

In 1979 a considerable boost for the conservation of nature in the north was the creation of the Taimyr Reserve, larger than any other in the USSR, occupying 5,206 sq miles (13,483 sq km). It has 16 species of mammals and 50 birds, including about 2,000 to 3,000 of the total population of Red-breasted Geese (*Rufibrenta ruficollis*), which breed only in the USSR (see pages 62 and 79–80).

5 THE LARGEST FOREST IN THE WORLD

Vast green oceans of coniferous forest, stretching over 6,000 miles (10,000 km) from the Baltic in the west to the Sea of Okhotsk in the east, cover over a third of the Soviet Union's land surface. This great belt of coniferous forest is commonly known by its Russian name, *taiga*. The taiga has a severe beauty all of its own, and is full of memorable sensations: the exhilarating smell of the pinewoods on a spring morning; the drumming of a Black Woodpecker carrying half a mile or more; the clear cry of a Nuthatch ringing through the trees; the tracks of a Brown Bear imprinted in the moss; the sight and sound of the mighty Siberian rivers as they roar and tumble through the forests; and the blue of Lake Baikal in summer, where the taiga meets the Mongolian steppe.

Taiga accounts for about 80 per cent of the whole wooded area of the USSR. This is the realm of mesophilic conifer trees (those that thrive in moderate conditions of temperature and humidity): the evergreen spruces, firs and pines, and the deciduous larches. Over large areas of the taiga, especially along the rivers of Western Siberia, the ground is covered with a springy carpet of sphagnum moss, which holds water like a sponge.

The different communities of animals and plants that live in any type of forest make up an extremely complex, delicately interwoven system. Nevertheless, the purely evergreen forest of the taiga is a simpler environment than the mixed forest. It is poorer in both animal and plant species, and its overall productivity is lower. Also, it is not so distinctly divided into different layers, or tiers, as the mixed forest.

Although there are various different types of taiga, depending on the latitude, soil type and other conditions, each type may extend for many hundreds of miles. The forest usually consists of vast tracts of one or two tree species only, except along the rivers, where there is more variety. So there are fewer different niches for animals to exploit compared with mixed or deciduous forests.

Winters in the taiga are long and cold, while summers are short and often very warm. There are two main regions of taiga, a relatively small western area in European Russia, and the much larger Siberian part, extending east of the Ural Mountains as far as the Sea of Okhotsk.

In the western taiga, the climate is cloudier, with far more rain and snow than in the east. Annual rainfall averages 20 in (500 mm), and can reach as much as $27\frac{1}{2}$ in (700 mm) in the south.

LEFT *Part of the great coniferous forest belt, or taiga, on the slopes of the South Mui Mountains, north-east of Lake Baikal.*

The strong anticyclone centred on the eastern taiga from October to March is responsible for its different, more continental-type climate. Here the skies are clearer and the winters are severe, but with far less rain and snow, typically only 6 to 12 in (150 to 300 mm) a year. It is sunnier here in summer than in the western taiga and temperatures can reach remarkable heights for so northerly a region.

The eastern taiga is subjected to the biggest annual range of temperature anywhere in the world. At Verkhoyansk (latitude 67° 33′N), the temperature plummets to −90.4°F (−68°C), making it the coldest place in the Northern Hemisphere (see also page 27), but in summer it can soar to almost 100°F (38°C). These are extremes, but the average temperature in the eastern taiga in summer is 66°F (19°C), higher than anywhere else in the world at comparable latitudes. These conditions allow the Russians to grow crops such as wheat, barley and rye. As well as this huge seasonal range, there can be a great range of temperature in a single day in summer in the eastern taiga, when the nights can still be as cold as 41°F (5°C).

Plant distribution in the taiga

The evergreen conifers are superbly adapted to life in the harsh conditions of the taiga. They can make food by photosynthesis all year round, as they do not shed their leaves in winter. Also, their waxy, needle-like leaves enable them to resist the drought that results from the combination of relatively low rainfall, much of it locked up as snow and ice, and drying winds. Their familiar conical shape is an adaptation for shedding snow easily, so that their branches are not damaged by the weight of a large fall.

The western taiga is dominated by dense, gloomy stands of Norway Spruce (*Picea abies*), Siberian Spruce (*P. obovata*), Siberian Fir (*Abies sibirica*) and Siberian Stone Pine (*Pinus sibirica*). To the north, the Siberian Larch (*Larix sibirica*) is abundant in many places. On light, sandy soils, various pine trees grow, especially the Scots Pine (*Pinus silvestris*). Where there has been extensive felling, Silver Birch (*Betula pendula*) soon takes advantage of the opportunity afforded by the disappearance of the conifers. Birches also grow naturally along the northern fringes of the taiga, where they meet the tundra.

To the east of the Yenisei River, the dominant trees are larches, though here the Daurian Larch (*Larix dahurica*) replaces the Siberian species, hybridizing with its western relative in a transition zone between the two regions. Daurian Larches are able to tolerate a wide range of soil

types, from sandy or peaty soils to sparse stony or gravelly soils. Daurian Larches are remarkably undemanding trees, able to grow further north than any other. They have evolved a particularly shallow root system, enabling them to draw water from the surface layers, beneath which a thick layer of permafrost prevents water from percolating any further.

Further to the east, the vast forests are occasionally broken up by areas of grassy steppe. The lower slopes of the great mountain ranges of eastern Siberia are clothed with dense forests, but these thin out higher up, to form a belt of dwarf Siberian Stone Pine and birches, clinging to the steep rocky terrain. The topmost zone is bare mountain tundra.

In the Far East, in the Amur River basin, on the island of Sakhalin and on the more southerly of the Kuril Islands, huge areas are covered with taiga, but in the rugged Ussuri region, north of Vladivostok, the taiga clothes only the summits of the mountains.

As well as the differences between the taiga in the west and in the east, there is a north–south variation. In the northern taiga, the undergrowth consists of small shrubs, most of which also occur in the tundra. These commonly include dwarf birches (*Betula*), Cranberry (*Vaccinium oxycoccus*) and Bilberry (*V. myrtillus*). The delicate scent from the lush carpet of mosses and lichens mingles with the stronger aroma of the resin from the conifers.

The central taiga contains dense stands of timber, and here the trees are able to grow very tall in the less extreme climate, even though the soils are not as rich as in the north. Brilliant green mosses clothe the forest floor, but lichens are common only in pine forests.

In the southern taiga, the trees are even closer together, and the increased temperature enables them to grow more vigorously, so there are many dead and decaying trunks

TOP *Winter in the taiga is long and harsh. Temperatures fall to* $-90.4°F$ ($-69°C$) *in parts of eastern Siberia, and snow lies deep in the western forests, as here in Estonia.*
RIGHT *The sun's rays barely penetrate the dense, gloomy spruce forests. Austere and often oppressively silent, they conceal a variety of wild creatures.*

and branches, which provide a home for fungi and a whole range of animals. There is generally less undergrowth than in the central taiga; typical species are Cranberries, Bilberries and the delicate white-flowered Wood Sorrel (*Oxalis acetosella*). The southern taiga is of great economic importance; it produces the best quality timber, and also provides rural people with a harvest of wild berries and a variety of fungi.

ABOVE *The delicate little white flowers of the Wood Sorrel appear in spring everywhere in the spruce taiga. They are able to thrive in the deep shade cast by their giant neighbours.*

ABOVE *Primitive, spore-bearing horsetail plants, whose ancestors formed the world's great coalfields, many of them in the USSR, grow in damp clearings in the taiga.*

Spruce and fir forest

Let us now look in more detail at the various types of conifer that make up the taiga. Spruce and fir trees have the densest foliage and create the deepest shade. Both need to tolerate shade themselves to be able to survive. Relatively few plants can grow in the gloom cast by these trees, and those that do have certain features in common. There are virtually none of the annuals so characteristic of deciduous forests, which are able to concentrate their main growth into a brief spurt in spring before the leaves appear. This is impossible in the permanent shade cast by the evergreen spruces and firs.

Rather than concentrating all their efforts into producing one crop of flowers and seeds before they die, like the annuals, the perennial plants of the spruce and fir forests reproduce by vegetative means as well as by seed. Many of them produce branching underground shoots, called rhizomes, which bear buds at their tips. These soon emerge from the soil as it warms up in spring, and grow into new plants. The flowers of the dark forests are often white or near-white, so that they stand out dramatically against the dark backcloth of conifer leaves.

Other plants deal with the problem of the dense shade, which provides very little light for photosynthesis, by abandoning this method of making food. They are the saprophytes, pale because they contain no green chlorophyll, which live by feeding on rotting vegetation. The great majority of saprophytes are not plants at all, but fungi, which occur in great variety in the spruce and fir forests, in particular.

Apart from the two species of spruce already mentioned, there are eight other species. The most important are the Oriental Spruce (*Picea orientalis*), found in the Caucasus; Schrenck's Spruce (*P. schrenckiana*) and the Tien-Shan Spruce (*P. tianshanica*), which replace the Oriental Spruce in parts of Central Asia; and the Yeddo Spruce (*P. jezoensis*) of the Far East.

There are six species of fir beside the Siberian Fir mentioned above. The Caucasian Fir (*Abies nordmanniana*) is restricted to the forests of the Caucasus; the Turkestan Fir (*A. semenovi*) grows in Central Asia; the Amur Fir (*A. nephrolepis*) and Manchurian Fir (*A. holophylla*) are found in the Far East; while the island of Sakhalin has its own species, which is called the Sakhalin Fir (*A. sachalinensis*) — as does the Kamchatka Peninsula (*A. gracilis*).

Stretching over 6,000 miles (10,000 km) from the Finnish border in the west to the Pacific coast in the east, the vastness of the Russian taiga conifer forest is hard to comprehend. Here the Podkamennaya Tunguska River carves a path through the dense taiga near Krasnoyarsk in south-central Siberia. This part of the taiga is dominated by pine and larch trees, forming a living green ocean.

Pine and larch forests

These are light, open places compared with the dense spruce and fir forests, and many more plants are able to grow beneath the trees. This is especially true of the pines, which can tolerate a wider range of soil types and other conditions than the larches, and allow even more light through their more open branches. Pine forests are usually dry, and the plants that grow in them are adapted to cope with this, having reduced or waxy leaves and other adaptations.

Pines are the most widely distributed trees in the Soviet Union. They grow almost everywhere in the European part of the country, apart from the tundra and the most southerly steppes. In Asia, they are absent only from the north-east, including Kamchatka. Remarkably undiscriminating, they thrive on rich loamy soils and chalky soils alike, and even manage to grow in stony ground and boggy regions.

Besides the abundant Scots Pine, there are 12 other species in the USSR. The only one with a wide distribution is the Siberian Stone Pine (*Pinus sibirica*), which the Russians call the Cedar. It covers the whole of the West Siberian Plain and the Yenisei Basin, including the upper reaches of the River Lena. Various rare and endemic species of pine grow in the Caucasus, and there are three species in the Far East: the Mourning Pine (*P. funebris*), which is registered in the Red Data Book of the USSR, the Korean Cedar Pine (*P. korainensis*) and the Japanese Dwarf Pine (*P. pumila*), which is characteristic of the mountain ridges of the Far East and eastern Siberia.

There are four species of larch in the USSR, including the widespread Siberian and Daurian Larches discussed above. The other two, the Kamchatka Larch (*Larix kamschatica*) and the Korean Daurian Larch (*L. olgensis*) are found only in the Ussuri region in the Far East.

Animals of the taiga

Animals are limited by the harsh winters and the small number of different habitats. Fossil evidence indicates that most taiga animals evolved in eastern Siberia, spreading both eastwards and westwards from their centre of origin. They appear to have evolved earlier than the animals of the Arctic region. During the Upper Pliocene and Lower Pleistocene periods, between about three million and one-and-a-half million years ago, the warmer climate allowed mixed forests to extend in a broad strip along the Arctic coast of Russia. The taiga of eastern Siberia subsequently passed through several distinct phases. In the first half of the Pleistocene period, up to about a million years ago, it consisted mainly of dark spruce and pine forests. In the second half of the Pleistocene, this was gradually replaced by the lighter, more open larch forests. These changes had a profound effect on the animal populations of the taiga.

The insect life is far richer than in the tundra. A whole range of different types attack the wood of the conifers. These include Pine Sawflies (*Lophyrus*), Bark Beetles

ABOVE *The Goshawk is a typical taiga bird of prey. It dashes through the trees, twisting and turning as it hunts down pigeons, Hazel Grouse, hares and other prey. Although Goshawks may wander south in search of food in severe winters, they are mainly year-round residents.*

(Scolytidae), Wood Wasps (*Urocerus gigas*) and the caterpillars of various moths.

As in the tundra, few species of amphibians and reptiles manage to survive the cold winters of the taiga. Amphibians include the widespread Common Toad (*Bufo bufo*), the Common Frog (*Rana temporaria*) in the European taiga, and the Amur Frog (*Rana amurensis*) in Siberia. The only common reptiles are the Common Viper or Adder (*Vipera berus*) and the Viviparous Lizard (*Lacerta vivipara*), both of which give birth to live young — essential in a habitat where there is not enough sun to warm eggs.

Birds are much more successful. As in the tundra, they are either resident all the year round and adapted to feeding in the taiga in winter as well as summer, like the capercaillies and Siberian Jay, or summer visitors only, feeding on the swarms of insects that fill the forests during the warmer months. Summer visitors include a variety of songbirds such as warblers and thrushes.

Here, I would like to describe some of the birds that are adapted to life among the trees. The taiga includes several other habitats as well as forest: marshes, rivers and areas of steppe. The birds that occur there are no less interesting, and they are described in the appropriate sections of this book, in Chapters 8 (pages 167–175) and 9 (pages 195–207).

ABOVE *The Honey Buzzard is a summer visitor. Although it is often found in the taiga, it prefers mixed forests, where it finds more of its odd diet of wasp and bee grubs.*

An Edible Snail glides down a tree trunk; these impressive molluscs, whose shells may measure as much as 2 in (5 cm) across, are found in the middle belt of the taiga.

GAMEBIRDS

The large grouse called capercaillies are among the most typical of all the taiga birds. There are two species in the USSR – the Western Capercaillie (*Tetrao urogallus*), which ranges from the extreme west of the region to central Siberia, and the smaller, darker Black-billed Capercaillie (*T. parvirostris*), which replaces its close relative in eastern Siberia. East of the Yenisei River, there is a large area of overlap between the two species, and they often interbreed to produce hybrids known to the Russians as dark grey capercaillie. The males of these hybrids, at least, are fertile, indicating the closeness of the genetic relationship between the two species.

Capercaillies are impressive birds; a cock Western Capercaillie is the size of a turkey and can weigh more than 14 lb (6.4 kg). Disturbing one on the ground is an unforgettable – and heart-stopping – experience, as it explodes almost vertically upwards on loud, whirring wings. As with other most gamebirds, the females are much drabber and smaller.

Western Capercaillies prefer the oldest, darkest, most inaccessible areas of forest, with a dense undergrowth of ferns and other plants, and including mossy swamps and clearings where the vegetation has been burned. Such areas provide them with a wide range of different habitats, to suit their changing needs throughout the year, and guarantee them food and protection from predators.

During summer and autumn, Western Capercaillies favour areas that provide them with the maximum protection and supplies of food, especially berries and grasses. Various types of forest are suitable, including mixed pine and spruce taiga, with plenty of shrubs and other undergrowth, areas consisting purely of spruce, or birch forests with tall grasses. In the Urals and in western Siberia, they also breed in forests of Siberian Pine (*Pinus sibirica*) interspersed with marshes and felled or burned areas where there is new growth. In the more mountainous east, the Siberian Pine forest is more common and forms the main breeding grounds.

Black-billed Capercaillies breed mainly in the sparse larch forest found over much of eastern Siberia and Sakhalin. They like areas of forest separated by large felled and burnt-out clearings or broad rivers. They may also occur in pine forests.

The lifestyle and behaviour of the two species are similar. In summer, both spend much of their time on the ground, though they keep mainly to the trees during the breeding season. They are able to survive the harsh conditions of winter by feeding on conifer shoots and buds

*The size of a small turkey, a male Western Capercaillie,
his tail fanned and head pointing skywards, performs his
remarkable mating display from a prominent perch.*

and becoming much less active. Western Capercaillies alternate short bursts of feeding in the trees with long periods of rest in snug holes which they dig out of the snow. Here, they can digest their food in peace, protected from both the cold and predators. They normally feed twice a day, but during the hardest weather may leave their snow holes only once.

The Black-billed Capercaillie is more active in the depths of winter, as its east Siberian homeland has relatively little snow to prevent it from moving over the ground. In the early part of winter, however, when it is even colder than in the west and there is no snow, the birds are unable to dig themselves in, and they must perch motionless on the branches to conserve energy, and are then vulnerable to predators, such as wolves, Goshawks or owls.

When spring begins to melt the surface layer of snow, Western Capercaillies begin their extraordinary courtship rituals. These take place in the same places year after year; some of them have been known to local people and naturalists for decades. In English, they are called 'leks'. Male capercaillies are highly territorial, and normally try to avoid each other except during the courtship rituals when they gather together at the lek in small groups with a band of admiring females.

During their rituals, the capercaillie may be oblivious of anything but their displays, and even ignore shots fired at them by hunters. This is why the Russian word for capercaillie is the same as that for a deaf person.

It is hard to imagine the taiga without the Northern Hazel Grouse, or Hazelhen (*Tetrastes bonasia*), which has a wide distribution right across the taiga belt. About the size of a partridge, Hazel Grouse have mottled grey-brown plumage with dark barring, rust-coloured flanks and a conspicuous black and white band at the end of the large tail. The larger cock bird is further adorned with a black and white throat patch and a short crest.

In places, the Hazel Grouse is common, and in areas where it is not hunted, it is often seen, even on the outskirts of large cities. It is most abundant in the taiga of the plains, although it extends up river valleys onto the lower slopes of mountains, as far as the upper limit of the forest. During the breeding season, it prefers the moister areas of dark spruce (*Picea*) or mixed spruce and larch (*Larix*) forests, with scattered birches (*Betula*), alders (*Alnus*), willows (*Salix*) and aspen (*Populus*), thick undergrowth, patches of tall grass and berry-bearing bushes. This habitat provides it with both suitable nest sites and a varied diet. It feeds mainly on the leaves of birch and other deciduous trees in summer, eating large quantities of berries in autumn, alder catkins in winter and alder buds in spring. After nesting, the birds may wander short distances in search of food. In eastern Siberia, they migrate vertically from the lower mountain slopes with a sparse covering of snow to higher levels where the snow lies deeper.

As soon as spring brings warmer weather and longer and clearer days, and the south-facing slopes of the river valleys reveal thawed patches, the male Hazel Grouse begin to give their courtship song. This is a simple affair, consisting of a high-pitched, long-drawn-out whistle, followed by a trill. The hens reply with a simpler version of the trill. The snow reveals the marks made by the males' wings and fanned tails as they drag them along in the simple courtship display.

Unlike capercaillies and black grouse, Hazel Grouse do not indulge in collective courtship displays or polygamy. They are strictly monogamous, and the cock defends the pair's territory fiercely against rival males. As the temperature rises in spring, so does the number of courting pairs. There is a great deal of fighting between males, who chase the females and mate with them. A male, on hearing the whistle of a rival, hurries to the source of the sound, ready to do battle. This behaviour is exploited by hunters, who attract the birds by blowing a whistle, and find it easy to shoot the birds as they fly to within a few yards of them.

During the courtship period, the males stay up in the trees almost all the time, eating little, so that soon they become quite emaciated. Their drop in weight coincides with an enlargement of their testes in preparation for breeding. The female, by contrast, remains mainly on the ground, where she feeds frequently, and her weight increases in preparation for egg laying. Her mating behaviour is delayed by a cold, late spring, ensuring that the eggs are not laid until after the ground has thawed.

The nest is a simple pit scraped in the ground beneath a shrub or a tree, sometimes against a fallen trunk. The hen usually lays between 6 and 10 glossy, buffish-yellow eggs, sometimes as many as 15. She does not start incubating until after she has laid the last egg. Then she sits tightly for about three weeks, leaving the nest silently if disturbed, but, like the capercaillies, relying mainly on her superb camouflage to avoid detection.

The Northern Hazel Grouse, or Hazelhen, is one of the most widespread of the gamebirds found in the taiga. In winter it digs itself into the snow to escape the severe cold.

After hatching, the chicks dry their down under their mother's wings. They are able to run immediately, and the following day, she leads them out to a sunny clearing where they can find small insects to eat, although in a few weeks they will become as vegetarian as their parents. A large number of eggs and chicks succumb to predators, disease or late frosts.

Like capercaillies and black grouse, Hazel Grouse renew their courtship behaviour in autumn, after the chicks have grown up and the family has separated. The old pairs break up and new liasons are formed, involving young birds of the season. In late autumn and winter, Hazel Grouse usually stay in couples or are solitary. At first, they remain near the nest site, but when the snow starts to fall, they move to the trees along river valleys and stream sides.

They feed in the alder, birch and other trees during the short winter days, spending the nights perched on the lower branches of the spruce trees or huddled on the ground beneath. When the cold is intense and the snow lies deep, the birds tunnel holes in it, and sleep in them, insulated against the freezing temperatures. When the air outside is as cold as −40°F (−40°C), the temperature 8 in (20 cm) down in the snow-hole is as much as 5°F (−15°C). The Hazel Grouse dig out new sleeping holes every night. When it is especially cold, they may spend as much as 19 hours underground, emerging only for brief feeding sessions.

The flesh of the Hazel Grouse is prized as food both in the USSR and in other countries, and it has the greatest

An Eagle Owl brings food to its offspring in taiga near the Pacific coast of the USSR; this fierce owl, one of the world's biggest, is much rarer than it was, and is mainly restricted to the more remote coniferous forests.

economic importance of all the taiga gamebirds. Hunting still accounts for large numbers, though nothing like the annual bag of some five or six million birds taken in Russia at the end of the nineteenth century.

Unlike the widespread Hazel Grouse, the Siberian Spruce Grouse (*Falcipennis falcipennis*) has a restricted distribution. It lives in southeastern Siberia — in southern Yakutia, on the coast of the Sea of Okhotsk, in the Amur River basin, in the Ussuri district and Sakhalin, inhabiting

dense forests of larch, spruce, or mixed spruce and fir. It is resident the year round, although in mountainous regions it wanders up and down to some extent. As its name and habitat suggest, it lives chiefly on conifer buds, shoots and needles, supplementing this diet with berries, insects and spiders, when these are available.

The size of a crow, the Spruce Grouse is brownish-black, spotted with white on the back and with a pattern of white bands on its breast; the black tail is tipped with a white stripe. Females are browner with pale stripes and lighter underparts. Like the Hazel Grouse, Spruce Grouse are monogamous. During the spring courtship ritual, the males may shake their wings, fan their tails and leap into the air with outstretched necks, giving a raucous call.

The nest is well concealed and the six to 10 brownish, delicately mottled eggs are laid at the end of May. The female is very reluctant to leave the nest during the 17-day incubation period, and she may be literally trodden on before she reveals her presence by a low, coarse crackle. The males play no part in incubation or care of the chicks, spending the summer separately from their families.

The Spruce Grouse has an unfortunate combination of tasty flesh and remarkable tameness. If disturbed in the forest, the birds make no attempt to hide, but fly down to the lower branches of the trees to investigate the cause of the intrusion, often perching only a couple of feet away from people. They are easily caught by hunters armed with nooses.

WADERS AND CUCKOOS

Various species of wader are found in the taiga, but two that are particularly adapted to this habitat in the breeding season are the Green Sandpiper (*Tringa ochropus*) and the Grey-rumped Sandpiper or Grey-tailed Tattler (*Heteroscelus brevipes*). Both these waders often take over the old nests of Blackbirds and other thrushes to raise their own young. They migrate long distances southwards in winter, Green Sandpipers to central and southern Asia, the Transcaucasus, the Mediterranean and Africa, and Grey-tailed Tattlers to Indonesia, the Philippines, Polynesia, Australia and Tasmania. Another typical forest wader is the Eurasian Woodcock (*Scolopax rusticola*), which nests on the ground and winters in the Transcaucasus and throughout much of Central Asia.

Two species of cuckoo breed in the taiga: the Eurasian Cuckoo (*Cuculus canorus*) and the Oriental Cuckoo (*C. saturatus*). The Eurasian Cuckoo has a very wide distribution, being found throughout the USSR except for the north, as well as right across the rest of Europe. It is

common in the taiga, and also occurs in a variety of other habitats: deciduous and mixed forests, wooded steppe and steppe, mountains, parks and gardens. It migrates to Africa and southern Asia for the winter. The Oriental Cuckoo, which is very similar to the Eurasian species but darker and more heavily barred beneath, breeds in the thick, old dark forests of eastern European Russia, Siberia and the Far East, and winters in Indonesia, New Guinea, Australia and the Solomon Islands. The song of the Eurasian Cuckoo, from which the bird gets its name, is too well known to need further description. The Oriental Cuckoo makes a quite different sound, a soft, three-note hooting, reminiscent of the call of the Hoopoe (*Upupa epops*). In other respects, the two species have very similar lifestyles, laying their eggs in

The Siberian Spruce Grouse is found only in the USSR, in the dense coniferous forests of southeastern Siberia. Remarkably tame, it allows people to approach it to within a few feet.

the nests of various small songbirds, such as warblers, flycatchers and accentors.

OWLS

The Great Grey Owl (*Strix nebulosa*) is one of the world's biggest owls, some individuals being even longer, at 30 in (76 cm), than the Eagle Owl (*Bubo bubo*), illustrated opposite, though only about half the latter's weight. It is widely distributed throughout the taiga of Europe, Asia and North America. In the USSR, it is most common in eastern Siberia and rarest in European Russia.

Great Greys are imposing creatures. They have massive heads as much as 20 in (51 cm) in circumference, with concentric circles of barred feathers around the small fiercely blazing yellow eyes, feathered legs as thick as a human wrist, and long, wedge-shaped tails. They are often remarkably tame, allowing human observers to walk right up to them. They start breeding at the end of March or the beginning of April. During the courtship period, the deep, melancholy hooting song of the male echoes through the still, dark forest at dusk or during the night. The owls usually use an unoccupied nest of a bird of prey, such as a Goshawk (*Accipiter gentilis*) or Buzzard (*Buteo buteo*), in a tree high above the ground. In April, the female lays three to five white eggs and incubates them for 28 days, beginning with the first egg. She sits tightly and if scared away, returns at the earliest opportunity.

Great Grey Owls protect their nests with considerable zeal after the chicks have hatched. The male hunts while his mate stands guard. If anyone attempts to climb the tree and approach the nest, the owls' fury is boundless, the female being the more aggressive. They are completely fearless, diving at the intruders and striking them on the back or the neck with their talons. Naturalists studying the breeding behaviour of this aggressive bird have to don protective clothing and crash-helmets with visors to avoid serious injury; those who have approached the nest without such precautions have suffered deep gashes, broken legs from being knocked out of a tree, and have even been blinded by the owl's slashing, razor-sharp talons. It is not surprising that no predators, not even bears, normally attempt to attack the young owls.

The Great Grey Owl feeds mainly on small rodents, especially voles. Like other birds that depend on such a diet, including the Snowy Owl (*Nyctea scandiaca*) and Rough-legged Buzzard (*Buteo lagopus*) of the tundra (pages 84–5), the owls' population fluctuates in response to the cycles of abundance and scarcity of their prey. In years when the rodent population 'crashes' to a low level, many pairs of Great Grey Owls do not even attempt to breed, waiting instead for better times.

Three other species of owls live in the taiga: the Ural Owl (*Strix uralensis*), the Eurasian Pygmy Owl (*Glaucidium passerinum*) and the Tengmalm's, or Boreal, Owl (*Aegolius funereus*). None of these is rare, but because of their secretive lifestyle they are rarely seen.

WOODPECKERS

These are among the birds most adapted to life in the forests, but of the 13 species which nest today in the USSR, most are found in deciduous or mixed woodland, and only four are particularly linked to the taiga. These are the Black Woodpecker (*Dryocopus martius*), the Northern Three-toed Woodpecker (*Picoides tridactylus*), the Great Spotted Woodpecker (*Dendrocopos major*) and the White-Backed Woodpecker (*D. leucotos*). The latter is found mainly in birch woods.

The Black Woodpecker prefers tall, old forests with mossy swamps. It is the largest of the USSR's woodpeckers and one of the biggest in the world, the size of a crow, at 18 in (45 cm) long. Both male and female are almost entirely black; the male is adorned with a brilliant crimson crown tapering to form a crest at the back of the head which the bird erects when it is excited. The female's red patch is much smaller and restricted to the back of the head. Both sexes have pale yellow eyes and whitish dagger-like bills.

Black Woodpeckers lead a solitary life, except for the breeding season, which begins early in the year, in February and early March. Although mainly silent and elusive during winter, the birds become noisy and conspicuous, drumming loudly and rapidly with their powerful bills against the tree trunks to produce a sound that is clearly audible for well over half a mile (1 km). The birds also utter a variety of calls, including a ringing laughing call, a series of high chattering notes and a plaintive nasal whistle. They chase each other through the trees, the male usually pursuing the female. She flies to perch on a tree-trunk near the ground, and gives a quiet call. The male responds loudly and flies to join his prospective mate, usually perching below her. He bends his neck gracefully, showing off his handsome red crest, and looks up at the female. Then they begin a complex dance, the female leading the male in spirals up the trunk.

Soon after they have paired, the birds move into the thickest part of the forest. Here, they excavate their nest holes high up in the trunks of large trees, inaccessible to predators. Unlike some woodpeckers, they often make them in perfectly healthy trees rather than in decaying wood, a habit that does not endear the birds to foresters. The male does most of the work, hacking away at the hard bark with his powerful bill so that chips of wood fly out in all directions, while his mate watches. The entry hole measures about 4 in (10 cm) across by 6 in (15 cm) from top to bottom. As with the nests of other woodpeckers, there is no lining to the bare hollow within, apart from the few wood chips not removed by the woodpeckers during its excavation. The female lays her three to five glossy white eggs directly onto this hard surface, and both sexes take it in turns to incubate the eggs for 14 to 16 days.

The blind, naked chicks cheep persistently for food from deep in the nest hollow. They have white-tipped beaks, which may help their parents locate them quickly in the gloom of the nesting chamber. As they grow larger, the chicks start to poke their heads out of the hole. Then their cries are audible for as much as 100 yards (90 m) away, and it is an easy matter to find the nest. After 24 to 28 days, the young fledge and jockey for position at the entrance hole. They usually spend several nights in the open before they manage to find roosting holes, and at this stage are very vulnerable to predators such as the Goshawk (*Accipiter gentilis*) and various owls.

Black Woodpeckers feed on large wood-boring insects, including beetles and their larvae and ants, reaching them by hacking out the decaying wood in which they live, sending chips of wood as much as 9 in (23 cm) long showering onto the ground below. The insects are extracted on the barbed tip of the woodpecker's remarkable tongue. As in other woodpeckers, this is coiled up like a spring inside the bird's skull, being suddenly shot out by the contraction of powerful muscles to a length of up to 8 cm (3 in). The woodpeckers may supplement their winter diet with berries and conifer seeds, and in spring they sometimes drill holes into the trees to drink the sugary sap beneath the bark.

ACCENTORS AND THRUSHES

One of the most unobtrusive and little-known birds of the taiga is the Siberian Accentor (*Prunella montanella*), which is endemic to the Soviet Union, breeding only in the taiga of northern and eastern Siberia. Sparrow-sized, it has streaked brown upperparts, with black on the head, and ochre-coloured underparts, and is best identified by its sweet warbling song, given from the top of a spruce or larch tree. It lays four to six pale blue eggs in a neat nest hidden in a tree close to the ground, and feeds on insects. In winter, Siberian Accentors migrate to eastern China and Korea.

'Did you ever hear a thrush sing?' asks a popular Russian song. For those Russians who live in the taiga belt, the answer must be 'Yes', for here there lives an impressive variety of thrushes, and their melodious songs fill the air in spring and summer throughout the vast forests of Siberia. They are hardy birds, penetrating as far north as the wooded tundra of the Taimyr Peninsula.

One of the smallest thrushes of the USSR, the Redwing (*Turdus iliacus*) is widely distributed throughout the taiga, chiefly in areas of forest where spruces alternate with patches of alder and other deciduous trees.

A White-backed Woodpecker at its nest hole; although widespread throughout the taiga, it is most common in the mixed forests of the Ussuri region in the south-east.

Other common thrushes include the Song Thrush (*Turdus philomelos*), the Mistle Thrush (*T. viscivorus*) and the Fieldfare (*T. pilaris*). All these are familiar to European birdwatchers. In Russia, they migrate south in winter, the Song Thrush to the Crimea and Transcaucasus, the Mistle Thrush to North Africa, southwest Asia and Asia Minor, and the Fieldfare to the Crimea, the Caucasus, Tadzhikistan and southwestern Asia.

As well as these four, the taiga contains a number of little-studied, rare or exotic species of thrush, but the greatest variety occurs in the mixed and broad-leaved forests, so they will be described in detail in the following chapter on that habitat (on pages 130–1).

The taiga also contains some beautiful, smaller relatives of the thrushes, including the Red-flanked Bluetail (*Tarsiger cyanurus*), the Whistling Nightingale (*Luscinia sibilans*) the Siberian Rubythroat (*Luscinia calliope*) and the Daurian Redstart (*Phoenicurus auroreus*).

Many species of warbler spend summer in the taiga, breeding over huge areas of forest. Common species are the Arctic Warbler (*Phylloscopus borealis*), the Greenish Warbler (*P. trochiloides*) and the Willow Warbler (*P. trochilus*). They are all about $4\frac{1}{2}$ in (11 cm) long, with

Redwing (Turdus iliacus)

Dusky Thrush (Turdus eunomus)

Greenish Warbler (Phylloscopus trochiloides)

Siberian Accentor (Prunella montanella)

Red-flanked Bluetail (Tarsiger cyanurus)/*male*

Unlike the tundra, the taiga is home to a variety of perching birds in summer, when they migrate from the south to breed. The Siberian Accentor breeds only in north and east Siberia. More widespread are the thrushes, such as the Redwing, familiar to Europeans as a winter visitor, and Dusky Thrush. A smaller relative is the lovely Red-flanked Bluetail, which breeds in the southern taiga. The many warblers include the Greenish Warbler.

brownish-grey or brownish-green plumage and delicate, insect-eating bills. Despite their small size and apparent fragility, they migrate huge distances to their wintering grounds in Africa, the Middle East, India and Southeast Asia, and are among the USSR's most northerly songbirds. Although they resemble one another closely in their appearance and general behaviour, their songs are as different as night and day, and afford the best means of distinguishing them.

TITS AND NUTHATCHES

Various species of the tit family live in the coniferous forests of the USSR, while others are found in mixed or deciduous woods and some in the mountains. One of the most typical and abundant taiga species is the Willow Tit (*Parus montanus*). This partly resident, partly migratory bird is widespread in both lowland and mountain forests of the USSR, and is also found over much of western Europe. The size of a Blue Tit (*Parus caeruleus*), it has greyish-brown upperparts, a large, dull black crown and black bib, buff flanks and paler underparts.

The nuthatch family, which contains 31 species worldwide, is represented in the taiga of the USSR by a single widespread species, the Eurasian Nuthatch (*Sitta europaea*), a pretty blue-grey and buffish-yellow bird which occurs throughout the forested parts of the country, except in Central Asia and Kazakhstan. Outside the USSR, it is a common and well-known species in much of western Europe. Unlike the tits, it can walk down trunks as easily as climbing up them.

A Eurasian Nuthatch feeds its young near the Pacific coast in June. This attractive bird, which ranges throughout Europe and Asia, is found in nearly all the forests of the USSR, from the western border to the Far East.

The Nutcracker is a member of the crow family that is common in the taiga. It is highly adapted to life in the taiga, feeding chiefly on conifer seeds. It regularly buries caches of food to see it through the hard winters.

CROSSBILLS

The most highly adapted of all the taiga's perching birds are the crossbills, a small group of finches which, as their name implies, have bills with crossed tips, evolved for extracting the seeds from the cones of conifer trees with the delicacy of a pair of tweezers. Three species are found in the forests of the USSR: the smallest, the size of a sparrow, is the White-winged Crossbill (*Loxia leucoptera*) and the largest, $1\frac{1}{2}$ in (4 cm) larger than the White-winged, is the Parrot Crossbill (*L. pytyopsittacus*); the other is the medium-sized Red Crossbill (*L. curvirostra*). The males are a striking rosy-red colour, while the females and young have more sober greenish-grey plumage.

The distribution of the three species is partly related to the size of their bills, each adapted for extracting seeds from different-sized cones. The slender-billed White-winged Crossbill eats mainly seeds of the small, soft cones of larches, the medium-billed Red Crossbill concentrates chiefly on the larger spruce seeds, while the heavy-billed Parrot Crossbill can cope with the large, hard cones of pine trees. The White-winged and Common Crossbills are widely distributed throughout the Soviet taiga, but the Parrot Crossbill is restricted to northwest European Russia.

If the season's crop of cones is good, more crossbills survive to breed the following spring, but if this plentiful harvest is followed by a poor cone crop, the large populations of birds soon eat all the available seeds and are forced to travel in search of food. These 'irruptions' take the birds far to the west or south of their usual haunts.

FOREST CROWS

Two species of the crow family are characteristic of the taiga: the Siberian Jay (*Perisoreus infaustus*) and the Nutcracker (*Nucifraga caryocatactes*). The Siberian Jay prefers the denser spruce/fir and pine/larch forest, and breeds throughout the taiga zone of the USSR, and also in Scandinavia. It is similar in appearance and general behaviour to the familiar Eurasian Jay (*Garrulus glandarius*), although it is smaller and less brightly coloured, its greyish-brown plumage relieved only by rusty red wing patches, rump and outer tail feathers. It is a year-round resident, although it may wander to a certain extent outside the breeding season in search of food. Its feathers are fluffier than those of the Eurasian Jay, as a protection against the extreme cold of the northern winter.

The Nutcracker is widespread throughout the taiga zone. About $12\frac{1}{2}$ in (31 cm) long, it has chocolate brown plumage peppered all over, apart from the crown and the nape, with conspicuous white spots, a patch of pure white feathers under its short black tail, blackish, rounded wings and a noticeably undulating flight.

Nutcrackers are equally at home in the trees and on the ground, where they hop about clumsily searching for insects and berries as well as their staple diet of pine or spruce seeds. When dealing with conifer seeds, they do not have the surgical precision of the crossbills; they often simply smash the entire cone against a rock or tree with their powerful pointed beaks, so that the seeds spill out, although they can also remove the seeds with the pointed tips of their beaks. In winter, Nutcrackers are easily seen, noisy birds, with harsh calls, but as the breeding season begins (as early in the year as the beginning of March, except in the north) they fall silent and become very secretive, hiding in the densest parts of the forest. They build cup-shaped nests of twigs and lichens, lined with moss and soil, usually siting them on the branch of a conifer tree 12 to 20 ft (3.7 to 6 m) high. The female lays between two and five eggs, which are pale turquoise and bear fine grey speckles. She incubates them for 16 to 18 days. The young are fed by both male and female, and leave the nest when about 4 weeks old, although they remain dependent on their parents for a further two or three months.

A remarkable habit of the Nutcracker, which provides a fine example of the ability of animals to adapt to life in the harsh conditions of the Siberian forests, is that of storing conifer seeds and nuts during autumn, to last them through the bitter winter and into spring. The birds gather large numbers of seeds in a pouch under the tongue; that of one Nutcracker was found to contain 120 seeds. Sometimes, they may spend all day, from sunrise to sunset, collecting the food and flying off to put it in their 'larders'. The Nutcrackers regurgitate their dry cargo with the help of unusually generous supplies of saliva, and then push the seeds or nuts into soft soil, into cracks in trees and beneath their bark, or into clumps of moss or lichen. Each larder may contain anything from three or four to 50 seeds. The birds have an uncanny knack of finding their hoards − or most of them − even though they often have to dig through as much as 2 ft (60 cm) of snow to reach them. How they do this is still a mystery to ornithologists, although their habit of arranging their larders in regular patterns near landmarks may mean that they remember where they are by visual clues.

Taiga mammals

A rather small number of mammals are linked closely with the taiga, but there are other, more flexible species that spend part of their time there. The most familiar taiga mammal is the Red Squirrel (*Sciurus vulgaris*). There are several different subspecies in the USSR. The rich rusty-red fur of the Siberian subspecies, or *teleutka*, as the Russians call it, is moulted to a beautiful silvery-grey coat in winter, though the long ear-tufts remain red and black. Squirrel fur is a valued natural resource in the Soviet Union, although hunting is forbidden in some areas.

The Siberian Chipmunk (*Eutamias sibiricus*), a small striped squirrel with a much less bushy tail than the Red Squirrel, is also widely distributed through the taiga. It stores food in its cheek pouches, like hamsters.

RODENTS

A number of rodents are common in the taiga. These are mainly voles, the most characteristic being the Common Red-backed Vole or Bank Vole (*Clethrionomys glareolus*), the Large-Toothed Red-backed Vole or Grey-sided Vole (*C. rufocanus*) and the Northern Red-backed Vole (*C. rutilus*). The first two are restricted to Europe and Asia, but the last named also occurs throughout Arctic North America. All voles, and especially forest species, are remarkably fertile; the female normally has three to five litters of between four and eight young each year. They are born in nests hidden under logs or among tree roots. The vole population fluctuates widely from year to year, depending on the weather and the amount of food available. Voles spend much of their time in shallow tunnels, but also appear above ground, especially when searching for food − seeds, leaves, shoots, roots, bulbs, the bark and buds of trees, as well as mushrooms and berries. In turn, they form an important part of the diet of many predators, from Red Foxes (*Vulpes vulpes*) to owls.

A Red Fox photographed near Moscow in January. Common in most of the USSR, this familiar mammal is one of the world's most widespread carnivores, ranging throughout the northern hemisphere, from remote forests to city centres.

An Arctic Hare speeds through the forest in its winter camouflage. In summer, its coat turns a lovely shade of grey-brown. Although common throughout the Soviet taiga, like most of its inhabitants, it is not restricted to this habitat, being found also in the tundra and on mountains.

WOLVES AND FOXES

Although the Wolf (*Canis lupus*) lives in a variety of other habitats, from tundra and mountains to steppes and deserts, the taiga is its stronghold. There are eight or nine subspecies of Wolf in the USSR – an indication of its great adaptability. Wolves avoid the denser parts of the forest in winter, as they find it difficult to run down their favourite prey, Elk (*Alces alces*) and other deer, in the deep snow. They hunt much more effectively in the open areas of forest, where the snow is lighter and more compacted. Except for the breeding season, Wolves spend most of their time in family groups, or packs, with a definite leader, and often show great cunning in outwitting their fast-moving prey when hunting together. They pair for life, or for many years at least, and the female gives birth to three, four or five cubs in a den dug out of soft ground or in a natural hollow among rocks or fallen trees.

The Red Fox (*Vulpes vulpes*), familiar to European and North American readers, is another typical inhabitant of the taiga, which is widely distributed throughout the USSR. It is even more variable than the Wolf, with 14 or 15 subspecies.

BEARS

The most impressive of all the taiga mammals is the majestic Brown Bear (*Ursus arctos*). In spite of extensive hunting, individuals weighing almost $\frac{3}{4}$ ton (750 kg) and measuring over 8 ft (2.5 m) from nose to tail can still be seen in the forests. Standing up on its hind legs, a full-grown adult is almost 10 ft (3 m) high. Brown Bears are found throughout the forests of the USSR. The largest bears live in the Soviet Far East and Kamchatka.

Brown Bears are remarkably variable in colour, from pale fawn to dark brown; these variations exist between individuals within a single area, as well as between widely separated populations, some of which are different enough to be considered separate subspecies. The bears' favourite habitat is dense taiga on gently undulating terrain, with plenty of fallen, decaying trees, interspersed with lakes, marshes and meadowland. The more open areas supply them with most of their food, while the taiga provides a refuge. Bears lead a solitary life for much of the year, and establish large territories. They may cover scores of miles in the course of their wanderings. They avoid contact with people as much as possible. A few of them, especially those living in the remote northern taiga, sometimes hunt large prey, such as Elk (*Alces alces*) or Wild Boar (*Sus scrofa*), tracking them tirelessly and using their great strength and surprising speed and agility to bring them down. Their main diet, however, consists of berries, nuts and other fruit, the leaves, stems, bulbs and tubers of various plants, fungi, birds' eggs, honey, insects, fish and carrion.

In autumn, the bears eat extra food to provide a store of fat that will see them through the long, cold winter, which they spend in their dens. In some areas, bears dig out deep dens in the earth, but often they make do with natural hollows among rocks or beneath fallen trees. In the depths of winter, when the snow covers the den, only a small opening remains for ventilation. The bears choose the most secure, hidden spots for their dens, often in an island of forest in the middle of a vast mossy bog. Contrary to popular belief, they are not true hibernators; they doze for long periods. The females and young stay in the den for as much as five or six months, although the solitary males usually leave earlier. Their heartbeat slows down and their body temperature drops by a few degrees, saving precious energy but allowing the bear to wake up quickly if danger threatens. Then, they leave the den and move to another. As they near their goal they take a complex, wandering route, creating many tracks that are difficult to follow.

Bears are sexually active from May to July. Normally silent, they roar loudly during the mating season, and bitter fights break out between rival males, sometimes ending with the death of one or other of them. The winner may even eat the loser. After a pregnancy of about six to eight months, the female gives birth in late winter to two, three or four cubs, very rarely five. They are surprisingly small, only the size of Guinea Pigs at birth. By spring, they have reached the size of small dogs and are weaned onto a diet of leaves, berries and insects.

The Wolverine, or Glutton, is the largest member of the weasel family. An extremely powerful and fierce predator, it is capable of killing prey as large as Reindeer.

THE WEASEL FAMILY

Most members of the weasel family (Mustelidae) are true forest dwellers. One widespread species in the Siberian taiga is the Siberian Weasel (*Mustela sibirica*). This little animal is valued by the Russians for its fur. It prefers the dark pine and larch forests, usually living near rivers or lakes, but is often seen on the edges of towns, where it may kill poultry, although it makes up for this by destroying large numbers of mice and rats. These form its main food, but it has a wide diet, including pikas (*Ochotona*), musk rats (*Ondathra*), Siberian Chipmunks (*Eutamias sibirica*), squirrels (*Sciurus*) and jerboas (*Allactaga*). If there are not enough of their usual prey, the weasels catch fish, but if food is particularly scarce, they may be forced to make mass emigrations. The breeding season is between February and April, and the female produces from four to ten young after a gestation period of 28 to 42 days.

The value and beauty of the smoky-reddish-brown and black fur of the Sable (*Martes zibellina*) are legendary – and the cause of its former rarity. This pretty relative of the weasels lives in the taiga from the upper Pechora River to the Soviet Far East. The Sables with the most valued fur come from Barguzin, on the eastern shores of Lake Baikal, Yakutia and Kamchatka. Sables prefer pine forests, where they can find an ample supply of rodents, which form a major part of their diet. They also eat pine seeds and, in

The Siberian Weasel, or Kolinsky, is common in the Siberian taiga. Like the Wolverine's, its fur is prized, but trapping of both species is strictly controlled.

summer, berries and insects. Sables are strongly territorial, leaving their hunting area only when forced to by winter food shortages or the necessity of feeding their young. They build a nest in a hollow tree stump or crevice in rocks or in the ground. They climb trees with ease, but catch most of their prey on the ground. In winter, they may dive beneath the snow in search of voles or other animals.

The young are born in April and May, and there may be only one or as many as seven in a litter. They leave the nest when they are six weeks old, and by August the family has split up. The low fertility of wild Sables and the high value of their fur have led to the introduction of fur farms containing many caged Sables.

DEER

The Elk (*Alces alces*) is the largest of the world's living deer, weighing up to half a ton or more (580 to 600 kg) and measuring over 9 ft (2.8 m) long and more than 7 ft (2.2 m) high at the shoulders. Elk have particularly long legs and a large, inflated muzzle which overhangs the mouth. Males have distinctive flattened antlers. They have a very wide distribution, from Scandinavia, Poland, northern European Russia and Siberia to northern USA (including Alaska) and Canada, where they are known as Moose.

In summer, Elk wander through the taiga in search of food, often travelling many miles in a single day. They prefer burnt or felled areas of forest, where succulent new shoots appear on the deciduous trees and there is plenty of lush, high grass. They also frequent swampy areas of taiga with quiet rivers and streams, feeding on water plants. In winter, they move to areas of conifer forest or mixed forest with dense undergrowth and a good growth of saplings. They remain in the forest, wandering little, as long as the snow is no deeper than 12 to 20 in (30 to 50 cm). They find it difficult to walk in deep snow, however, and are often forced to move to other areas. During such migrations, they try to keep off well-worn tracks and so avoid Wolves. In some areas, Elk are abundant; in the Pechoro-Ilych nature reserve, for instance, an unusually dense population of about 250 Elk per sq mile (1,000 per 1,000 hectares) has been recorded.

Elk are less gregarious than other large deer, and often live alone. In August and September, the males are on heat and their dull mooing echoes through the forest, especially at dawn. Males become sexually mature during their third or fourth autumn, females a year earlier. Rival males use their antlers in sparring contests, and chase away the young males. Unlike other deer, such as Reindeer (*Rangifer tarandus*), they do not collect a harem of females, but

LEFT *Epitomizing the wildness of the vast Russian coniferous forests, a pack of Wolves appears among the trees. The USSR is one of the last strongholds of these magnificent predators.*
ABOVE *European Bison and calf in Lithuania. Extinct in the wild by 1925, they have been reintroduced to the Soviet Union from captive breeding stock.*

usually have only one mate. Calving is in April and May, and there may be one or two young. If there are twins, the second-born often dies. Elk can live as long as 25 years.

They eat various kinds of vegetation, including grass. In summer, they browse on the leaves of various shrubs and trees, using their long, flexible muzzles. In winter, their diet includes the shoots of willow, aspen and birch, the shoots and foliage of pine, and raspberry canes. They also eat bark, especially of pine and aspen. In 24 hours, an adult Elk can eat about 26 to 33 lb (12 to 15 kg) of food in winter, and as much as 77 lb (35 kg) in summer. It is easy to appreciate that a large population of Elk can do considerable damage to a forest, particularly to the young saplings.

The numbers of Elk are controlled by hunting; as in Alaska, Canada and other countries, they are important game animals in the Soviet Union.

In this chapter, I have been able to describe only a selection of the rich variety of wildlife that inhabits the taiga. A list of characteristic birds and mammals appears in the appendix (pages 211–12).

Forest nature reserves

Most of the USSR's nature reserves – and the largest ones – are in the taiga. The nature reserves of the more southerly mixed forests and of the Far East are described in the next chapter (on pages 136–7). Vast areas of forest have been set aside for conservation, including nature reserves and national parks. Scientifically based forestry management is combined with the conservation of nature in large areas of forest, so that they are completely free from exploitation. The largest reserves are in Siberia; those in European Russia are relatively small.

In 1979 the Baikal State Nature Reserve was created in the Buryat Autonomous SSR, in the central part of the Khamar–Daban mountain range, on the south-western shores of Lake Baikal. It has an area of 640 sq miles (1,657 sq km), of which 453 sq miles (1,172 sq km) is taiga. On the northern slopes of the range, dark fir and Siberian Stone Pine forest predominates, while on the southern slopes there is a light conifer taiga of larch and pine. Vegetation in the reserve includes 800 species of flowering plants; there are also 37 species of mammal and 260 species of birds and a wide variety of other animals.

About 200 miles (320 km) to the north lies the Barguzin State Nature Reserve, which was created in 1916, initially to protect the specially valuable local subspecies of Sable. Today, it is a superb refuge for the varied and fascinating flora and fauna of the Lake Baikal taiga. Occupying an area of 1,016 sq miles (2,632 sq km), it stretches for nearly 60 miles (100 km) along the shores of Lake Baikal and contains many of the region's famous healing hot springs, with

water at temperatures of 104 to 169°F (40 to 76°C). There are more than 600 species of flowering plants, 39 species of mammals, 4 of reptiles, 2 of amphibians and 243 of birds. There is a healthy population of the Barguzin Sable, with about 100 animals per 40 sq miles (100 sq km). In the lake itself lives the endemic Baikal Seal (*Phoca baicalica*), as well as many unique species of fish and other animals. This region is also described briefly on pages 52, 57.

The Bashkir Nature Reserve, created in 1945, is in the Southern Ural area, at the meeting point of the three regions of Kalinin, Yaroslavl and Vologda. A sub-zone of the southern taiga, it includes 190 sq miles (492 sq km) of forest and 179 sq miles (463 sq km) of water. The total area of the reserve is 435 sq miles (1,126 sq km), and it contains 530 species of flowering plants, 230 species of birds and 40 species of mammals within its boundaries.

BELOW *The map shows the USSR's forest reserves, including mixed forest reserves (page 134) as well as taiga reserves.*

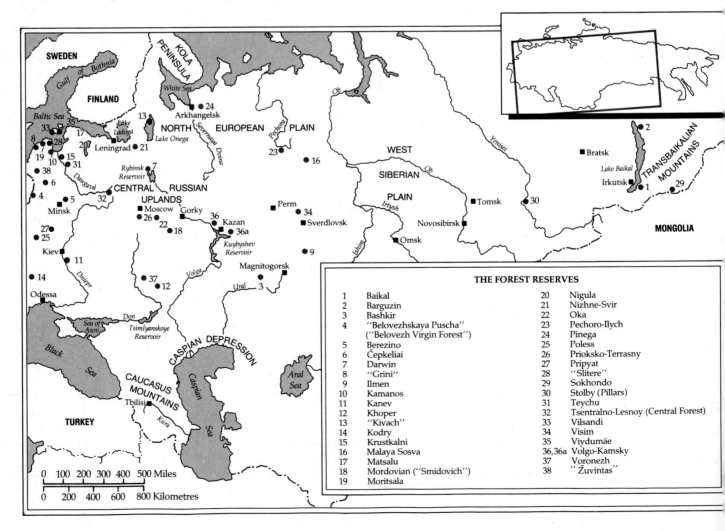

On the eastern slopes of the southern Ural Mountains is the Ilmen Nature Reserve. Named after Lenin, it has an area of 117 sq miles (304 sq km). The different taiga of Karelia is represented in the 'Kivach' Nature Reserve in the Lake Onega region, which occupies 41 sq miles (105 sq km). In 1976, the large 'Malaya Sosva' Nature Reserve was created along a tributary of the River Ob, with an area of 359 sq miles (929 sq km), of which 84.1 per cent is forest. This belongs to the sub-zone of the central taiga (see page 92). In 1985, a large reserve was established in Central Siberia, in the middle of the course of the great River Yenisei. This includes almost 3,860 sq miles (10,000 sq km) of virgin taiga.

The Mordovian Autonomous SSR, in the Upper Volga area, contains the 'Smidovich' Nature Reserve, with 124 sq miles (321 sq km) of land, including 119 sq miles (309 sq km) of forest. In 1980, the Nizhne-Svir Reserve, with an area of 158 sq miles (410 sq km), was created in the Leningrad region.

The well-known Oka Reserve was established as long ago as 1935 in the Ryazan region, not far from Moscow. Its area is 88 sq miles (229 sq km), of which 75 sq miles (194 sq km) are forest. It contains 800 species of flowering plants, 230 species of birds and a number of rare animals, including the extraordinary, long-nosed Russian Desman (*Desmana*

The Russian Desman is an aquatic relative of the moles with dense waterproof fur, webbed feet, a flattened tail and a long, mobile snout; it is rare and fully protected.

moschata), illustrated above. The central ornithological station of the USSR has been sited here since 1956.

In 1930, the Pechoro-Ilych Reserve was created in the Komi Autonomous SSR, on the western foothills of the northern Urals. It includes 2,412 sq miles (6,246 sq km) of taiga in its total area of 2,785 sq miles (7,213 sq km). There are 204 species of birds and 43 of mammals. The Pinezh Reserve in the Arkhangelsk region, created in 1975, has an area of 159 sq miles (412 sq km), of which 90 per cent is forest.

The large Sayano-Shushen Reserve, in the mountains of south-central Siberia (map, page 162), with a total area of 1504 sq miles (3,896 sq km), was established in 1976. Forest covers 59.3 per cent of this reserve. The Sokhondo Reserve in the Chita region consists of 815 sq miles (2,110 sq km) of taiga. On the spurs of the eastern Sayan Mountains is the 'Stolby' Reserve, occupying 182 sq miles (472 sq km), of which 454 sq km are forest.

A further increase in the already impressive area of nature reserves set aside in the taiga of the USSR is likely to be announced in the near future.

6 MIXED FORESTS

Forests are the most complex natural communities in the world. They are also the most valuable – both in terms of richness of species and use to man. In the USSR, forests cover almost 3 million square miles (7.7 million sq km), or 35.5 per cent of the total land area.

Most of the USSR's forest are coniferous, forming the great taiga belt (see Chapter 5). The remainder, although it includes some purely broad-leaved deciduous forest, consists mainly of a mixture of coniferous and broad-leaved trees. The European part of the USSR and the southern Soviet Far East contain the two largest regions of mixed forest.

Forests are particularly complex environments: no other plant communities develop so diversely, spread so widely, and, alas, disappear so fast as the forests. Most mixed forests suffer considerably from human exploitation, and there are very few which the naturalist can still see in their virgin state – although several areas of original forest in the USSR are protected in nature reserves and national parks.

The forest provides food and homes for countless animals. Warblers and tits comb the trees in search of a wealth of caterpillars and other insect food; squirrels leap from branch to branch; bees buzz from flower to flower; ants march through the undergrowth; and huge numbers of other invertebrates live among the rotting leaves that carpet the forest floor.

Mixed forests can be clearly separated into tiers or stages, from the leaf litter at ground level to the crowns of the tall, old trees. Only a few of its inhabitants make use of all these layers in their choice of nesting sites or their search for food. And even these avoid competition with other species by taking different kinds of food from different parts of each layer, and tend to favour a certain layer. This neat, extremely subtle arrangement has been found to operate among tits, for example.

There are four main layers in broad-leaved and mixed forests. The first is the ground layer. The leaf litter and soil teem with invertebrate life. Above, on the forest floor, live countless other invertebrates, and a variety of mammals, from tiny shrews to deer or Wild Boar (*Sus scrofa*); various bird species feed here, and there are also forest-dwelling snakes.

LEFT *The mixed forest zones of the USSR, especially those of the Ussuri region and other areas of the Far East, contain a rich variety of plants and animals, including this White's Thrush, seen here with a brood of chicks at its nest on Kunashir Island, just to the north of Japan.*

The next layer, which is not always present, is the understorey. If the shrubs and other undergrowth are well developed and dense, with a rich crop of berries and other fruit, it will provide food for a variety of mammals and birds. Many animals use the understorey as a refuge and birds build their nests there.

The third layer is that of low trees, which can survive in deep shade. Many specialist forest dwellers, especially birds, live and nest here, spending most of their time in the trees, as do squirrels and other rodents, martens and other mammals.

Finally, the uppermost branches of trees, thrusting up into the sunlight, is the home of birds such as orioles and cuckoos. Some butterflies, such as hairstreaks (*Zephyrus*), also reach these higher levels, rarely descending to lower layers. The sky above the forest is the province mainly of birds of prey and some strong-flying insects.

A Steller's Sea Eagle chick adopts a threatening pose in its nest on Sakhalin Island in the Far East.

Many forests contain clearings of various sizes, created naturally by storms or artificially by felling or fire. Unless kept open, these areas quickly become overgrown with shrubs and finally revert to forest. The fauna and flora of such communities vary from year to year, depending on the speed of the succession of vegetation.

The forests of the middle latitudes of the USSR are remarkably homogeneous. Some consist almost entirely of one or two tree species, others being rare and growing in widely separated areas. This is in great contrast to the complex forests further south. In the USSR, the mixed and broad-leaved forests of the southern Far East, along the Amur and Ussuri river valleys and the Pacific coast, have a great variety of trees and other plants.

Ussuriland

I shall consider this particular area in detail in the rest of this chapter. The central European type of mixed forest in European Russia is well known to readers in many countries and has been described in numerous books. But the Ussuri River region of the Far East contains a wealth of endemic and exotic animals and plants, and has rarely been described except in scientific journals.

Ussuriland is a vast area of the southern Soviet Far East, extending southwards from the mouth of the River Amur to the border with China and Korea. It is bounded on the west by the great Ussuri River, and on the east by the many picturesque bays and inlets of the Sea of Japan. It is one of the world's most interesting natural regions, containing a unique combination of flora and fauna from the northern taiga and the southern subtropics.

Much of Ussuriland consists of high mountains and wide plains. The Sikhote–Alin mountain range stretches some 600 miles (1,000 km) from the mouth of the River Amur in the north to the southern coast of the Sea of Japan in the south.

In the river valleys and on the low, densely forested hills, Leopards (*Panthera pardus*) stalk through the undergrowth, and the beautiful Asian Paradise Flycatchers (*Terpsiphone paradisi*) flit restlessly among the branches. Lianas and other tropical plants flourish, and there are many exotic butterflies. Higher up the mountains, the bright southern birds are left behind in an enchanting sea of sounds, scents and colours. In their place stands the more solemn but equally beautiful world of the coniferous taiga, where the cool silence is perhaps broken only by the simple but sweet song of a Pallas's Warbler (*Phylloscopus proregulus*). The forest is dense and unbroken over much of these higher altitudes. Various other typical taiga species live here, such as the Siberian Spruce Grouse (*Falcipennis falcipennis*), the Black-billed Capercaillie (*Tetrao parvirostris*) and the Brown Bear (*Ursus arctos*).

In many parts of this mountainous terrain there are plateaus formed by the outpourings of basaltic lava in recent geological times. The Sikhote–Alin Range rises, on average, only 2,600 to 3,300 feet (800 to 1,000 m), and few summits exceed 6,600 ft (2000 m). The eastern side of the range, facing the Sea of Japan, is more dramatic, and because it lies close to the sea, its rivers are shorter and more torrential than those of the Ussuri basin to the west, including the Khor, Bikin and Great Ussurka, are generally large and placid.

To the south-west of the area lies the vast Khanka

The Funeral Pine is found in parts of the Far East, but is so scarce that it is listed in the Red Book of the USSR.

lowland, most of which lies only 80 ft (25 m) above sea level. The low ground is covered with meadow and meadow-steppe vegetation, while the long hills bear scattered oaks and forests of pine and apricot trees. This area, together with the marshes of Ussuriland, are described in Chapter 9 (on page 197).

In southern Ussuriland, the forests are of the gigantic Black, or Manchurian, Fir (*Abies holophylla*), with a second tier of Hornbeam (*Carpinus*) and many southern trees and shrubs, such as *Kalopanax* and Purple-bloom Maple (*Acer pseudosieboldianum*), while various species of *Actinidia* lianas and other twining shrubs form the undergrowth. Some of these plants are found throughout the forests of east Asia, while others are typical only of the Manchurian forest region.

Mixed forests of pine and deciduous trees are widespread, and contain rich communities of plant species. The pine is Korean Pine (*Pinus korainensis*), and the deciduous trees include the Manchurian Ash (*Fraxinus mandshurica*), the White-barked Elm (*Ulmus propinqua*), the Manchurian Walnut (*Juglans mandshurica*) and the Amur Cork Oak (*Phellodendron amurense*). The second tier contains various

RIGHT *A view of the dense Ussuri forest from one of the mountains of the Sikhote-Alin Range, which runs some 600 miles (1,000 km) in a north-south direction.*

Codonopsis ussuriensis

Corydalis repens

Cypripedium macranthum (*Lady's Slipper Orchid*)

Panax ginseng (*Ginseng*)

Adonis amurensis

Lychnis fulgens (*Brilliant Campion*)

endemic species, including the Amur Lilac (*Syringa amurensis*) and the Amur Maackia (*Maackia amurensis*). The undergrowth is very varied, with three species of honeysuckle (*Lonicera*), the mock orange *Philadelphus schrenkii*, Small-flowered Deutzia (*Deutzia amurensis*) and viburnums (*Viburnum*). The lianas include the widespread Amur Grape Vine (*Vitis amurensis*), the Kolomikta Vine (*Actinidia colomicta*) and the Chinese Magnolia Vine (*Schisandra chinensis*). The herb layer also contains a wealth of endemic southern species, including the legendary Ginseng (*Panax ginseng*), Amur Columbine (*Aquilegia amurensis*), Lemon-yellow Day Lily (*Hemerocallis flava*), the Amur Jack-in-the-Pulpit (*Arisaema amurensis*), various peonies (*Paeonia*), stitchworts (*Stellaria*) and many others.

The spruce/fir forests, consisting chiefly of Yeddo Spruce (*Picea jezoensis*) and Khingan Fir (*Abies nephrolepis*),

ABOVE *The mixed forests of the Ussuri region contain a great wealth of beautiful plants, some of them rare and many of them found nowhere else. They include the lovely* Codonopsis ussuriensis, *in the bellflower family; the bright* Corydalis repens, *a member of the poppy family; the orchid* Cypripedium macranthum, *which has relatives in Europe and North America; the Ginseng, whose root is renowned throughout the Far East for its curative and restorative properties; the cheerful* Adonis amurensis, *a member of the buttercup family; and the flame-red Brilliant Campion.*

are far poorer in plant species. Usually, the second tier contains the Yellow Maple (*Acer ucurunduense*) and the Amur Mountain Ash (*Sorbus amurensis*). The undergrowth includes *Spiraea*, currant bushes (*Ribes*) and Manchurian Alder (*Alnus mandschurica*). There are many mosses and lichens, and several species of ferns characteristic of the taiga. In the spruce forests of the south of Ussuriland grows a rare plant, the Devil's Club (*Echinopanax elatum*).

The high-mountain vegetation above the tree-line consists of three zones, which are described in Chapter 7, on mountains (pages 139–41).

The larch (*Larix*) forests, uncommon in Ussuriland, also contain relatively few species. The undergrowth includes Willow-leaved Spirea (*Spiraea salicifolia*), Manchurian Alder (*Alnus mandshurica*) and Daurian Rhododendron (*Rhododendron dahuricus*). The ground cover is usually of Cranberry (*Vaccinium oxycoccus*), Bog Whortleberry (*V. uliginosum*) and other low-growing plants.

The rich fauna of Ussuriland

The geological history of the region and the variety of its ecological conditions, climate and relief, have all had a hand in moulding the evolution of the interesting and varied fauna of Ussuriland. There are many endemic and relict species of animals as well as plants. These have been able to survive in the region because it formed a safe haven, free from glaciation and other natural events that wiped out many species in other regions. Also, both northern and southern species invaded Ussuriland. The north–south orientation of the Sikhote–Alin Range allowed northern species to penetrate right to the southern edge of Ussuriland, as far as the source of the Great Ussurka River. The valleys of the large rivers, as well as the broad lowlands, facilitated the dispersal of the southern species.

As a result, Ussuriland is the meeting point of two major groups of animals, the Chinese and Siberian faunas. Within these two groups it is possible to single out a group of species peculiar to the region, called the Manchurian fauna. This contains many relicts and species endemic to Ussuriland. A secondary influence on the Ussuri fauna came from influxes of species from Indo-Malaya, Mongolia and Europe.

Deciduous and mixed coniferous forests occupying vast areas of Ussuriland contain faunas which are mainly Chinese. The southern part of the area is occupied by dark forests of conifers and hornbeams (*Carpinus*), especially rich in lianas. The Sika Deer (*Cervus nippon*), the Amur race of the Leopard (*Panthera pardus orientalis*) and, in oak

ABOVE *The Amur Chicken Snake is one of the most beautifully marked of the many species of reptiles that live in the Ussuri region; it eats eggs as well as birds.*

ABOVE *The great variety of exquisite butterflies that grace the lush forests of Ussuriland includes species that originated in the tropics, such as this* Brahmaea certhia.

forests, the very rare Siberian Red Dog, or Dhole (*Cuon alpinus*) live here. There are many birds, chiefly representatives of the Chinese and Indo-Malayan faunas. There are also many reptiles in the south, including the Amur Chicken Snake (*Elaphe schrenkii*), the Patterned Snake (*E. dione*), the Tiger Snake (*Natrix tigrina*), two species of Ussurian Mamushi (*Agkistrodon halys* and *A. blomhoffi*) and the Korean Long-tailed Lizard (*Tachydromus wolteri*). Typical amphibians are the Far Eastern Tree Frog (*Hyla japonica*), the Far Eastern Fire-bellied Toad (*Bombina orientalis*) and the Lungless Newt (*Onychodactylus fisheri*).

A strong flyer, Limenitis moltrechtii *is a typical butterfly of Ussuriland. Many of the butterflies, moths and other insects of the region are found nowhere else.*

Ussuriland is home to a whole world of unusual and beautiful insects. Especially lovely are the butterflies, such as *Epikopaea hainesi* and Westwood's Elcysma (*Elcysma westwoodi*) and the giant silk moths *Rhodinia fugax* and *Caligula boisduvali*. There are various endemic species of harlequin beetles, tiger beetles and ground beetles, such as *Carabus jankowskii* and many others. There are also rare and striking species of cicadas (Cicadiidae) and praying mantises (*Mantodea*).

The fauna changes as one travels northwards or climbs the mountains. The number of southern species diminishes dramatically. Above 1,640 ft (500 m) the warmth-loving Chinese and Indo-Malayan members of the fauna begin to be succeeded by northern animals of the mixed pine/deciduous forests, with fewer species than at lower levels.

As well as mixed conifer and deciduous forests, there are unforested areas of marsh, meadowland and steppe. Characteristic mammals of this patchwork landscape are the Ussurian race of the Wild Boar (*Sus scrofa ussuricus*), the Manchurian race of the Red Deer (*Cervus elaphus xanthopygus*), the Far Eastern Wild Cat (*Felis euptylura*), the Siberian race of the Tiger (*Panthera tigris altaica*), the Amur race of the Eurasian Badger (*Meles meles amurensis*) and the

Yellow-throated Marten (*Martes flavigula*). Other common species include the Manchurian Hedgehog (*Erinaceus amurensis*), the Lesser White-toothed Shrew (*Crocidura suaveolens*) and the related species *C. lasiura*, the Oriental race of the Siberian Chipmunk (*Eutamias sibiricus orientalis*) and the Manchurian race of the Red Squirrel (*Sciurus vulgaris mandshurica*).

Typical insects include Schrenck's Butterfly (*Apatura schrenckii*), many large species of hawk moths (Sphingidae) and geometrid moths (Geometridae). There are also many unusual beetles, including the large ground beetle *Carabus schrenckii*, which feeds mainly on small forest molluscs.

The fauna of the Mongolian Oak forests is sparser. Typical mammals are the local races of the Roe Deer (*Capreolus capreolus ochracea*), the Wolf (*Canis lupus tschiliensis*) and the Fox (*Vulpes vulpes dahurica*), and the Brown Bear (*Ursus arctos*). The caterpillars of many species of butterfly, including hairstreaks (*Zephyrus* and *Zygaena*) and members of the large family Nymphalidae, depend on the leaves of the Mongolian Oak for food. Apollo butterflies (*Parnassius bremeri*) are found on steep, scree-covered slopes, and unusual beetles, such as the large Radde's Beetle (*Neocerambyx raddei*) also occur.

The Siberian element of the Ussuriland fauna can be divided into the Okhotsk and the East Siberian sub-groups. The Okhotsk fauna, found among the spruce/fir taiga, dwarf birch woods, high grass meadows and creeping Korean Stone Pine (*Pinus pumila*), is concentrated mainly in the north of Ussuriland, in the Sikhote–Alin Mountains. It includes many species which are common to the Eurasian taiga fauna as a whole, but are represented in Ussuriland by local subspecies. As well as the Brown Bear (*Ursus arctos lasiotus*) and Lynx (*Felis lynx stroganovi*), there are the Wolverine (*Gulo gulo sibiricus*), and the Stoat, or Ermine (*Mustela erminea transbaicalica*). Typical birds are the Arctic Warbler (*Phylloscopus borealis*), the Yellow-browed Warbler (*P. inornatus*), the Coal Tit (*Parus ater*), the Red Crossbill (*Loxia curvirostra*), the Siskin (*Carduelis spinus*), the Siberian Jay (*Perisoreus infaustus*) and Nutcracker (*Nucifraga caryocatactes*). The few species of reptiles and amphibians include the Viviparous Lizard (*Lacerta vivipara*) and the Siberian Frog (*Rana cruenta*).

The Okhotsk fauna contains a group of endemic species, including the Siberian Spruce Grouse (*Falcipennis falcipennis*), the Japanese Waxwing (*Bombycilla japonica*), Middendorff's Grasshopper Warbler (*Locustella ochotensis*) and the Sakhalin Viper (*Vipera sachalinensis*).

The East Siberian, or Angara, subfauna is concentrated in the larch forests and vast sphagnum-moss bogs with stunted trees, which are best developed in the Sikhote–Alin Mountains. It includes the Musk Deer (*Moschus moschiferus*), the Eye-browed Thrush (*Turdus obscurus*), the Dark-sided Flycatcher (*Muscicapa sibirica*), the Mugimaki Flycatcher (*Ficedula mugimaki*) and the Grey-breasted Bullfinch (*Pyrrhula cineracea*).

I will now go on to describe some of the Indo-Malayan, Mongolian and European elements of the Ussuriland fauna in more detail, paying particular reference to the birds.

Reptiles and amphibians of Ussuriland

Russia's only soft-shelled turtle is the Chinese Trionyx (*Trionyx chinensis*). Within the USSR, it occurs only in Ussuriland; elsewhere, it is found in eastern China, Korea, Japan, and various islands of the North Pacific. Its completely flat, rather elongated shell is up to 1 ft (30 cm) long and covered with long rows of small nodules. It lacks the horny plates that cover the bone of the shell in other turtles and tortoises.

The Trionyx lives in the larger rivers and lakes, with muddy and sandy beds, water plants and gently sloping banks. It spends most of its life in the water, and is a skilful and elegant swimmer. On land, too, it is agile. Timid and difficult to spot, it drops into the water at the slightest sign of danger, dives to the bottom, and digs itself into the mud or sand. The Trionyx uses a combination of superb camouflage and stealth to catch its prey. Its shell resembles the lake or river bed so closely that the turtle is virtually invisible when lying motionless at the bottom. It waits there patiently, head thrust out of its shell, until a suitable meal appears. As well as fish, the Trionyx eats insects, molluscs, crustaceans and worms. At night, it adopts a different hunting technique, actively seeking out its prey.

The turtles spend the winter buried deeply in the bottom mud. They awake from their torpor in April or May, and soon start breeding. The females lay two or three batches of eggs each season in a small pit which they dig in the bank. Each batch contains between 20 and 70 eggs. The tiny turtles hatch after one and a half to two months.

In the southern part of Ussuriland lives one of the most elegant grass snakes, the Tiger Snake (*Natrix tigrina*). It grows up to $3\frac{1}{2}$ ft (110 cm) long, and prefers damp areas of deciduous or mixed forest near water, feeding mainly on frogs and toads, and the occasional fish.

Schrenck's Grass Snake (*Elaphe schrenckii*) is up to $6\frac{1}{2}$ ft (2 m) in length. It lives in forest or bushy scrub, hiding in tree holes, tree stumps, among stones or in rodent burrows. It climbs high into the trees and even onto the roofs of

Tristram's Bunting is a small seed-eating bird that ranges widely over the different levels and habitats of the Sikhote Alin Range; it winters in southeastern China.

houses in search of birds' eggs; it also eats chicks and adult birds, and small mammals.

Birds of Ussuriland

Ussuriland has an extremely rich bird fauna. More than half of the USSR's 796 breeding species of birds have been recorded in the region, including 244 species that breed there and another 20 for which nesting is suspected but not yet proven. This impressive total increases almost every year.

Most of the birds live in the lush Manchurian taiga. They include representatives of tropical families, such as white-eyes (Zosteropidae), drongos (Dicruridae) and mini-vets (Campephagidae), which do not occur elsewhere in the USSR. In terms of numbers of individuals, the commonest bird families in the region are the buntings (Emberizidae), Old World flycatchers (Muscicapidae), thrushes (Turdidae) and cuckoos (Cuculidae).

The different environments of the eastern and western river valleys of the Sikhote–Alin Range contain distinct bird communities. Along the fast-flowing eastern rivers live the Chinese Merganser (*Mergus squamatus*) and Long-billed Plover (*Charadrius placidus*), while the broader, placid rivers of the west contain birds such as the Manchurian Red-footed Falcon (*Falco amurensis*) and Blakiston's Fish Owl (*Ketupa blakistoni*).

The dark conifer forests of the Okhotsk taiga contain relatively few birds, either in number of species or individuals. A number of species are typical of the oak forests, including the Forest Wagtail (*Dendronanthus indicus*) and Yellow-billed Grosbeak (*Eophona migratoria*).

Some species range widely over the different altitudes and habitats of the Sikhote–Alin Mountains. These include White's Thrush (*Zoothera dauma*), the Short-tailed Bush Warbler (*Urosphena squameiceps*), Pallas's Warbler (*Phylloscopus proregulus*) and Tristram's Bunting (*Emberiza tristrami*). Most species, however, are confined to a certain habitat and altitude; for instance, the Olive-backed Pipit (*Anthus hodgsoni*), the Pacific Water Pipit (*A. rubescens*), the Siberian Accentor (*Prunella montanella*) and the Eyebrowed Thrush (*Turdus obscurus*) are characteristic of the bare summits.

MANDARIN DUCKS
One of the pearls of the Far East's birdlife, the little Mandarin Duck (*Aix galericulata*) lives along the fast forest streams. It returns from its wintering quarters in south-east China and Japan at the end of March, as the ice starts to thaw. By mid-April, when all the ice has melted, the ducks take part in dramatic courtship displays. The males are at their most splendid, with handsome green and white crests and elongated chestnut wing feathers raised like sails. Mandarins lay their 7 to 12 eggs in tree holes, at heights of up to 50 or 65 ft (15 to 20 m), occasionally beneath a windblown or rotten tree trunk. The chicks leave their unlined nest hole almost immediately after hatching, leaping down to the ground and setting off after their mother on the water. In October, the Mandarins leave for the south.

BIRDS OF PREY
The diminutive Besra Sparrowhawk (*Accipiter virgatus*) lives along river valleys with tall trees. It is the most vocal of all the Ussuri birds of prey, giving its screeching 'tai-tai-naletai' alarm calls and flying from tree to tree to draw the intruder away from its nest, usually at the top of a tall elm (*Ulnus*) or Korean Willow (*Chosenia macrolepis*). Near the tree, however, the bird behaves very quietly – until the small nest is actually located, when the female makes persistent dive-bombing attacks. The birds are late breeders, not laying until early June. The chicks, which are fed almost entirely on small birds, fledge in mid-August. Besra Sparrowhawks spend the winter in South-east Asia.

The Grey-faced Buzzard-Eagle (*Butastur indicus*) is widespread in Ussuriland, north-east China, Korea and Japan, although it is a local bird and the total population is quite small. It migrates from its winter quarters in South-east Asia, arriving in Ussuriland in early April, to breed in mixed or deciduous forests near meadows and hummocky bogs with scattered trees. The nest, remarkably small for a bird almost the size of a Buzzard (*Buteo buteo*), is built in a tree. From mid-July, the 3 or 4 chicks give loud cries as they stretch their heads out of the nest and beg for food. Buzzard-eagles eat mainly rodents, lizards, snakes, toads and frogs. By September, they are on the way back south.

Several scarce birds of prey live in Ussuriland, including this handsome Grey-faced Buzzard-Eagle, seen here at its nest in the 'Kedrovaya Pad' Reserve in the extreme south.

The buzzard-eagles' habitat is shared by the secretive Crested Honey Buzzard (*Pernis ptilorhynchus*). This rare bird occurs from east of Lake Baikal to Malaysia and the Philippines. Like the Grey-faced Buzzard-Eagle, the Crested Honey Buzzard prefers the open spaces it needs for feeding. It returns late from its winter quarters in southern Asia already paired, and the birds set about nesting immediately in tall trees. They take time off for dramatic aerial displays, circling high in the air and hovering on raised wings. One or two eggs are laid in early June. The chicks are fed mainly on pieces of honeycomb containing wasp and bumble-bee larvae, brought by the male, who travels considerable distances to track down the insects' nests and dig them out of the ground or tear them

from the branches. The uneaten larvae hatch into adult wasps and bees, and the growing chicks amuse themselves trying to catch them. The female hunts close to the nest, bringing mainly frogs. The late nesting of this bird is doubtless timed to coincide with the appearance of the wasps, and the young do not fledge until late August. By September and October, the birds are on their way south.

One of the most interesting and one of the rarest birds of prey seen in Ussuriland is Horsfield's Sparrowhawk (*Accipiter soloensis*), which occurs only in the extreme south of the region, on the northern fringes of its range, which includes Korea and eastern China. It breeds in the areas of Mongolian Oak (*Quercus mongolica*). Only four nests have been found in the USSR, the most recent by my colleagues and me. Courtship rituals can be seen in May, and by the end of the month, these small hawks begin to build their nests of twigs lined with green leaves on a central or side fork of a tree. The 3 or 4 white eggs with muddy brown

One of the rarest of Ussuriland's birds of prey is Horsfield's Sparrowhawk. This picture, taken in July 1983, shows a female at her nest in the 'Kedrovaya Pad' Nature Reserve, on the northern edge of its range, which includes China, Korea and Indonesia. This nest, found by the author and his colleagues, is the fourth recorded in the USSR.

spots are laid very late, in the second half of June. Both parents incubate the eggs and feed the chicks. The male usually hunts well away from the nest. Flying in with his prey, he signals to the sitting female from a distance with loud, harsh calls reminiscent of the Eurasian Sparrowhawk (*Accipiter nisus*), and quite different from those of the Besra Sparrowhawk (*A. virgatus*). The female flies from the nest, takes the prey, and carries it back to the chicks. She also hunts, but stays near the nest.

CUCKOOS

The Ussuri taiga is particularly rich in cuckoos, with as many as five species. Although some of them look very similar, their calls are quite distinct, although that of the Oriental Cuckoo (*Cuculus saturatus*) resembles that of the Hoopoe (*Upupa epops*). The main host of the Ussuri Oriental Cuckoos is the Eastern Crowned Leaf Warbler (*Phylloscopus coronatus*), but they also parasitize the Pale-legged Leaf Warbler (*P. tenellipes*). The other cuckoos winter in South-east Asia, but the Oriental Cuckoo travels further south, as far as Indonesia, New Guinea and Australia.

The Eurasian Cuckoo is common, but avoids the dense taiga, living along river valleys and in water meadows. At the end of May, the Little Cuckoo (*Cuculus poliocephalus*) arrives in the south of the region, preferring deciduous forest alternating with open spaces. The Little Cuckoo is more noticeable than its relatives, often flying from one group of trees to another. In some areas, several males can be heard calling together. The Little Cuckoo's favourite host is the Chinese Bush Warbler (*Horeites diphone*), which lives in tall-grass meadows overgrown with thick shrubs.

The most secretive cuckoo in Ussuriland is the Fugitive Hawk Cuckoo (*Hierococcyx fugax*). This fairly rare bird leads a secretive life in the treetops. Usually, the only clue to its presence is its penetrating call, but if it is glimpsed, it is easily distinguished from the other cuckoos by its unbarred breast, pink in the male. It usually lays its eggs in the nest of the Blue-and-white Flycatcher (*Cyanoptila cyanomelana*).

OWLS AND NIGHTJARS

Ussuriland is home to a variety of owls. The Ural Owl (*Strix uralensis*) occurs in deciduous and mixed forest on the slopes of the conical hills. It nests early, in late March or the beginning of April, in a tree hole, usually high above the ground, and some areas contain dense populations, with three or four courting males visible from a single spot, but many owls die during hard winters or when their rodent prey is scarce. In the northern and middle parts of Ussuriland, the commonest owl is the Eastern Scops Owl (*Otus sunia*). These owls live in deciduous and mixed forests, nesting in May and June in tree holes at various heights and feeding mainly on insects, and occasionally on rodents. Unlike the Ural Owl, it is not a year-round resident, migrating to South-east Asia in winter.

The Brown Hawk-Owl (*Ninox scutulata*) is an exotic Indo-Malayan species which is generally a rare breeder in Ussuriland, although locally common. It arrives from its southern wintering grounds in early May. Until recently,

little was known of its biology. Although it is larger than the Boreal Owl, it feeds mainly on insects. It nests in tree holes, usually between 30 and 45 ft (10 to 14 m) above ground, chosing only trees that allow an easy approach flight. Here the 3 eggs (occasionally 2 or 4) are laid in late May or early June.

In the mixed forests live two particularly interesting species of owls. The Collared Scops Owl (*Otus bakkamoena*) nests in tree holes at any height above the ground. The male, which is considerably smaller than the female, hunts within a radius of 650 to 1,300 ft (200 to 400 m) from the nest. While the female incubates the eggs, the male brings her small rodents once or twice nightly. The female flies to meet him outside the nest hole, but often keeps him waiting some time. Both parents feed the growing owlets. Collared Scops Owls allow humans to approach closely, relying on their superb camouflage and ability to elongate their bodies, pressing them against a tree-trunk so that they melt into the bark.

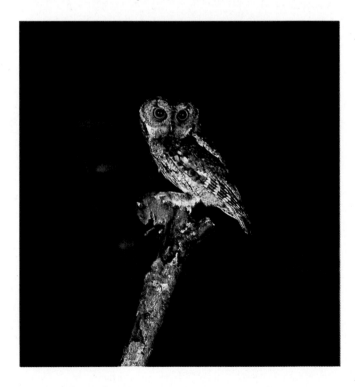

ABOVE *The Collared Scops Owl is one of a number of species of owls that live in the Ussuri forests.*
RIGHT *A Pale-legged Leaf Warbler, at its nest in the 'Kedrovaya Pad' Reserve with an Oriental Cuckoo chick, which, like that of the familiar Eurasian Cuckoo, ejects its host's own chicks or eggs.*

A shy and little-studied owl of the region is Blakiston's Fish Owl (*Ketupa blakistoni*). This impressive bird, which is as big as an Eagle Owl (*Bubo bubo*), lives along the large, slow-flowing rivers to the west of the Sikhote—Alin Range, especially in areas where there are ox-bow lakes, shallow inlets, shingle spits and springs that remain unfrozen in winter. They are generally rare. A pair of owls will remain in their chosen territory for life, leaving it only during the hardest winters, when they may join with four or five other individuals in search of food.

The owls do not start breeding until they are three years old. Courtship is most intense in the second half of February, and one or two muddy-white eggs are laid in mid-March in a tree-hole high above the ground, while it is still carpeted with a thick layer of snow. It is likely that the female alone incubates, with her mate feeding her from 3 to 5 times a night. While the owlets are small and the nights still frosty, the female rarely leaves the nest. By early May, she is able to take some time off for hunting, sometimes travelling quite far from the nest, and usually returns with fish for the hungry owlets, which she snatches from the water like an Osprey (*Pandion haliaetus*) and carries in her feet. The male, on the other hand, hunts close to the nest, and usually brings frogs to the offspring in his bill. Most of the fish seem to be caught at night, and the frogs mainly at dusk. In autumn and winter, the owls' diet includes many

ABOVE *The most elusive and least-known of the Ussuri owls is Blakiston's Fish Owl, one of the world's largest owls. Living along slow-flowing rivers west of the Sikhote-Alin Range, it specializes in hunting fish, frogs and toads. It snatches these from the water like an Osprey, creating a cascade of spray. Like an Osprey too, it has sharp scales on the undersides of its toes and long talons to hold its slippery prey. It also catches crayfish and small mammals. This bird has caught a frog.*
LEFT *One of the tributaries of the middle reaches of the Bikin River, a favourite haunt of Blakiston's Fish Owl, photographed in February.*

ABOVE *The Japanese Pygmy Woodpecker is a resident bird restricted to a small area of southern Ussuriland. It has a similar lifestyle to the Lesser Spotted Woodpecker, which is widespread across Eurasia, including Ussuriland.*

WOODPECKERS AND ROLLERS

Although Ussuriland is not far from South-east Asia, which is renowned for the diversity of its woodpeckers, only one of the exotic Indo-Malayan species has penetrated the region. This is the Grey-headed Pygmy Woodpecker (*Dendrocopos canicapillus*). It is fairly rare in Ussuriland, and ornithologists can count themselves lucky if they find a nest of this exciting bird.

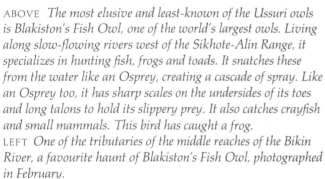

crayfish and other crustaceans, as well as small mammals, such as voles and mice.

Outside the Ussuri region, Blakiston's Fish Owl occurs on Sakhalin Island, on the coast of the Okhotsk Sea, in north-east China and on Hokkaido, the northern island of Japan.

The Jungle Nightjar (*Caprimulgus indicus*) lives in the forests of central and northern Ussuriland. Its courtship song, a series of hoarse, muffled notes followed by a series of 'tuk-tuk-tuk' calls, resounds among the trees in spring. It nests on the slopes of the conical hills, laying its two greyish-white eggs in June in a simple pit in the ground. The birds migrate south to spend the winter in Indonesia.

A close relative is the Japanese Pygmy Woodpecker (*Dendrocopos kizuki*). It is most plentiful in the southern parts of Ussuriland, where it is present throughout the year, like its relative. Nesting from the end of April, it chooses rotten trees to excavate its nest hole at a height of about 6$\frac{1}{2}$ to 10 ft (2 to 3 m).

One of the most exotic birds is the Eastern Broad-billed Roller (*Eurystomus orientalis*), found in wooded valleys with areas of open ground, chiefly in the western part of the Sikhote-Alin Range. It returns in mid-May from its wintering quarters in parts of southern Asia. Court-ship rituals involve elaborate head movements and drama-tic display flights, in which the pair give loud, harsh calls as they perform loops and other aerobatics. The nest-hole is in a tree, often high above the ground. The eggs are laid in

ABOVE *One of the brightest of all the birds of Ussuriland is the Eastern Broad-billed Roller, an invader from the tropical Indo-Malayan region, seen here feeding its offspring.*

ABOVE *The Ashy Minivet is the USSR's sole representative of the family Campephagidae, otherwise restricted to the tropics. Like the roller, it is a summer visitor.*

early June, but the young do not fledge until the end of July or early August. Broadbills eat insects, chiefly beetles, dragonflies and damselflies. In the evening, they gather in flocks of up to 30 birds over placid reaches of the river, often accompanied by Manchurian Red-footed Falcons (*Falco amurensis*). Together, they hawk for insects until dusk turns to night. By early September, the rollers are on their way back south.

UNFAMILIAR SONGBIRDS

The Ussuri forests contain a wealth of perching birds (passerines), unlike the USSR's northern taiga. There are many familiar European species, although the subspecies are often different. Among others, these include the Long-tailed Tit (*Aegithalos cauadatus*), Marsh Tit (*Parus palustris*), Common Treecreeper (*Certhia familiaris*) and Eurasian Nuthatch (*Sitta europaea*). But many of the Ussuri songbirds are unfamiliar to most of us.

The Forest Wagtail (*Dendronanthus indicus*) is one of the few species that lives in the sparse Ussuri oakwoods clothing the conical hills; this bird is also found in north-east China and Korea. It prefers areas of scree, building its nest in an oak tree, some $6\frac{1}{2}$ to 23 ft (2 to 7 m) above ground, and laying 4 or 5 eggs.

Sometimes, one hears a song like the tinkling of a little silver bell ringing out from the tops of the tall Korean Willows (*Chosenia macrolepis*). The singer is the Ashy Minivet (*Pericrotus divaricatus*), the sole breeding representative in the USSR of the tropical minivet family (*Campephagidae*). This bird arrives in early May and begins nesting in mid-May, building a compact nest embellished with lichens on a high branch. Minivets spend most of their time in the treetops, rarely visiting the ground. They move south in early October to winter in Taiwan, the Philippines and Indonesia.

FLYCATCHERS

Seven species of flycatchers breed in Ussuriland. In the deciduous forests, along the groves of trees that flank the rivers, lives the beautiful Asian Paradise Flycatcher (*Terpsiphone paradisi*). It likes dense scrub with thick under-growth and often nests in apple orchards. It is generally uncommon, but as many as 16 to 19 birds per mile (10 to 12 per km) have been found breeding in favoured locations. There is a good deal of variation in plumage, especially of the long-tailed males, and the white form is much scarcer than the brown one. The flycatchers do not appear until the end of May from their wintering grounds in South-east Asia, and start nesting in early June.

ABOVE *A splendid male Asian Paradise Flycatcher. This bird is of the brown form; there is also a 'white' form, with less brown in its plumage. The male's two central tail feathers are very long, resembling somewhat the ornamental plumes of the birds of paradise, which accounts for the 'paradise' part of their name. Like other flycatchers, they catch insects on the wing.*

ABOVE *Another of the seven species of flycatchers that breed in Ussuriland is the Blue-and-White Flycatcher. This is a brilliantly coloured male; females are mainly brown.*

The Asian Brown Flycatcher (*Muscicapa latirostris*) is a fairly common bird in the deciduous and mixed forests, which builds a nest similar to that of a Chaffinch (*Fringilla coelebs*). The Blue-and-White Flycatcher (*Cyanoptila cyanomelana*) is an east Asiatic species with a restricted breeding range in Ussuriland. Its favoured nesting site is among large rocks overgrown with ferns and damp moss at the foot of a hill, usually near a river. The exquisite males, their heads and backs of a brilliant shade of blue, perch on the branches and sing their song, a combination of whistling and trilling notes. The nest is beautifully camouflaged, as it is made of the same moss that surrounds it. This species winters in Indochina, the Philippines and Borneo.

The Yellow-rumped Flycatcher (*Ficedula zanthopygia*) is common in the Ussuri river groves and mixed or deciduous forests. In some areas, there may be as many as 260 pairs per sq mile (100 pairs per sq km) of forest. They nest in tree-holes, but readily take to nest-boxes. The Yellow-rumped Flycatcher leaves the Ussuri region to winter in Indochina, Indonesia and the Philippines.

ABOVE *A male Yellow-rumped Flycatcher at its nest-hole in the 'Kedrovaya Pad' Nature Reserve, in the extreme south of Ussuriland.*

ABOVE *A female Grey-backed Thrush at her nest. The male is extremely similar. The taiga and mixed forest zones of the USSR are particularly rich in thrush species.*

THRUSHES

One of the finest songsters of the Ussuri forests is the Grey-backed Thrush (*Turdus hortulorum*), whose sad but melodious whistling trill rings through the deciduous woodland along the river valleys. The males usually choose the highest branches for their songposts. These thrushes winter in south-east China, returning to Ussuriland in late April. The nest is often sited in a dense bush, and sometimes beneath a fallen tree. There is usually more than one brood, compensating for the losses inflicted by predators.

Occasionally, the naturalist is lucky enough to hear the quiet whistling song of White's Thrush (*Zoothera dauma*), an uncommon, shy species that lives in the dense conifer taiga and deciduous forests, arriving to breed in mid-April from its winter quarters in South-east Asia. It feeds largely on earthworms.

One of the most beautiful of all the Ussuri birds is the Daurian Redstart (*Phoenicurus auroreus*). This is a common species, found in all types of forest and showing little fear of man. Arriving from its Japanese and South-east Asian wintering quarters in early April, it begins nesting at the end of the month, choosing tree-holes or holes in walls or other parts of houses. The six eggs may be pale blue or pale

ABOVE *The Japanese Robin is a very local breeder in the Soviet Far East, nesting on Kunashir Island, southernmost of the Kuril Islands, which lies to the north of Japan.*

A dapper Radde's Warbler watches warily from its domed nest, built low down among grass in the 'Kedrovaya Pad' Nature Reserve. This is a common breeder in Ussuriland.

grey with brick-red mottling. The first brood leaves the nest early in June, and are then fed by the male while the female quickly builds another nest for her second brood. The birds fly south in mid-October.

The Siberian Blue Robin (*Luscinia cyane*) is a common bird of the region. It lives in both the coniferous and mixed forests, and prefers well-lit areas with dense shrubs and herbaceous undergrowth. It winters in South-east Asia, and by mid-April its melodic whistling song resounds through the woods. The nest is skillfully camouflaged under a fallen tree, on a cliff-side or the slope of a hill, and is very hard to find.

In places where there are many fallen trees, on steep banks of rivers in the dense taiga, one can hear a song reminiscent of the chirping of a cricket. The singer is the Pale-legged Leaf Warbler (*Phylloscopus tenellipes*), a shy little bird about which little was known until recently. It now seems, as is often the case, that it is not as rare as it seemed to be. It has an uneven distribution, with concentrations in the most suitable habitats. My colleagues and I recently found nests among fallen trees and along river banks in dense forest, both deciduous and mixed. The little warblers arrive in early May from their wintering grounds in Indo-China, and lay 5 or 6 white eggs in early June. The spherical nest, with a side entrance, is like that of other *Phylloscopus* leaf warblers in structure, but is much better camouflaged; indeed, it is almost buried in the ground. In 1981, we were lucky enough to find a nest containing a young Oriental Cuckoo (*Cuculus saturatus*). The warbler's eggs hatch after 12 days' incubation and the young leave the nest 10 or 11 days later. The birds return south in August and September.

One of the most numerous inhabitants of the Ussuri forests is the Eastern Crowned Leaf Warbler (*Phylloscopus coronatus*), whose song is heard everywhere. It lives in various types of woodland, from the small copses that dot the fields to the densest conifer forests. After arriving from Indochina and Indonesia at the end of April, it builds its nest and lays its 4 to 6 eggs in May. It is often parasitized by the Oriental Cuckoo (*Cuculus saturatus*).

BUNTINGS AND GROSBEAKS

Tristram's Bunting (*Emberiza tristrami*), which breeds in the valleys of deciduous, mixed and sometimes coniferous forest, is a typical, though quite scarce, summer visitor to Ussuriland, which winters in south-east China. By contrast, the Black-faced Bunting (*E. spodocephala*) is one of the most numerous birds of the region, and is also found in south central Siberia, Sakhalin Island and the southern Kuril

ABOVE *The Azure-winged Magpie, one of the most beautiful members of the crow family, has a puzzling distribution, living only in the Far East and south Spain and Portugal.*

ABOVE *Close relatives of the crows, the orioles are brightly coloured birds; this is a female Black-naped Oriole at her nest in Ussuriland. The male is even brighter.*

Islands. It avoids dense forest, preferring clearings and forest edges or areas of thick shrubby undergrowth along river valleys. It winters in South-east Asia.

The Yellow-billed Grosbeak (*Eophona migratoria*) is common only in the south of Ussuriland, and is also thinly distributed over north-east China and Korea. It is one of the few birds to be seen in the oak forests. It winters in south-east China.

ORIOLES AND MAGPIES

The Old-World Orioles are medium-sized relatives of the crow family, in which the males are much more brightly coloured than the females. The Soviet Far East is home to the Black-naped Oriole (*Oriolus chinensis*), illustrated on the previous page. It migrates south for winter after breeding.

The Azure-winged Magpie (*Cyanopica cyanopica*), one of the most beautiful member of the crow family (*Corvidae*), has a world distribution that is hard to explain – it occurs only in the Far East and thousands of miles to the west in southern Spain and Portugal. For a long time, ornithologists and zoogeographers regarded this bird as a relict species, citing its curious distribution as an indication that it ranged from the Pacific to the Atlantic in prehistoric times. Some scientists, however, are now inclined to believe that the birds were brought to Spain and Portugal by sailors returning home from the east, and then escaped or were deliberately released.

In the Ussuri, the Azure-winged Magpie is common along river valleys, in deciduous forests and shrubby thickets. It nests in small colonies of up to a few dozen pairs, usually at the foot of a shrub or no higher than $6\frac{1}{2}$ to 10 ft (2 to 3 m) among its branches.

The table on pages 212–13 lists the most typical bird species of the Ussuri forests. It does not include those that are widespread throughout Europe and northern Asia, such as the Magpie (*Pica pica*), the Jay (*Garrulus glandarius*), various woodpeckers, and many others.

Mammals of Ussuriland

The mammal faunas of the mixed forests of European Russia generally resemble those of similar forests in other parts of Europe, especially east and central Europe; as with the birds, these familiar creatures will not be described here. By contrast, the mammals of the southern part of the Soviet Far East, like the birds, include various exotic species. Also like the birds, both northern and southern elements are present in Ussuriland. There are northern species, such as the Brown Bear (*Ursus arctos*) and the

Wolverine (*Gulo gulo*) as well as exotic species of southern origin, such as the Amur races of the Tiger (*Panthera tigris altaica*) and the Leopard (*Panthera pardus orientalis*).

HEDGEHOGS, MOLES, SHREWS AND BATS

Many of the mammals live in the forest's lower tiers; in the upper layer of the soil, in the leaf litter, or on the surface of the ground. Most of them belong to the order of insect-eaters (*Insectivora*), including the Manchurian Hedgehog (*Erinaceus amurensis*) and the large Japanese Mole (*Talpa robusta*), the largest of the world's moles, weighing about $8\frac{3}{4}$ oz (250 g). The Ussuri forests also contain many species of shrews (*Soricidae*). One of these is the tiny Pygmy Shrew (*Sorex minutissimus*), one of the world's smallest mammals, weighing no more than 1/10 oz (3 g). One family of insectivores have freed themselves from the ground layer – these are the bats (*Chiroptera*), of which there are 15 species in the Ussuri forests. In winter, some of them migrate south, while the rest hibernate in caves and other sheltered places.

HARES AND RODENTS

Two species of hare live in Ussuriland: the Arctic Hare (*Lepus timidus*), described on pages 88 and 107, and the Manchurian Hare (*L. mandshuricus*). The second, the smaller of the two, weighs no more than $4\frac{1}{2}$ lb (2 kg). It prefers the slopes of the conical hills, overgrown with grass and sparse, stunted oak trees, and with areas of scree at their summits. During the day, it hides under stones or a fallen tree. The female produces two litters a year, each containing from 2 to 6 leverets.

Among the many species of rodents is the Siberian Flying Squirrel (*Pteromys volans*), whose range extends from Finland right across to Korea and Japan. Along each side of its body, it has a furred flight membrane, or patagium, running from each forepaw to the hindpaws. The membranes are folded up neatly while the animal is climbing trees, but when it leaps from a high branch, they are held out taut between the extended legs, forming a parachute with which the squirrel can make a controlled glide. Flying squirrels are nocturnal, and are rarely seen.

RIGHT *Largest of the eight subspecies of tiger, and the largest of all the world's cats, the magnificent Siberian Tiger has an extra-thick coat to withstand the cold winters of the Soviet Far East. Completely protected throughout its range, the population is currently estimated at over 200 individuals. Largely solitary, each tiger needs a hunting territory of about 150 sq miles.*

BEARS, MARTENS AND CATS

The Asian Black Bear (*Selenarctos thibetanus*), whose range extends from Iran to Japan, is found in the mixed forests of the Ussuri. It is smaller than the Brown Bear (*Ursus arctos*), and rarely weighs more than 330 lb (150 kg). Its long curved claws enable it to climb trees with ease. It has a very varied diet, including plants, acorns, nuts, insects, molluscs and honey. The females are on heat during June and July. During autumn, it builds up large reserves of fat to see it through its winter sleep in a snug den in a hollow tree, beneath the permanent snow cover. In late winter, the female gives birth to one or two cubs, which leave the den as soon as the weather gets warmer in spring.

The Yellow-throated Marten (*Martes flavigula*), the largest marten in the world, occurs in the Ussuri region, where it preys on rodents, chipmunks and hares, and also hunts animals as large as Musk Deer (*Moschus*) and goats.

The Far Eastern Forest Cat (*Felis euptylura*) is a small nocturnal predator. It is very shy and rarely seen, although its tracks are often found. The females are on heat in February and March. In April or May they give birth to as many as five kittens, which become independent before winter. Forest cats eat birds and small rodents, occasionally taking prey as large as hares and squirrels.

The Siberian race of the Tiger (*Panthera tigris altaica*) is the largest and most powerful of the world's wild cats, record-breaking males weighing as much as 845 lb (384 kg). The small but stable population of tigers in the southern Far East region is now estimated to contain more than 200 individuals. This subspecies is included in the Red Book of the USSR and in that of the IUCN.

The great cats are solitary for most of their lives, each occupying a hunting territory of about 150 sq miles (400 sq km) of forest. A tigress with cubs patrols a territory of about 6 to 8 sq miles (15 to 20 sq km), gradually enlarging it. The tigers rove constantly around their large territories, and in winter clear smooth paths which make the journey easier. They hunt mainly hooved mammals, including Wild Boar (*Sus scrofa*), wild goats and deer. If there is not enough game, they may kill domestic cattle and dogs. They are largely nocturnal, and their roars can often be heard echoing through the night.

Even in the harsh climate of the Far East, their breeding is not confined to a particular season. After a pregnancy lasting 95 to 112 days, the female gives birth to 2, 3 or 4 cubs, in a well-hidden den. She guards her offspring for 2 or 3 years until they become fully independent. They do not become sexually mature until they are 4 years old, and, throughout her entire life, a tigress gives birth to 20 cubs at the most, no more than half of which manage to survive.

The Amur subspecies of the Leopard (*Panthera pardus orientalis*) is a very rare animal, included in the Red Books of the USSR and the IUCN. It lives in the southern Ussuri forests, mainly in the 'Kedrovaya Pad' Nature Reserve (see page 137). The leopards pair off in winter. The den is sited among large boulders or in areas of scree. After a pregnancy lasting three months, the female produces from one to three cubs. They are born blind and spotted. They mature quickly, and usually after two years they are fully grown and sexually mature. Males are larger than females. The Leopard population in Ussuriland is currently estimated at no more than 50 individuals.

SIKA DEER

The Sika Deer (*Cervus nippon*) is also a rare animal, registered in the Red Books of the USSR and IUCN. This small, elegant deer weighs no more than 220 lb (100 kg), and lives in valleys and mixed forests on the slopes of the conical hills. In the deep snow of winter, it often descends to the river valleys. It has a very varied vegetarian diet, eating grass, the shoots of trees and shrubs, and fruit. In October, and November, the deer are on heat, and the roaring of the males can be heard at dusk and dawn. They fight over the females, the victors acquiring a harem of three or four females. In spring, usually in May, each female bears a single calf, which remains with its mother until the following spring. The males shed their antlers in April, and in May the new growths sprout, brittle, bleeding and covered with the soft fur-covered skin, or velvet. The deer then become very timid, retiring to the densest parts of the forest, where they lie low.

Sika Deer also occur in the wild in north and south-east China, Korea, Japan, Formosa and Vietnam, and they are kept in captivity in many places, including the USSR. Their antlers are valued as a source of the medicinal preparation pantocrin. Sika have also been introduced to countries as far away as New Zealand, Great Britain and the USA.

Mixed-forest nature reserves

If you glance at the map of the forest nature reserves on page 112, it will be apparent that many of them are in the mixed-forest zone. The major conifer forest (taiga) reserves are described on pages 111–13.

The following nature reserves of the European part of the USSR are all in the mixed-forest zone. The Voronezh Reserve, created in 1927, occupies 120 sq miles (310 sq km), of which 110 sq miles (285 sq km) are woodland. It contains 973 species of higher plants, 8 each of reptiles and amphibians, 185 of birds and 51 of mammals, including Beavers (*Castor fiber*). To the east of the Voronezh administrative region is the Khoper Reserve, with an area of 63 sq miles (162 sq km). Created in 1935, this reserve contains the rare Russian Desman (*Desmana moschata*), an aquatic relative of the moles.

The Tsentralno-Lesnoy Nature Reserve was created in 1931 in the Kalinin administrative region, with an area of 82 sq miles (213 sq km), of which 77 sq miles (199 sq km) are wooded. In the south of the Moscow region is the Prioksko-Terrasny Biosphere Nature Reserve, with an area of 19 sq miles (49 sq km), mostly wooded; it contains a herd of European Bison (*Bison bonasus*).

The map shows the nature reserves that have been established in the Soviet Far East. The mixed-forest reserves created in the rest of the Soviet Union appear on the map on page 112, together with those in the coniferous forest (taiga) zone. Some of the mountain reserves (pages 162–5) contain forests.

The nature reserves of the Ukrainian SSR are also in the mixed forest zone, some of them in wooded steppeland. The Poless Reserve has an area of 78 sq miles (201 sq km). Some mixed-forest reserves are located in the Belorussian SSR, including the Berezina Biosphere Nature Reserve on the Berezina River, with an area of 294 sq miles (762 sq km), of which 245 sq miles (635 sq km) are wooded; the Pripyat Reserve, with an area of 240 sq miles (622 sq km), of which 197 sq miles (511 sq km) is forest; and the dense primaeval forest of the 'Belovezhskaya Pushcha' Reserve, with an area of 338 sq miles (876 sq km). When this is translated from the Russian, its name means 'Belovezh Virgin Forest'.

In the Baltic republics, most of the nature reserves were established for the conservation of areas of marshland, but as they all contain large areas of mixed forest, they are listed here. There are three reserves in Lithuania: 'Žuvintas', established in 1937, with an area of 21 sq miles (54 sq km); Kamanos, occupying 14 sq miles (37 sq km); and Čepkeliai (Chyapkyalyai), with an area of 33 sq miles (85 sq

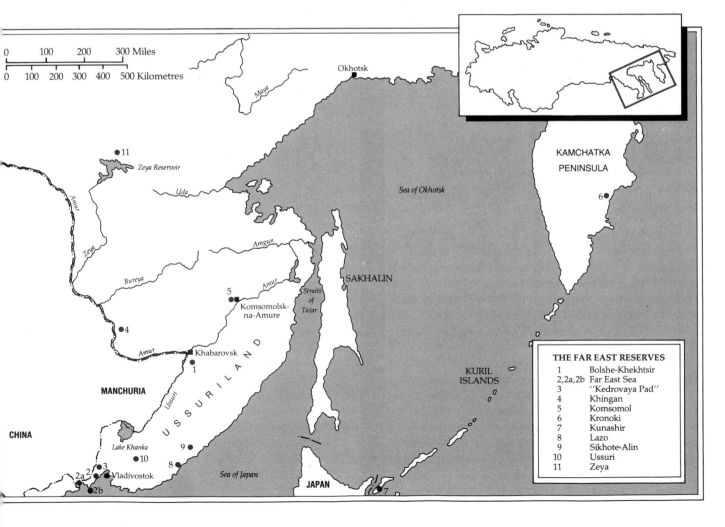

THE FAR EAST RESERVES

1	Bolshe-Khekhtsir
2, 2a, 2b	Far East Sea
3	''Kedrovaya Pad''
4	Khingan
5	Komsomol
6	Kronoki
7	Kunashir
8	Lazo
9	Sikhote-Alin
10	Ussuri
11	Zeya

The rushing sound of small waterfalls is a feature of the landscape along the Tyurina River in the nature reserve created on Kunashir, southernmost of the Kuril Islands.

km). Latvia has the $4\frac{1}{4}$ sq mile (11 sq km) 'Grini' Reserve; the 11 sq mile (28 sq km) Krustkalni Reserve; the 3 sq mile (8 sq km) Moritsala Reserve; the 58 sq mile (149 sq km) 'Slitere' Reserve; and the 73 sq mile (190 sq km) Teychu Reserve. Estonia has the following reserves: the $2\frac{1}{4}$ sq mile (6 sq km) Viydumyäe Reserve; the 41 sq mile (107 sq km) Vilsandi Reserve on the islands of the same name in the Baltic Sea, one of the oldest reserves in the USSR, established in 1910; and the 153 sq mile (397 sq km) Matsalu Reserve, created in 1957, which in 1975 was incorporated into a wetland reserve of international importance – the 'Matsalu Gulf of the Baltic Sea Reserve', with a total area of 188 sq miles (486 sq km). On the boundary between Estonia and Latvia is the Nigula Reserve, with an area of 11 sq miles (28 sq km). Lithuania, Latvia and Estonia each have a national park containing a nature reserve.

Far East reserves

A network of large nature reserves has been established in the Soviet Far East to protect its rare wildlife.

In 1934 the Kronoki State Nature Reserve was created on the Pacific coast of Kamchatka to conserve the peninsula's unique wildlife. Within its 3,722 sq miles (9,640 sq km) live some 800 species of higher plants, 179 of birds and 33 of mammals. Kamchatka is a volcanic region, and the reserve includes the peninsula's second highest volcano, Kronots, 11,575 ft (3,528 m) above sea-level. Most of the geysers and hot springs are in the reserve. In the Valley of the Geysers, established in 1941, 22 separate geysers have been counted; the most powerful shoots a stream of hot water 165 ft (50 m) into the air.

The Zeya Reserve was created in 1963 in the north of the Amur region, with an area of 319 sq miles (826 sq km), of which forest covers 90.7 per cent. More than 500 species of higher plants, 133 of birds and 37 of mammals have been recorded there.

The Komsomol Reserve, created in 1963, is in the lower part of the basin of the River Goryun, a large tributary to the west of the River Amur. In 1981, after a large fire, its area was increased, and, at 236 sq miles (612 sq km), is now almost twice that of the old reserve.

In 1963 the Bolshe-Khekhtsir Reserve was created on the Bolshoi Khekhtsir mountain range near Khabarovsk, on the junction of the Amur and Ussuri rivers. This has an area of 173 sq miles (449 sq km). The 755 species of higher plants include many rare ones registered in the Red Book of the USSR. This reserve has 11 species of reptiles and amphibians, 191 of birds and 35 of mammals.

The Khingan Reserve has existed since 1963 in the foothills of the Lesser Khingan Range, near the middle reaches of the River Amur. It has an area of 317 sq miles (822 sq km), 47 per cent of it forested. Much of the rest is marsh. There are some 500 species of higher plants, 103 of birds and 44 of mammals.

The Biosphere Nature Reserve of Sikhote-Alin was created in 1935 on the eastern and western slopes of the Sikhote–Alin Range, with an area of 1,342 sq miles (3,475 sq km), of which 99 per cent is forest. The highest land is 5,250 ft (1,600 m) above sea-level. The flora includes about 940 species of higher plants, and there are 340 species of birds and 61 of mammals.

In the southern part of the Sikhote–Alin Range, on the coast of the Sea of Japan, the nature reserve at Lazo, named after L. G. Kaplanov, was created in 1937, with an area of 450 sq miles (1,165 sq km). The land is mountainous and about 96 per cent of it is forested. There are about 1,000 species of higher plants, including many rare and endemic species. The animals are many and varied, including 8 species of amphibians, 9 species of reptiles, 286 species of birds, and 48 species of mammals.

In the extreme south of Ussuriland lies the nature

By comparison with the great stands of conifer trees, the mixed forests of Ussuriland are more complex natural communities, with a rich shrub layer that includes many species of twisting, climbing lianas, giving them something of the appearance of the tropical rainforests.

reserve of 'Kedrovaya Pad', occupying 69 sq miles (179 sq km), created in 1916. It lies in the basin of the Kedrova River, with conical hills rising 1,970 to 2,300 ft (600 to 700 m) above sea-level. As many as 17 plants grow here that are registered in the USSR's Red Book, including Ginseng (*Panax ginseng*) and *Rhododendron schlippenbachii*. There are 817 species of higher plants, 250 of birds (118 of which breed in the reserve) and 57 of mammals, including the very rare Amur race of the Leopard (*Panthera pardus orientalis*). The insect population is rich in endemic species of tropical origin, such as Maack's Swallowtail Butterfly (*Papilio maackii*) and Schrenck's Purple Emperor Butterfly (*Apatura schrenckii*).

In 1932 the Ussuri Reserve was created on the southern spurs of the Sikhote–Alin Range, with an area of 156 sq miles (404 sq km), of which 99 per cent is forested. A total of 824 species of higher plants have been found in the reserve, and the animals include many Far-Eastern relict species. In 1978, the USSR's first marine nature reserve was created in the Gulf of St Peter the Great, in the extreme south of the Soviet Far East, with an area of 249 sq miles (644 sq km), 243 sq miles (630 sq km) of which is sea. The reserve, called the Far East Sea Reserve, has three separate areas of sea and land, including islands as well as coastline. The islands contain large colonies of seabirds.

In 1985, a new nature reserve was created in the Far East, on the southernmost of the Kuril Islands, Kunashir. This large island has a most interesting community of plants and many rare and interesting animals, including some known only from the islands. Two of these are the Far East Skink (*Eumeces letiscutatus*) and the Kunashir Island Grass Snake (*Elaphe climacophora*).

7 MOUNTAINS

Although the USSR is a country of enormous plains, it also contains many mountain ranges. These are remarkably varied in area, height, vegetation and animal life. Mountains and hills cover just over a third of the Soviet Union.

The author has been fortunate to have wandered hundreds of miles over these regions on foot and on horseback, getting to know the changing faces of the peaks with the seasons. Unforgettable sights and sounds include dramatic thunderstorms, spectacular sunsets and peaks shrouded permanently in cloud and mist; Apollo butterflies floating slowly over the alpine meadows like huge snowflakes; the beautiful song of the Whistling Thrush; the penetrating calls of the marmots, and the unmistakable silhouette of a Golden Eagle as it scans the mountainsides for prey.

The grandeur and wildness of mountains and the physical challenges they pose have increasingly drawn people to them as a retreat from the pressures of urban life. Mountains are enigmatic and powerful, yet fragile and easily harmed. Conservationists are right to warn us of their vulnerability. Fortunately, the mountain ranges of the

USSR are now receiving the official protection they so justly deserve.

I will begin this chapter by taking a look at the general features of mountain vegetation, and then go on to examine the highest and most interesting of the USSR's mountain ranges — the Caucasus, Tien Shan, Pamir, Gissaro-Alai and Altai — which have the most highly developed vegetation and the greatest diversity of animals.

In each case, a description of the physical features of the mountain range is followed by an account of the most typical plants to be found there. The second part of the chapter deals with the animal life of the mountains. The plants and animals of the cold mountains of Siberia and the Far East range of Sikhote-Alin have already been described in detail in the sections on taiga and mixed forest, as they are more characteristic of those habitats.

High-mountain vegetation

Vegetation in the high mountains resembles that of the Arctic, but there are some important differences, which increase the further south the mountains are. So the mountain vegetation of the northern Urals and of the eastern Siberian chain is similar to tundra vegetation, but the southern mountains of the Caucasus and Central Asia have quite different plants, which are more truly alpine.

A common feature of tundra and alpine climates is their short growing season. However, there are also considerable differences between conditions in the mountains and those in the Arctic tundra. In the mountains, there is no permafrost, so there is more available moisture in the form of rain or snow. Also the sunlight is more intense, and because of this alpine plants have developed special anatomical features, such as a strongly developed protective layer of palisade tissue in the leaves to protect the sensitive chloroplasts which carry out photosynthesis.

Zonation

One of the most striking features of mountains is the separation of the plants and animals that live on them into horizontal belts, or zones, at different altitudes. This is most noticeable as one climbs one of the peaks of the major ranges, such as the Caucasus, Tien Shan or Pamir. The vegetation zones are determined largely by temperature and humidity which, in turn, are affected by both the altitude and latitude of the mountain. In the northern mountains, covered with snow or tundra for their whole

ABOVE *One of several species of wild onion to be found in the mountains of the USSR, the Karatau Onion grows in the western Tien Shan Mountains.*
LEFT *The Soviet Union contains some of the world's most impressive and beautiful mountains, such as this one in the great Pamir range, which includes the country's highest peaks and largest glaciers.*

All these influences, which can vary dramatically over short distances within a particular mountain, are responsible for the great variety of zonation patterns. Basically, however, there are two distinct zones of true mountain vegetation above the tree line: the subalpine and alpine belts. The lower limit of the mountain vegetation in different mountain ranges varies greatly, due to the geographical orientation of the range, its latitude and the direction of its slopes. The distribution of rainfall or snowfall is also very important. In the Altai, for example, the lower limit of high-mountain meadows is between 4,360 and 8,200 ft (1,330 and 2,500 m) in the north but lies at 7,870 ft (2,400 m) in the south. In the Tien Shan this limit is at 4,920 ft (1,500 m) in the north but rises to 8,200 ft (2,500 m) in the west.

SUBALPINE MEADOWS

There is a great difference between the plant species of alpine and subalpine meadows. Subalpine meadows in full bloom are a mass of bright colours. They have an almost complete plant cover of grasses and wild flowers. In several Central-Asian mountain areas there may be as many as 100 species of flowers in the grassy subalpine meadows. Over the whole of the Central Asia mountain area, the subalpine belt may contain as many as 200 plant species, and an area of only 264 sq ft (25 sq m) has been found to contain no fewer than 57 species.

Not all the mountain chains of Central Asia have a subalpine meadow belt, however. Its distribution is linked primarily to the amount of rain or snow that falls and to its seasonal variation. For this reason, there are none in the secluded parts of the central Tien Shan, nor in many areas of the Pamir and Gissaro-Alai, where the general dryness of the climate is one of the chief reasons for the formation of the unusual high-altitude steppes that occur there. It is in the outlying ranges of the Central Asian mountain system that the most colourful subalpine meadows are found.

ALPINE MEADOWS

If the subalpine vegetation shows many features characteristic of mountain plants, the alpine plant community reflects the real austerity of life at high altitudes – a short growing season affected by extremes of temperature. Low temperatures and constant winds have encouraged the formation of ground-hugging creepers and cushion plants. Many of the plants have leaves of rosette pattern with almost no stem, and most of them reproduce themselves asexually by means of tubers, rhizomes and other vegetative organs. Those that do reproduce sexually have

A view of the foothills of the Talass Alatau Range in the western Tien Shan Mountains, which show a particularly striking vertical zonation of vegetation.

height, the temperatures at the base and summit do not differ markedly. In the southern ranges, however, temperature differences between various levels can often be quite considerable.

Apart from the height above sea level, the direction in which a slope faces plays an important part in the distribution of plant and animal life. Most of the USSR's mountain ranges run in a predominantly east–west direction. Lower, older mountains, such as the Carpathians, whose summits have suffered millions of years of erosion, are wooded to the very top; but the jagged, rocky summits of the Caucasus and Gissaro-Alai, for example, are covered with snow and have large glaciers.

unusually bright colours to attract the relatively small number of pollinating insects that can survive at high altitudes.

The alpine meadows of Central Asia in full bloom are among the most beautiful sights in the whole of the Soviet Union. They dazzle the eye with their brightness, freshness and luxuriance. At first the meadows are covered with pale green foliage, then, by early summer, the flowers begin to open; delicate blue Forget-me-nots, pale pink Crowfoots, golden Globeflowers, pale yellow Alpine Poppies and many others. The upper boundary of this highest zone of vegetation in the Central Asian mountains can be as high as 12,500 ft to 14,800 ft (3,800 to 4,500 m).

A classic example of zonation: the Tien Shan

A classic example of horizontal zonation at different heights can be found in the Tien Shan. The mighty Tien Shan is a vast mountain range in Central Asia, running in an east–west direction for 1,520 miles (2,450 km), of which 745 miles (1,200 km) lie in the Uzbek, Kazakh and Kirgiz republics of the USSR, and the rest in China. The Tien Shan Range is linked by ridges to the Dzhungar Alatau and Pamir-Alai systems, which also run in a mainly east–west direction. The highest peaks are in the central Tien Shan, on the border with China. These are Pik Pobedy (Victory Peak), 24,406 ft (7,439 m) high, and Han Tengri, which reaches 22,950 ft (6,995 m). The longest ridges of the Tien Shan in the USSR are the Zaiiliskii, Kungei, Terskei, Kirgiz, Talass Alatau and Chatkal.

The landscape of the Tien Shan mountains bears unmistakable signs of having been carved out by glaciers to create corries and troughs, with large amounts of rock debris dragged along to form screes and moraines. In the foothills, the snow lies for a mere two to three months of the year, halfway up it stays for six to seven months, and just below the glaciers, which in the Tien-Shan cover the huge area of 3,939 sq miles (10,200 sq km), it remains for as much as nine to ten months.

The dry, continental-type climate of the Tien Shan allows only the hardiest plants to thrive. Over much of the range, steppe vegetation occurs intermittently at a height of 3,300 to 9,800 ft (1,000 to 3,000 m), intermingled with areas of coniferous scrub and meadowland. From 9,800 to 10,500 ft (3,000 to 3,200 m) lie the subalpine and alpine belts, while above 11,500 ft (3,500 m) the scene becomes a harsh landscape of rocks, glaciers, snowdrifts and scree.

The northern Tien Shan shows a particularly clear pattern of zonation. The foothills rise from the surrounding

Altai Globeflowers grace a mountain stream in the Katun Range of the vast Altai Range in south-west Siberia.

desert, from about 500 to 2,100 ft (150 to 660 m). Their lower levels have semi-desert, slaty soil, clothed with drought-resistant, salt-tolerant plants, such as tamarisks (*Tamarix*) and Camel's Thorn (*Alhagi camelorum*). The upper foothills are a region of wormwood (sagebrush) desert, dominated by the species *Artemisia sublessingiana*. At about 3,900 ft (1,200 m) they give way to deciduous forests. This broad-leaved forest belt, from 2,000 to 5,250 or 5,900 ft (600 to 1,600 or 1,800 m) has the richest, most varied flora, with about 40 species of trees and shrubs, dominated by the Wild Apple (*Malus sieversii*) and Apricot (*Armeniaca vulgaris*), the endemic Goat's Wheat (*Atraphaxis muschketovii*) and maple (*Acer semenovii*), and many thorny shrubs, such as roses (*Rosa*) and barberries (*Berberis*). The ground layer of plants features a rich growth of grasses, and includes various species of tulips, some of them endemic or exotic (such as *Tulipa kolpakovskiana* and *T. ostrovskiana*) various species of desert candle (*Eremurus*), the daisy-like, yellow-flowered Golden Rays (*Ligularia macrophylla*), and many others.

In the highest part of the broad-leaved forest belt grow copses of Aspen (*Populus tremula*) and Hackberry (*Celtis caucacisa*) and the aromatic Dittany (*Dictamnus turkestanicus*), renowned as a cure-all herbal remedy. Birches, including the White Birch (*Betula tianshanica*), and Sea Buckthorn (*Hippophae rhamnoides*), grow in the river valleys. Of some 1,200 species of higher plants characteristic of this part of the northern Tien Shan, no fewer than 600 are established in the lower belt.

At 5,600 to 5,900 ft (1,700 to 1,800 m), the broad-leaved forest is replaced by a zone of spruce trees. This is dominated by thick stands of Tien Shan Spruce (*Picea tianshanica*). The lower part of the spruce belt features a thick layer of undergrowth, including Aspen (*Populus tremula*), birches (*Betula*) and the endemic rowan *Sorbus tianshanicus*, together with many shrubs, such as currant bushes (*Ribes*), roses (*Rosa*) and honeysuckles (*Lonicera*). Beneath these grows a variety of herbaceous plants, including a corydalis (*Corydalis semenovi*) a cranesbill (*Geranium rectum*) and an interesting member of the orchid family, the helleborine *Epipactis latiuniflora*. In the upper part of the spruce belt the number of species of trees and shrubs diminishes rapidly, but various species of grass take their place, notably Cock's-foot (*Dactylis glomerata*), Tufted Hair-grass (*Deschampsia caespitosa*) and Meadow-grass (*Poa pratensis*), among which appear such lovely flowers as the monkshood *Aconitum excelsum*, Lesser Meadow Rue (*Thalictrum minus*) and the buttercup *Ranunculus grandiflorus*.

In turn, the spruce belt gives way to a subalpine belt of dwarf juniper bushes (*Juniperus sibirica* and *J. turkestanica*). Honeysuckles (*Lonicera karelini* and *L. humilis*) grow here as well as in the spruce forest belt, together with various grasses, aconites (*Aconitum nemorum* and *A. rotundifolium*) and other herbaceous plants. In the clearings grow the poppy *Papaver croceum*, the globe-flower *Trollius dshungaricus* and the aster *Aster alpinus*. The juniper zone extends up to about 9,800 ft (3,000 m), where a zone of alpine meadows of various types takes over. These consist chiefly of small areas of meadow surrounded by rocks. The alpine zone is dominated by the following herbaceous plants: *Primula algida*, the Altai Violet (*Viola altaica*), *Trollius dshungaricus*, Alpine Blue Grass (*Poa alpina*), the sedge *Carex melanantha*, the knotweed *Polygonum nitens, Anemone protracta*, the gentians *Gentiana algida* and *G. kaufmanniana* and the louseworts *Pedicularis violascens* and *P. songarica*. The drier areas of alpine meadow typically contain sedges, such as *Cobresia capilliformis*, which form a dense turf.

These alpine meadows are interspersed with desert-like areas, clothed in many places with drought-resistant grasses, such as the meadow grass *Poa relaxa*. Even more highly adapted to the dry, windswept terrain are the remarkable cushion-forming plants. These include *Saxifraga alberti* and the rock jasmine *Androsace villosa*. Their

Many species of violets grow in the mountains, most of them in the damp climate of the Altai, especially in the alpine meadows near the upper limit of the trees.

long runners twine about each other to form dense, dome-shaped clusters of foliage. This curious growth habit enables the plants to tolerate the strong mountain winds and conserve heat. Also, the whole surface of the cushion soaks up water. When growing in an exposed position, the cushions often begin to wither on the side of the prevailing wind. An entire miniature garden of less hardy plants may develop within the protection afforded by the cushion.

The most widespread cushion-forming plant in the Tien Shan and Pamir ranges is the Prickly Thrift, or Prickly Heath (*Acantholimon diapensioides*). Its branches, pressed close to the ground, bear numerous short twigs, densely covered with tiny succulent leaves, forming a lichen-like encrustation. When the summer shoots have reached an inch or two (3 to 5 cm) high, the central portion stops growing and the edges of the plant grow rapidly, so that the whole plant slowly but surely spreads across the ground, continuously leaving behind a dead, inner core.

Another cushion-former is the moss-like *Thylacospermum caespitosum*, which grows as turf-like cushions so dense that one can sit or even stand on them with no visible effect on the plant. Sometimes, the south-facing side of the cushion bursts into bloom, its entire surface covered with tiny, delicate, whitish flowers. Another species, a member of the rose family (Rosaceae), is *Dryadanthe tetranda*. It is endemic to the Tien Shan and Altai ranges, and forms such a tight cushion that it is hard to believe it is a higher flowering plant. Other species are even more unusual, resembling stones, so densely packed are their highly adapted pale greyish stems.

ABOVE *One of the loveliest of all mountain flowers, with blooms 3 in (7.5 cm) long. Greig's Tulip is scarce and local, and is listed as endangered in the Soviet Red Book.*

ABOVE *Another of the wild onions of the Soviet mountains (see also page 139), the Pskem Onion grows only in the western Tien Shan, and is listed in the Soviet Red Book.*

Around the snow-fields grow such beautiful alpine flowers as the whitlow grasses *Draba oreades* and *D. intermedia, Lloydia serotina*, and the globe-flower *Trollius lilacinus*. Among the rocks grow plants such as Chives (*Allium schoenoprasum*) and *Paraquilegia grandiflorum*. The upper limit of vegetation, growing among the large boulders on the glacial moraines, includes plants such as the honeysuckle *Lonicera glauca*, the meadow grass *Poa lipskyi*, the sedge *Carex griffithii*, the dandelion *Taraxacum lilacinum* and the chrysanthemum *Pyrethrum leonthopodium*. The summits are lifeless regions of glaciers, bare rock and perpetual snow.

The entire Tien Shan area boasts a vast wealth of plant species, a number of which are rare and confined to small remote areas. Among the most beautiful flowering plants are the tulips, whole fields of which carpet the mountain-sides in spring. The most dramatic species is the large Greig's Tulip (*Tulipa greigi*) which is endemic to the western Tien Shan. This grows in clumps on dry, gravelly slopes among stands of juniper at altitudes of up to 7,870 ft (2,400 m). Its broad greyish-green leaves, marbled with bronze-purple, may grow 6 in (15 cm) long and the single, large, cup-shaped, brilliant scarlet-orange flower is so impressive that it is easy to see how the plant acquired its popular name, 'king of the tulips'. As long ago as 1877 the Dutch awarded this species a first class diploma as an outstanding cultivated tulip. Unfortunately, its beauty has proved its undoing. People still thoughtlessly pick the splendid flowers. As a result, this lovely tulip is endangered and has been registered in the Soviet Red Book. Also listed there is another rare tulip from the western Tien Shan, Kaufmann's Tulip (*Tulipa kaufmanniana*). Sometimes called the Water-Lily Tulip, it has delicate white flowers flushed with red and gold on the outside, and its petals open out almost flat, so that they resemble those of a water-lily. Fortunately, this species has a more widespread distribution and grows at a greater range of heights.

The western Tien Shan is also home to another early-spring flower, the lily *Korolkowia severtsovi*. Originally described botanically in 1873, it was first grown in St Petersburg (now Leningrad) from bulbs sent from Karatau by General Korolkov, after whom it is named. It grows on shady damp slopes at up to 8,200 ft (2,500 m). In Kazakh-stan it is called *tau agla*, which means 'wild potato', a reference to its large tubers, which contain over 40 per cent of starch.

One of the rarest plants in the Tien Shan is the Pskem Onion (*Allium pskemense*). Up to 20 in (50 cm) high, with a large globe of greenish-white flowers, it grows in rocky areas along high river valleys. The onions are large – the size of a clenched fist – and taste rather sweet. The Pskem Onion is important as a wild stock from which cultivated onions can be bred, and it is protected throughout its range in the mountains.

Another characteristic mountain plant of these parts is the Minkwitz Primula (*Primula minkwitsiae*) which grows at altitudes above 9,840 ft (3,000 m). Its favourite habitat is on damp rocky slopes near glaciers on the Talass and Kirgiz ridges of the Tien Shan.

Islets in Lake Kara-Kul, in the eastern Pamir Mountains, 13,120 ft (4,000 m) above sea-level, provide nesting sites for Brown-headed Gulls, Common Terns and Bar-headed Geese.

The Pamir-Alai

Another large mountain system in Central Asia is the Pamir-Alai, which includes the highest mountain range in the USSR, the Pamir, as well as the Tadzhik Depression and the Gissaro-Alai Mountains. The great Pamir mountain region measures approximately 155 miles (250 km) from north to south and 170 miles (275 km) from east to west, though geographers and biologists disagree on a precise definition of its boundaries. It boasts the USSR's highest mountains, including Pik Kommunisma (Communism Peak), at 24,600 ft (7,495 m), and also contains the largest glacier in the Soviet Union, the Fedchenko Glacier, about 50 miles (77 km) long.

The relief of the Pamir varies from east to west. In the east, the mountain ranges are mostly very old, with softly rounded outlines. The heights of the peaks range from 13,120 ft (4,000 m) to 19,680 ft (6,000 m), with a few, including Pik Kommunisma, soaring higher still. In the western Pamir, the mountains are broken up by ridges of the alpine type, and snow and glaciers alternate with deep narrow ravines, through which tumble torrential rivers. The peaks here are of more modest heights, mostly between 9,850 ft and 16,400 ft (3,000 and 5,000 m). Much of the landscape is bare rock and scree.

The Pamir has a severe, markedly continental climate, and contains a total 3,240 sq miles (8,400 sq km) of ice. In the harsher eastern Pamir, particularly, there are few plant and animal species, although one hardy animal inhabitant is the Brown-headed Gull (*Larus brunnicephalus*), which nests on the shores of some of the high mountain lakes. The western Pamir, by contrast, is extremely rich in both plant and animal species. This is an area which has experienced much erosion in relatively recent geological times, carving out deep valleys which plunge from a height of about 13,000 ft (4,000 m) down to about 6,600 or 5,600 ft (2,000 or 1,700 m). The watersheds are long and rocky and the rivers torrential. Trees and shrubs are practically absent, while drought-resistant plants are as much of a feature of the dry mountain slopes as in the Tien Shan. Many species of the cushion-forming prickly thrifts (*Acantholimon*) have a widespread distribution, along with the thorny *Cousinia*, a member of the daisy family (*Compositae*), and other species.

As in the Tien Shan, there is a clear division into vegetation zones with increasing altitude. Four belts are generally distinguished. First, there is a Mediterranean type of gravelly desert, dominated by species of drought-resistant, salt-tolerant glassworts (Salicornia). This is succeeded by a zone of open steppe, with prickly thrifts (*Acantholimon*), wormwoods (*Artemisia*) and needle-grasses (*Stipa*). Above this lies a belt of subalpine Eurasian steppe, with needle-grasses and the fescue grass *Festuca sulcata*. The highest zone is one of alpine meadows, with many similar species to those in the Tien Shan Range. Some botanists divide the western Pamir into only three belts, regarding the two steppe zones as one.

The Gissaro-Alai

The Gissaro-Alai Range, 560 miles (900 km) long and 50 to 90 miles (80 to 150 km) wide, lies to the east of the Tien Shan and north-east of the Pamir Range. Its main ridges, the Zeravshan, Gissar, Alai, and Turkestan, rise to over 16,400 ft (5,000 m). The plants and animals of this region include a wealth of varied species. Many of these are also found in the Tien Shan and Pamir mountains, but there are also endemic plants, such as the giant umbellifer *Ferula badrakema*, which yields resin, the Scurf Pea (*Psoralea drupacea*), and sage-like *Phlomis* species.

The Caucasus

Nearer, better known and more accessible than the great Central Asian ranges are those of the Caucasus, which occupy a total area of about 170,000 sq miles (440,000 sq km) between the Black Sea and the Caspian Sea, extending from the Kumo-Manych Depression in the north to the USSR's frontiers with Turkey and Iran in the south.

The ridge of the Great Caucasus extends from the Taman Peninsula in the north-west to the Apsheron Peninsula on the Caspian Sea. To the southeast lie the folds of the Talysh Mountains, which rise to 8,136 ft (2,477 m). In the middle and western part are the Little Caucasus and the volcanic highlands of Armenia.

The mountain system of the Great Caucasus can be divided into three parts: western, central and eastern. The northern slopes of the Great Caucasus are gentler than the southern. The two largest ranges, with sharp crests, are the Glavny (main) and Bokovoi (side) Ranges. The highest point of the Caucasus is Mount Elbrus, at 18,500 ft (5,642 m). Glaciation is widespread in this region, especially on the main ridges, and there are well over 2,000 glaciers. The animal and plant life of the Caucasus is of great interest, being rich in relict and endemic species. The endemic plants come from a wide variety of families. Among the most beautiful are the orchids and lilies which grow among the mixed forests of fir, beech and other trees which clothe many of the lower slopes. These forests contain many endemic tree species, especially conifers.

Dense thickets of rhododendron (*Rhododendron caucasicum*) occur in many parts of the Caucasus. In the extreme west these magnificent shrubs can cover an entire slope, but they become progressively rarer as one travels towards the drier east. The rhododendron thickets alternate with subalpine meadows, and are often so thick as to be practically impassable.

True subalpine meadows form a fairly wide belt above the tree line, both in the Great and the Little Caucasus. Tall grasses and other herbaceous plants are a feature of the Caucasus's subalpine meadows, especially of its western parts, although there are few in the Little Caucasus. They form a luxuriant sward up to 8 ft (2.5 m) high and include giant buttercups (*Ranunculus*), larkspurs (*Delphinium*) and umbellifers, the last-named with flower-heads as big as dinner-plates. A huge variety of different species is found, as many as 1,600 in a single nature reserve.

At an average altitude of around 6,560 ft (2,000 m), the subalpine meadows merge into those of the alpine type, which here consist mainly of relatively low grasses and sedges, growing to a height of 4 to 12 in (10 to 30 cm).

ABOVE *The Caucasian Lily is one of the most beautiful high-mountain flowers of the Caucasus region, restricted to the most remote areas.*

ABOVE *This columbine,* Aquilegia olympica, *is a common flower of the upper forest belt and subalpine belt of the Caucasus Mountains.*

Alpine meadows in the Caucasus also contain carpets of beautiful rosette- and cushion-forming flowers. These are similar to some of those found in the Central Asian mountains. In the Caucasus, as in the mountains of Central Asia, considerable areas of the alpine and subalpine belts are covered with boulders and screes. Cushion-forming plants grow among the boulders, while screes contain plants with long underground stems, which can tolerate burial from rocky debris.

The Altai

The Altai is a vast mountain region lying to the south of western Siberia. It forms a clearly defined geographical unit with an interesting climate and unusual sedimentary rocks. Its ecology is also quite distinct.

The clearest boundaries of the Altai are to be found in the north and west where the mountains border the plains. To the south and east, however, the distinction is blurred by other, lesser mountain ranges. To the southeast lies the Mongolian Range, which originates in Mongolia and China. The highest of the many peaks of the Altai mountain system is Mount Belukha in the Katun Range, rising to 14,783 ft (4,506 m).

Thanks to their position, the northerly Altai are

distinctly alpine at lower altitudes than are mountains to the south. As low as 9,842 ft (3,000 m) there is a true alpine landscape with snow, glaciers, bare rocks and scree. Strangely enough, climbers do not seem to suffer as much from lack of oxygen as they do at similar altitudes in the Pamir, Tien Shan or Himalayas. The Altai are also notable for their abundant rivers, streams, lakes, springs, and waterfalls, all adding to the impression of a rain-sodden, water-filled landscape.

Mount Belukha, in the Katun Range, at 14,783 ft (4,506 m) the highest peak of the Altai Mountains, has a sheer, inaccessible wall of ice and snow, which is held in awe even by the most experienced mountaineers.

The alpine and subalpine belts are well defined in the Altai Mountains. The lower boundary of the subalpine belt fluctuates considerably between about 3,640 ft (1,110 m) and 7,870 ft (2,400 m) in various parts of this vast mountain system. In the southern and eastern parts of the Altai, the boundary is higher.

Because of their northerly location compared to the other great mountain ranges of the USSR, the Altai Mountains show many similarities with the Arctic. Out of a total of some 300 species of flowering plant from the Altai, as many as 39 per cent closely resemble those found in the Arctic regions. The remaining 61 per cent are genuine mountain species.

A distinctive feature of the Altai is the presence, and usually the predominance, of the mountain tundra zone, which occupies a much greater area than the lower alpine and subalpine meadows. This extensive zone is due both to the northerly location and to the considerable area of flat plateau which continues uninterrupted for up to 100 miles (160 km) with its scant cover of mosses and lichens.

In the subalpine belt of the Altai, meadows of tall grass alternate with forests of Siberian Stone Pine (*Pinus sibirica*) and larch (*Larix*). Near the upper limit of the trees, the meadow grasses become shorter and the meadows change to a narrow belt of true alpine meadows. Particoloured violets, large-flowered columbines, and bright orange globe-flowers delight the traveller who ventures into these remote parts.

The Urals, Sayan and Carpathians

Some of the less dramatic, lower mountains of the USSR are the Urals, the Sayan and the Carpathians. More than 1,242 miles (2,000 km) long, the Urals, unlike most of the country's mountain chains, run from north to south. They include steppe, forest and bare mountain zones. As a rule, the animals do not differ from those in the neighbouring plains. Few species are endemic. The three highest peaks are 6,560 ft (2,000 m), 6,217 ft (1,895 m) and 6,161 ft (1,878 m).

In the Sayan Mountains to the north-east of the Altai, there are even fewer truly alpine species of plants (only 150) and the proportion of plants common to the Arctic region reaches 55 per cent. In the eastern Sayan, the sub-alpine belt begins at an altitude of 3,940 to 5,900 ft (1,200 to 1,800 m), while the alpine belt occurs above 6,230 to 7,220 ft (1,900 to 2,200 m). Many plant species common to the Altai also live here. Above the alpine meadows of the Sayan are the rocky snowless summits.

As for the Carpathians, most of this range lies outside the USSR, in Romania and Czechoslovakia. The main peaks are in the west of the country and are no higher than 1,640 to 3,280 ft (500 to 1,000 m). The animals found there are typical woodland species, but the vegetation does include some endemic species.

Eastern Siberian Mountains

In the mountains of Yakutia and other eastern Siberian regions, including the Verkhoyansk, Chersky, Kolyma and Chukotsk ranges, the lower slopes are mainly clothed in conifer woodland. It is difficult to distinguish an alpine zone, partly because the peaks are not high enough, but also because of the arid climate. The landscape most often takes the form of a stony scree, with areas resembling true tundra. These tundra-like areas become more common as the mountains approach and merge into the true tundra in the north.

In the Soviet Far East lie the mountains of the North Pacific region, including the volcanoes of the Kuril Islands and Kamchatka. The Klyuchev volcanoes of the vast Kamchatka Peninsula, which is 745 miles (1,200 km) long and 142,870 sq miles (370,000 sq km) in area, include the cone of Mount Klyuchev itself, at 15,583 ft (4,750 m) one of the world's highest active volcanoes. Other major mountain ranges in the North Pacific region include those of Chukotka, the Anadyrskii High Plateau, the Koryaks Highlands and the Komandor Islands. The climate is cold and the distant Pacific trade winds make the summers dull, overcast and sometimes foggy.

In the Sikhote-Alin Mountains, the lower slopes are covered with forests, of coniferous trees in the northern mountains and predominantly of broad-leaved trees in the southern ranges. A rich undergrowth of trees, shrubs and herbaceous plants is found in the south, including many Japanese, Korean and Chinese species, such as the Chinese Magnolia Vine (*Schizandra chinensis*), whose Russian name, *limonnik*, refers to the strong scent of lemon emitted by its bark, Japanese Yew (*Taxus cuspidata*), Japanese Stone Pine (*Pinus pumila*) and Manchurian Filbert (*Corylus mandshurica*). This unique mountain flora is described in more detail on pages 117–19 of the chapter on Mixed Forests.

Higher up, this rich community of plants is replaced by forests of Khingan Fir (*Abies nephrolepis*) and Yeddo Spruce (*Picea jezoensis*), with prolific growths of moss. Above this is a subalpine zone, with stunted groves of Creeping Japanese Stone Pine (*Pinus pumila*). Among these can be found Bush Honeysuckle (*Diervillea praecox*), a relative of

The Tolbachik volcano in the Kamchatka Peninsula in the Soviet Far East. There are many active volcanoes in this unstable region of the earth's crust; of the 30 or so volcanic cones lying to the east of the main central chain of mountains in Kamchatka, about a dozen are currently active. The chain of volcanoes continues southwards from Kamchatka down to the Kuril Islands and Japan, forming one section of the great Pacific 'ring of fire'.

the weigelas loved by European gardeners, Golden Rhododendron (*Rhododendron aureum*), Alpine False Spiraea (*Sorbaria alpina*) and the endemic dwarf conifer *Microbiota decussata*, a juniper-like shrub, growing to 2 ft (60 cm) tall, which is the sole representative of its genus.

Next there is a belt of rocks with tall grass meadows and copses of dwarf Stone Birch (*Betula lanata*). The highest levels are covered with mountain tundra dominated by lichens and including a variety of low-growing heaths, Cowberry (*Vaccinium vitis-idiaea*), *Cassiope* and other tundra plants.

Mountain birds and other animals

In Soviet mountains, as in mountains elsewhere, animal life is diverse. Many animals that live there are also found in other habitats, such as the plains, forests, tundra and desert areas that occur within the mountain ecosystem. Typical of these 'general purpose' animals are the Rock Ptarmigan (*Lagopus mutus*), the Horned Lark, or Shore Lark (*Eremophila alpestris*), and the Reindeer (*Rangifer tarandus*). The true mountain species, by contrast, are real specialists. The splendid snowcocks, for example, which are described and illustrated on pages 151–2, are so intimately tied to the mountains that they cannot tolerate life in the plains, even in captivity.

Research on how animals adapt to life in the harsh conditions of the mountains poses some interesting ecological problems. For example recent investigations of birds in the Tien Shan Range have revealed new facets of their breeding behaviour, including relations between the sexes, details of their nest building and the rearing of other birds' young. Some birds of high altitudes can successfully rear two or even three broods in one season, a feat normally associated with birds of gentler habitats, and one which is achieved only by a clear division of labour between male and female. Clearly, many secrets of mountain life remain to be discovered. In some of the more remote ranges, the nests of various bird species have yet to be found.

The high and jagged crags are deceptively alive, particularly along the ridges of the Caucasus and in Central Asia. Among the most beautiful of all mountain creatures are the many species of Apollo butterflies (*Parnassius* spp.). Although some species, such as the Black Apollonius (*Parnassius mnemosyne*) also live as relict populations on the plains, most of these butterflies live in the high mountain meadows, where they float lazily over the brightly-coloured flowers. In the Tien Shan, their caterpillars feed on plants called golden root (*Radiola*). As many as ten species of *Parnassius* are registered in the Red Book of the USSR.

Because they are cold-blooded, few species of reptiles can survive in the cold, dry air at high altitudes. But in the arid mountains of desert type, such as the Kopet-Dag Range in Southern Turkmenia, there is a great variety of species, some of which are described in the chapter on Deserts (on pages 178–83).

ABOVE *Many beautiful Apollo butterflies live in the mountains of the Caucasus and Central Asia; this is* Parnassius apollo, *a common species in the Caucasus.*

ABOVE *The Golden Root, which grows on the slopes of the Tien Shan Mountains, is the food plant of the caterpillars of Apollo butterflies. This attractive plant, a member of the flax family, is greatly valued in the Soviet Union as a medicinal herb, which contains a wide variety of curative and stimulating substances.*

The most interesting mountain birds in the USSR live in the Caucasus, in Central Asia and in the Altai. Here, I shall also refer to birds from the Himalayas and Tibet, including several rare species, although most of the mountain ranges in these regions border on other states, so that few of their birds can be described as truly endemic to the USSR.

Among the most impressive of the USSR's insects is this mantis, belonging to the species Bolivaria brachyptera, *which was photographed in the western Tien Shan Mountains.*

ABOVE *This Himalayan Snowcock chick was photographed in June at the Aksu-Dzhabagly Nature Reserve, Tien Shan.*
RIGHT *A Caucasian Snowcock at the Teberda Reserve. All five species of snowcocks occur in the USSR; as well as the two illustrated, there are the Caspian, Altai and Tibetan.*

SNOWCOCKS

Any description of mountain birds must begin with the snowcocks, whose courtship call in spring epitomizes, more than anything else, the high mountain landscape of rocky screes, high peaks and deep canyons.

Related to the domestic fowl, this group of birds contains five species, all of which are found within the USSR. The Caucasian Snowcock (*Tetraogallus caucasicus*) lives only in the Great Caucasus; the Altai Snowcock (*T. altaicus*) inhabits the Altai Mountains; the Caspian Snowcock (*T. caspius*) is found on the ridges of the Little Caucasus and in Iran and Turkey; and the Himalayas have two species – the Himalayan Snowcock (*T. himalayensis*) and the Tibetan Snowcock (*T. tibetanus*). The former is found in the north-west Himalayas, occurring in the USSR in the Tien Shan and the Pamir-Alai ranges, while the range of the Tibetan Snowcock, which includes the Pamir plateau in the USSR, extends further south into the Himalayas.

There are various theories about the origin of these remarkable birds. Most biologists think that the genus *Tetraogallus* originated in the high Central Asian mountains, settling later in the mountain ridges to the north and west, and that the parent form then evolved into the five species we know today. Another theory is that their ancestors lived where the descendants live today, before the uplifting of the mountain ranges. Later, as the new mountains were slowly formed, the birds became isolated from each other and evolved into the present-day species.

Whichever of these theories is correct, the snowcocks have undergone a long process of evolutionary adaptation to life in the high mountains, enabling them to survive extremely harsh conditions.

Although they may be locally quite common, snowcocks are generally scarce birds, so it is always a great thrill to find one of their nests tucked away among stones and boulders. After the young hatch, several females may join together to protect their chicks and those of their neighbours. When disturbed, they will typically run for cover, but if pressed further, they cluck loudly and take to the air before gliding down the mountainside on bent, motionless wings. The fledglings follow close behind. Snowcocks are real masters of evasion and will not settle within sight of a human being.

It is only during the breeding season that there is a chance of studying their behaviour, observed from behind a camouflaged hide in one of their favourite haunts, large thawed patches on the snowline. The moving snowline is their true boundary, the birds ranging up and down the mountainside with the seasons, as the snow advances and retreats.

Snowcocks rise from level ground with difficulty. Pushing against the snow with their feet, they launch themselves down the mountainside, then switch over to a gliding flight, with frequent side-slipping. Then, thanks to their inertia, they climb abruptly and disappear over the nearest ridge.

Snowcocks spend much of their time in small flocks, pairing off to mate in spring. They nest on the ground, beneath an overhanging rock, in a cliff-crevice or beneath a lone pine tree. The female sits tightly on her 6 to 11 spotted brownish-grey eggs, allowing an observer to approach closely. At all other times, though, snowcocks are extremely wary birds. One of the most interesting aspects of their life in the high mountains is their partnership with mountain goats and wild boars which can dig away the snow, ensuring a supply of onion and crocus bulbs and other plant food for the snowcocks, even in the severest winters. All five species of snowcock have a very similar diet.

The most northerly species is the Altai Snowcock. The Altai Mountains experience particularly severe winters, and the birds rarely climb higher than 9,840 ft (3,000 m) in winter, and may even move down into the river valleys. The Tibetan Snowcock lives at the highest altitudes, in Pamir, at heights of up to 17,760 ft (5,400 m). The withdrawal of this species to such high levels is related to its need for plenty of moisture, which it finds on the mountain-tops. The Himalayan Snowcock, by contrast, ranges far more widely down the mountains, sometimes nesting as low as 3,280 ft (1,000 m) above sea-level. This species is clearly more flexible than the others. The Caspian Snowcock lives between 5,900 and 11,480 ft (1,800 and 3,500 m), having a preference for dry slopes. Even in the harshest of winters these birds do not descend as far as the upper tree-line. Endemic to the USSR, the Caucasian Snowcock is closely tied to the alpine belt of the Great Caucasus. Its favourite haunts are inaccessible, rocky areas in the high mountains, between 8,530 and 12,140 ft (2,600 and 3,700 m), where there are meadows of grasses and flowers. In winter, the birds move down the mountainside to the warmer, south-facing slopes.

Of the five species, three are classified as endangered and listed in the Soviet Red Data Book. The Tibetan Snowcock occurs in the USSR on the edge of its range. The Caspian and Altai Snowcocks are rare species by comparison with the Himalayan and Caucasian species. The populations of the last two species are thought to be approximately equal.

In general, snowcocks do not cause conservationists serious concern, thanks to the inaccessibility of their haunts, their high degree of adaptation to their harsh environment and their extreme cautiousness. However, to ensure that their melodic whistling cries continue to combine with the wind in providing a unique background music to the mountains of the Caucasus and Central Asia, it is essential that their habitats are safeguarded by the creation of new nature reserves.

BIRDS OF PREY

Though found throughout the USSR, the Golden Eagle (*Aquila chrysaetos*) is most common in the Central Asian mountains and tundra. It is exactly as one would picture the king of the mountain birds, soaring over the magnificent landscapes and arousing anxious cries from colonies of marmots and other potential prey in the valleys far below.

I have often encountered this royal bird, but I particularly remember two occasions. At the end of April, my colleagues and I decided to visit a large nest among the rocks in the nature reserve of Aksu-Dzhabagli in the western Tien Shan, which had previously been occupied by a Eurasian Griffon Vulture (*Gyps fulvus*). Riding on horseback up the Sukhaya Balka Canyon, we slowly approached the nest. Only when we were up alongside it

ABOVE *A Golden Eagle with its prey in the northern Tien Shan Mountains. This large eagle is widespread over much of the USSR, but is scarce in most regions, It is still quite numerous in the high mountains of Central Asia.*
OPPOSITE PAGE *A Black Vulture at its huge nest in May in the Aksu-Dzhabagly Nature Reserve in the western Tien Shan Mountains. Even larger than the Golden Eagle, this imposing bird has a body 3½ ft (1.05 m) long and a wingspan of almost 9 ft (2.7 m). Although it may gather in flocks at carcases, it is not a common bird.*

did we see a large female eagle flap noisily off the nest. Straightening her wings, she flew off towards the setting sun. But the single egg was hatching, for it already had a fairly large hole on one side of it. We hurriedly took some photographs and left the mountain. The Golden Eagle was nowhere to be seen and the sky seemed empty, but we all knew that her keen gaze was following our every movement.

The following July, we revisited the nest and saw a feeble Golden Eagle fledgling which flapped clumsily from one rock to the next. Having witnessed its birth, we were delighted to see that the youngster had survived.

On another occasion in April 1983, in a similar locality at about 8,200 ft (2,500 m) we discovered a new nest in which there was an already fully grown eaglet. While we were photographing it, it became excited and to our astonishment tried to fly off. At first its wings trembled in the wind but it soon gained confidence and slowly wheeled higher and higher until it disappeared from view beyond a distant crag. It was a tremendously exciting and memorable moment.

Another magnificent mountain bird of prey is the Lammergeier or Bearded Vulture (*Gypaetus barbatus*). This powerful bird, with a wingspan of up to 8 ft (2.5 m), lives in all the large ranges of the Caucasus and Central Asia. It tends to be a carrion eater and rarely kills healthy prey, although marmots and the occasional mountain goat are taken. This lifestyle is accurately reflected in the legends of the mountain people in which the Lammergeier changed from a bird of prey into a carrion-eater.

Lammergeiers are also associated with magical powers. According to an old Kirgiz legend:

After incubation, an axe hatches from the egg. This axe has miraculous properties. There is nothing on earth which it cannot cleave and nothing on earth can smash it. It can disappear only if a bird swallows it. If a man finds this axe he has a miraculous weapon for life. But in the nest the axe can exist only for three days. After this time it changes into a puppy called Kumaik, who has white eyes like his parents. If a man finds the nest with a puppy in it he can rear a wonderful dog for himself, able to cope with the strongest wild animals, even a dragon. Not only that, but this dog can determine the owner's fate, making him a happy man. In the nest the puppy, too, can exist only for three days. After this time, if no one has taken him from the nest, he turns into the usual vulture fledgling.

Several other vultures live in the mountains of the USSR. The Eurasian Griffon Vulture (*Gyps fulvus*) nests in colonies; the Eurasian Black Vulture (*Aegypius monachus*) lives in isolated pairs; the Egyptian Vulture (*Neophron percnopterus*) is the most common vulture, found in the low mountains and desert foothills; finally, there is the rare Himalayan Griffon (*Gyps himalayensis*), about which very little is known, since it lives in the high mountains of Central Asia.

A RARE MOUNTAIN WADER

Perhaps the most exciting of all the mountain birds, because of its rarity and the mystery that surrounds it, is the Ibisbill (*Ibidorhyncha struthersii*). It is a very specialized wader, restricted to small areas of the high Central Asian mountains, and, until recently, little was known about it. A few photographers had managed to obtain mainly rather poor-quality photographs of the bird, and there were a few useful studies of its behaviour. Also, a colour film was made by Viacheslav Belyalov, but no colour photographs have been published in the West – until now!

In spring 1986, in the high mountains of the Zailiiski Alatau Range in the northern Tien Shan, together with Oleg Belyalov, I was lucky enough to study and photograph a pair of Ibisbills and their nest at about 8,200 ft (2,500 m). Our photographs, reproduced above, show clearly the appearance of this exciting bird.

The Ibisbill is unique among waders in its bill structure, feeding habits and plumage, as well as the fact that it is so intimately tied to such a restricted habitat in the high

ABOVE LEFT *A pair of Ibisbills patrol the shingly banks of a remote high-mountain river in the Zailiiskii Alatau Range in the northern Tien Shan. Despite their striking plumage, these rare and enigmatic waders are surprisingly difficult to see among the pebbles. Each pair defends a narrow territory, centred on the river. The birds use their curved bills to probe or rake for food.*

TOP *This picture of the Ibisbill's habitat, taken in May, gives an idea of its remoteness and harshness.*

ABOVE *Although they may look conspicuous here, the eggs are very hard to spot (see above left).*

mountains. It has usually been classified with the family of avocets and stilts (Recurvirostridae), but may be more closely related to the oystercatchers (Haematopodidae). Some ornithologists think it is so different that it should be placed in a family of its own, the Ibidorhynchidae. Because of the isolation or inaccessibility of its breeding grounds, it is difficult to give an accurate estimate of its population, but it is included in the Red Data Book of the USSR, which estimates the Soviet population of the Ibisbill to be probably more than 150 pairs.

The Ibisbill's bold grey, black and white plumage is remarkably effective in camouflaging it against its surroundings – an advantage particularly when it is incubating eggs or brooding chicks. The red bill is strongly downcurved, like that of an ibis (a feature which gives it its name) and it has long pinkish legs with slightly lobed toes. With a total length of about 15 in (38 cm), it is about the size of a Black-headed Gull (*Larus ridibundus*).

The Ibisbill occurs in a very restricted high mountain habitat, being confined to valleys, usually devoid of any vegetation, along which the rivers flow relatively slowly, forming broad pebbly shallows with scattered small boulders where it can nest and find its food. It eats insects and their larvae, small crustaceans, molluscs and small fish. It finds its prey by probing with its bill beneath the pebbles or by raking its bill from side to side through the pebbles to dislodge its prey. The curve of its bill fits neatly round the larger stones. It also feeds in the water with its head submerged, its long legs allowing it to wade into the river up to its belly. It sometimes also feeds on the river banks, probing into the soil or beneath the rocks. Because it is so tied by its chief method of feeding to the pebbly shallows, it avoids large areas of the mountains where there are sheer rock faces or large boulders and powerful, deep rushing streams.

Ibisbills begin nesting in May, when their loud piping courtship calls can be heard ringing out across the pebbly valleys. The nest, which is simply a little pit in the ground, lined with flat pebbles, contains from two to four beautifully camouflaged eggs, and is very hard to find against the pebble-strewn background. Indeed, the only way we spotted one was to climb high above the valley and scan the whole area through powerful binoculars. The incubation period is thought to be about one month, but as with many other details of the Ibisbill's life, we still have so much to learn.

In winter, the Ibisbill moves down to lower altitudes, where the conditions are less severe, although it never leaves its mountain habitat.

BROWN-HEADED GULLS

In the Pamir Range, 13,120 ft (4,000 m) above sea level, is the high-mountain lake of Kara-Kul, covering 147 miles (380 sq km). Here, on the islets of this remote, cold expanse of salt water are the nesting colonies of Brown-headed Gulls (*Larus brunnicephalus*). These islet nesting sites, the remains of flooded glacial moraines, tangled tree roots and various debris, are lodged on slow-flowing, buried ice. At the end of April, when the lake is still iced over and there are only a few small thawed patches of earth at the mouths of the rivers feeding the lake, the first Brown-headed Gulls fly in. A month later, they begin to build their nests. These are arranged in small, very dense colonies, and each gull lays from one to three brown-spotted, ochre eggs in late June or early July. The largest colonies contain about 50 nests, although many are smaller, and, recently, single nests have been found.

The gulls share the islets with Common Terns (*Sterna hirundo*) and Bar-headed Geese (*Anser indicus*), although these two species nest nearer the water. Brown-headed Gulls resemble the widespread and familiar Black-headed Gulls (*Larus ridibundus*), but they are larger, with a browner head in summer, and a black collar bordering the brown; also the entire wing tips are black, not just the tips of the primary feathers. In marked contrast to those of Black-headed Gulls, the colonies of Brown-headed Gulls are

A Brown-headed Gull with one of its chicks at Lake Kara-Kul, in the high Pamir Mountains, in July.

remarkably peaceful and the birds make little noise. Their main food on Lake Kara-Kul consists of sandhoppers (*Gammarus*) and caddis-flies (*Astratus alaicus*). The Brown-headed Gulls leave the Pamirs in October, migrating south to India, where they spend the winter along seashores and inland waters in low-lying country.

ACCENTORS

The accentors (Family Prunellidae) are a group of small, ground-feeding birds, most of which are mountain-dwellers. This purely Eurasian family contains only 13 species, eight of which live in the USSR.

The exclusively mountain members of the group are the Alpine Accentor (*Prunella collaris*) the Himalyan Accentor (*P. himalayana*), the Brown Accentor (*Prunella fulvescens*), the Black-throated Accentor (*P. atrogularis*) and Radde's Accentor (*P. ocularis*). In their behaviour and biology they provide impressive examples of adaptation to harsh mountain conditions. The Alpine Accentor has the widest range of all the accentors, ranging from southern and central Europe and northwest Africa to China and Japan,

The nest and eggs of the Brown Accentor, one of a family of small perching birds, most of which are restricted to mountain habitats. It nests as high as 11,500 ft.

but it has a patchy distribution and is only locally common, because it is tied to the high mountains. In the USSR, it occurs in the Caucasus, Central Asia, Southern Kazakhstan, the central Altai and the mountains of the Far East. It ranges higher than the other species.

The Himalayan Accentor prefers to live between about 9,200 and 11,480 ft (2,800 and 3,500 m), among large boulders or stony meadows of short grass. It has a patchy distribution, with only a few birds in the Altai and Central Asian mountains. In April, the accentor's song can be heard at the breeding sites, and they remain there until September, when they move down the mountains to areas where food is more plentiful. The nest is built on the ground, screened by a boulder, crag or grassy clump. Four to six pale-blue eggs hatch in the first half of June. Apparently, there is only one clutch a year.

The Brown Accentor of Central Asia is widespread and numerous in some areas. It nests in subalpine and alpine belts, from 7,900 to 11,500 ft (2,400 to 3,500 m). Recent observations of marked birds have shown that this species occupies quite a restricted area, wintering along the lower boundary of the nesting territory. Ornithologists have revealed its complex breeding biology – in some localities there may be three adult birds, one female and two males,

responsible for feeding a single brood of chicks. A pair of Brown Accentors has been known to rear three broods in a season. In the harsh conditions of the mountains such an achievement is possible only as a result of the clear division of responsibilities between the parents: as the young of one brood come close to fledging, they are fed almost exclusively by the male, while the female is already building another nest and laying the eggs. As with other accentors, the plumage of male and female is almost identical, although the males usually tend to be somewhat brighter.

The Black-throated Accentor is widespread in the mountains of Central Asia and the Altai, preferring open spruce forest at 4,600 to 9,200 ft (1,400 to 2,800 m), chiefly in sparse areas among shrubs, avoiding the densest cover. Unlike the Brown Accentor, which nests on the ground, the Black-throated Accentor builds its nest on the branches of trees or shrubs. It is usually sited less than $6\frac{1}{2}$ ft (2 m) above the ground, though nests have been found as high as 43 ft (13 m). The birds lay between two and six eggs in June or July; they are a delicate shade of blue, like those of the other accentors.

Radde's Accentor occurs in the USSR only at the edge of its range, in the Armenian plateau; this population also ranges across north-east Turkey and northern Iran.

MOUNTAIN THRUSHES AND BABBLERS

Two alpine members of the thrush family (Turdidae), the Himalayan Rubythroat (*Luscinia pectoralis*) and the White-throated or Persian Robin (*Irania gutturalis*), are especially beautiful. Neither species can be said to be common, although in some places they may be quite plentiful. These closely related birds occupy totally different habitats. The Himalayan Rubythroat is an inhabitant of the juniper forest on the Tien Shan range between about 8,200 and 11,480 ft (2,500 and 3,500 m). It is migratory and appears at the nesting site only when much of the snow has thawed. Breeding may be at the end of May or the beginning of June. As early as August the breeding grounds are deserted and the birds are on their way south to spend the winter in India.

The male has a brilliant red throat, contrasting dramatically with the blackish upper parts and breast. This striking colour combination, together with its attractive call, helped this bird to become adopted as the emblem of Tien Shan. The females and young are much duller.

The Rubythroat's nest is built on the ground among cover, usually the spreading branches of a juniper or a thick, overhanging clump of grass. The birds prefer to

settle on south or east-facing mountain slopes. The globular nest has a hole in the side, and the hen bird lays between two and six (usually four) pale blue eggs. Rubythroats are chiefly insect-eaters.

The White-throated Robin tends to breed at lower levels, at around 3,600 to 7,550 ft (1,100 to 2,300 m), preferring dry slopes with thickets of shrubs interspersed with boulders, crags and scree – a habitat that can become unbearably hot by early summer, when the grass may wither in the scorching heat. As with the Himalayan Rubythroat, the male of this species is brightly coloured, with ash-grey upperparts, a black and white head, and orange breasts and flanks. He is strongly territorial and guards the nesting site from rivals while singing loudly to attract the hen bird. Most nests are built in small, sparse bushes, such as honeysuckle. Three to five dirty green eggs are laid in May or June. Both parents feed the fledglings with various invertebrates. The population of this species can fluctuate dramatically from year to year. For example, we observed male and female White-throated Robins for five consecutive years in the nature reserve of Aksu-Dzhabagly. However, none were present in the 1960s. In places the population is now more plentiful than before the Second World War, although it is still a scarce species.

We had to wait five years to photograph the male. We first saw him in 1980 and from then on we tried to photograph this remarkably beautiful bird every year. We photographed the eggs, the nest, and the hen bird, but never the male. Then, in 1985, we finally tracked one down. With the help of our mentor at the Aksu reserve, Dr A. Ivashchenko, we found a nest that was perfectly sited for photography. It was on a stony eastern slope, overgrown with bushes and juniper and there were several

ABOVE LEFT *A Himalayan Rubythroat, photographed in June at the Aksu-Dzhabagly Reserve in the western Tien Shan.*
ABOVE *A male White-throated, or Persian, Robin at its nest in June at the Aksu-Dzhabagly Reserve.*

five-day-old chicks in it. The male quickly became accustomed to the hide, and in two days we had completed our task. We heaved sighs of relief, and experienced a mixture of pleasure and sadness that here was one more bird that had been captured on film in Aksu-Dzhabagly, the pearl of the mountain nature reserves.

The Streaked Laughing-thrush (*Garrulax lineatus*), although superficially thrush-like, is in fact a member of the babbler family (Timaliidae). It has the distinction of being the only member of its family to occur in the Soviet Union. The Streaked Laughing-thrush is found in overgrown thickets in the Pamir and Gissaro-Alai Mountains, where it occurs in small flocks, forming pairs only in the breeding season.

BIRDS OF MOUNTAIN STREAMS
Birds of mountain streams need special methods of study, due to the nature of the habitat – the water tumbles over the rocks and through ravines, and is often deep and treacherous. The lives of several mountain birds are intimately linked with these mountain torrents. In the Central Asian mountains live two species of dipper, the Eurasian Dipper (*Cinclus cinclus*) and the Brown Dipper (*Cinclus pallasii*), both of which hunt under the water for their prey – insect larvae and other small invertebrates. Other interesting water birds widespread in the Central Asian mountains are the Blue or Himalayan Whistling-thrush (*Myiophoneus caeruleus*); the Little Forktail (*Enicurus*

scouleri) the Grey Wagtail (*Motacilla cinerea*) and the White-capped, or Water Redstart, also called the River Chat (*Chaimarrornis leucocephalus*).

Like the Himalayan Rubythroat, the Blue Whistling-thrush is also regarded as a symbol of the mountains. Its very name in Russian, 'blue bird', conjures up an air of mystery; and in the wild places where this bird lives, the mystery becomes reality. A mountain waterfall crashes over the rocks, the air is filled with a fine spray, its margins covered with vivid, succulent green moss; while overhead a narrow strip of clear blue mountain sky is framed by the jagged cliffs. Suddenly the peace of this paradise is interrupted. A vivid dark blue bird flies to a crag, sits on a moss-strewn boulder, and begins to sing. Its melodious whistling trills are so piercing that they can be heard for considerable distances, even above the noise of the waterfall. Such moments make a mountain walk unforgettable. But, of course, one has to be in the right place at the right time.

The Blue Whistling-thrush builds its nest on rocky terraces and lays two to four pale bluish-brown eggs in May and June. It feeds on a variety of invertebrates which it finds on wet rocks and the banks of streams. It is a widespread, though not numerous, species in the mountains of Central Asia and though it may wander locally, does not migrate south in winter like many of the other mountain birds of the Soviet Union.

Mountain mammals

As can be seen from the table on page 215, there are some 40 mountain mammals in the USSR, including several less specialized species, such as the Stone Marten (*Martes foina*) and Forest Dormouse (*Dryomys nitedula*), which also live in lowland forests.

Among the most characteristic mountain mammals of the USSR are the marmots (*Marmota*), which live in the mountain ranges of Central Asia, Kazakhstan, the Altai, eastern Siberia, and Kamchatka. The various representatives of this genus form an extremely compact group of ecologically similar species. They belong to the squirrel family (*Sciuridae*), and are its largest members. There is a good deal of disagreement among zoologists as to how they should be classified.

However, most zoologists think there are seven species in the USSR. The Steppe, or Bobak, Marmot (*M. bobac*) is restricted to the plains. The Grey Marmot (*M. baibacina*) inhabits the mountains of Kazakhstan and southern Siberia. Two other species, the Long-tailed, or Red, Marmot (*M.*

ABOVE *The Long-tailed, or Red, Marmot is a typical mammal of the Tien Shan and Pamir Mountains. Superb burrowers, marmots are the largest of the squirrels.*

ABOVE *Menzbier's Marmot is the rarest of the USSR's seven species, restricted to two small areas of the Tien Shan.*

caudata) and Menzbier's Marmot (*M. menzbieri*), have a more westerly distribution. The Long-tailed Marmot lives in southern Central Asia and in the Pamir mountains. Menzbier's Marmot is the rarest species in the USSR, endemic to two separate regions in the Tien Shan, on the Talass and Chatkal ridges, which occupy an area of no more than 770 sq miles (2,000 sq km). The Common Marmot (*M. marmota*) is found in the Carpathian Mountains in the west. Eastern Siberia and Kamchatka are the home of the Kamchatka Marmot (*M. camtschatica*). The

Siberian Marmot (*Marmota sibirica*) inhabits the plains of Transbaikalia.

Marmots are stocky, thickset animals with a rather comical appearance. They have streamlined bodies and although they weigh about 9 lb (4 kg), are flexible enough to squeeze themselves into narrow spaces. They need this flexibility, for they are superb burrowers, digging out complex systems of tunnels, often full of sharp bends.

Most marmots prefer to live in open steppe or mountain terrain. Their territories are usually in the subalpine or alpine belt, where piles of boulders alternate with meadows. The altitude at which a particular species may live varies greatly – by as much as 10,000 ft (3,000 m).

Marmots are highly colonial animals adapted to a life in open spaces by having a large repertoire of visual and sound signals. Social communication plays an important part in a marmot's life. Neighbours are warned of impending danger by a loud piercing cry, whether the threat is from a Golden Eagle high in the sky or a group of travellers approaching on horseback.

The social life of marmots is complicated by a system of links between the sub-colonies that make up a 'township'. Above the burrows, between five and ten per cent of the ground area is taken up by the entrances. The burrows themselves vary considerably in shape and length, depending on the relief of the ground and the function of the burrow. There are distinct winter burrows and summer burrows, as well as the permanent system of tunnels. The nest chamber where the baby marmots are born is about 6½ ft (2 m) deep, while that used for hibernation may be as much as 23 ft (7 m) deep. The largest burrows are 197 ft (63 m) long but the average length is only 85 ft (25 m).

ABOVE LEFT *The attractive little Forest Dormouse is common in the forest belt of the Tien Shan Mountains.*
ABOVE *The Afghan Pika is one of several species of pikas, close relatives of the rabbits and hares, that live in the mountains and steppes of the USSR.*

Marmots hibernate for six to nine months of the year; with the mountain species, the waking period is shorter, but it increases with altitude. The energy outlay during sleep is reduced by a tenth. Without food, an active marmot loses about 3.7 per cent of its weight in a day, but during periods of sleep, this loss is reduced to as little as 0.02 to 0.12 per cent.

Marmots show no preference for particular plants, but always select the youngest, tenderest shoots. They are inefficient at chewing their food and extracting the nutrients, and animal food sometimes makes up for the deficiencies of their plant diet. Marmot stomachs have been found to contain molluscs, grasshoppers, caterpillars and ants' eggs.

The number of young in a marmot family depends on the total populations in the neighbourhood and varies from three to 14. Young marmots are very playful, and indulge in noisy, boisterous games, sometimes involving their mothers.

MOUNTAIN PREDATORS
Two of the most interesting mountain predators are the Tien Shan Brown Bear (*Ursus arctos isabellinus*) and the Snow Leopard, or Ounce (*Panthera uncia*), both of which are listed as endangered species in both the Soviet and the IUCN Red Data Books.

ABOVE *A Brown Bear, of the Tien Shan race, ambles across the mountain meadows in the Aksu-Dzhabagly Reserve.*
RIGHT *A ewe and lamb of the Turkmen race of the Argalis, a mountain sheep, at the Ustyurt Nature Reserve.*

Captive breeding, followed by release in the wild, may help to save the dwindling population of this magnificent animal before it is too late.

The Snow Leopard lives in high mountains, alpine meadows, dead-end ravines, and crags, and is only rarely encountered in the forest belts. Its diet consists mainly of mountain goats and sheep, and its favourite method of catching them is by ambush. Its den is in a cave or a crack in the rocks, where the female, after 90 to 100 days of gestation, gives birth to a litter of two to four young during the months of April or May.

MOUNTAIN GOATS AND SHEEP
In the USSR there are five species in the genus *Capra*: the Wild Goat (*Capra aegagrus*); the Siberian Mountain Goat (*Capra sibirica*); the Markhor (*Capra falconeri*); the West Caucasian Tur (*Capra caucasica*) and the East Caucasian or Dagestan Tur (*Capra cylindricornis*). The rarest is the Markhor, which lives in two isolated areas of Tadzhikistan, on the border with Afghanistan. The Wild Goat is found in the Caucasus, and in south Turkmenia in the desert mountains of Kopet-Dag. It lives on rocky mountain slopes between 3,280 and 8,200 ft (1,000 and 2,500 m), climbing as high as the snow line from time to time. The total population in the USSR is estimated at 5,000 to 6,000 individuals.

The Siberian Mountain Goat is the most widespread

Unlike most subspecies of the Brown Bear which live in forests, the Tien Shan Brown Bear lives in mountainous areas with a sparse tree cover, and occasionally even in completely treeless areas. It is restricted to the Tien Shan and Pamir-Alai ranges. Smaller than the other races of the Brown Bear, it is distinguished by its light-coloured, reddish fur. There are thought to be several thousand individuals within the Central Asian mountain system.

The Snow Leopard still roams the mountains of Central Asia, the Altai, and Sayan. At present this species is extremely rare and it is very difficult to give even an approximate estimate of its population. Some authorities suggest a rough estimate of 1,000 animals. Fortunately, the Snow Leopard has bred successfully in captivity in several zoos; for example, in the Kaunas Zoo, in Lithuania, a female gave birth to a litter of four, which is a world record.

Dagestan Turs descend from the high mountains in the early morning to feed in the sub-alpine meadows of the Caucasus; these ones are in the Severo (North) Osetin Reserve.

species. It ranges throughout the Central Asian, Altai and Sayan ranges. When walking in these mountains, one comes across them frequently, running along a ridge or lying in the snow, or one hears falling stones which they have dislodged. Old males are especially impressive, with their long beards and powerful horns. This fine animal is at home on the steepest slopes, strewn with large rocks and extensive screes. They can jump from rock to rock with deceptive ease and climb along the steepest and most inaccessible crags.

Goats usually live in herds, sometimes numbering 50 or more individuals. In winter they may descend to the middle belts of the mountain, returning to higher altitudes in summer. In spring they can often be seen at salt licks, the whole herd licking at the soil or even eating the salty earth.

The mating season of the Siberian Mountain Goat lasts from October to January, during which time a male may serve between five and 15 females. After a gestation period of 170 to 180 days, one or two kids are born between April and June.

The Caucasus contains two species of tur or mountain goat, though some biologists consider them merely subspecies. The West Caucasian Tur occupies the western part of the Great Caucasus and is well protected in several reserves, notably the Caucasus and Teberda nature reserves. The East Caucasian Tur has a shorter, broader beard, darker colouring and slightly different shaped horns.

There is also a great deal of confusion about the classification of mountain sheep. The true mountain sheep or Argalis is *Ovis ammon* and it has many subspecies registered as endangered. Another species of steppe and desert plateaux is the Asiatic Mouflon (*Ovis orientalis*). In the northern mountains lives a species of Siberian Bighorn (*Ovis nivicola*).

The Argalis is widespread in the mountains of the Altai, Sayan, Central Asia, and the remote Caucasus. Only some subspecies, for example the Tien Shan Argalis (*O. a. karelini*), prefer higher altitudes. Many live at the foot of

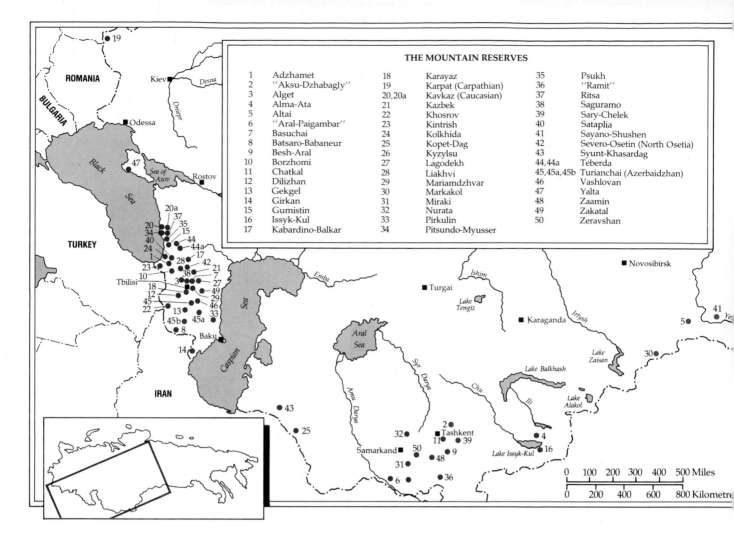

THE MOUNTAIN RESERVES

1	Adzhamet	18	Karayaz	35	Psukh
2	"Aksu-Dzhabagly"	19	Karpat (Carpathian)	36	"Ramit"
3	Alget	20,20a	Kavkaz (Caucasian)	37	Ritsa
4	Alma-Ata	21	Kazbek	38	Saguramo
5	Altai	22	Khosrov	39	Sary-Chelek
6	"Aral-Paigambar"	23	Kintrish	40	Sataplia
7	Basuchai	24	Kolkhida	41	Sayano-Shushen
8	Batsaro-Babaneur	25	Kopet-Dag	42	Severo-Osetin (North Osetia)
9	Besh-Aral	26	Kyzylsu	43	Syunt-Khasardag
10	Borzhomi	27	Lagodekh	44,44a	Teberda
11	Chatkal	28	Liakhvi	45,45a,45b	Turianchai (Azerbaidzhan)
12	Dilizhan	29	Mariamdzhvar	46	Vashlovan
13	Gekgel	30	Markakol	47	Yalta
14	Girkan	31	Miraki	48	Zaamin
15	Gumistin	32	Nurata	49	Zakatal
16	Issyk-Kul	33	Pirkulin	50	Zeravshan
17	Kabardino-Balkar	34	Pitsundo-Myusser		

the mountain or no further up than the middle slopes. In autumn and winter, the sheep form large herds, but at other times they live in small groups. They are less skilled than mountain goats at climbing rocks, preferring gentler slopes. Mountain sheep mate in the autumn and the beginning of winter; the gestation period is about five months.

PIKAS AND RODENTS

Two groups of mountain mammals tend to be restricted to the subalpine or alpine belts or the corresponding northern zones in Dauria or eastern Siberia. The first are the pikas (*Ochotona*) − interesting little animals which are related to hares and rabbits. The tail is usually very short and the ears rounded. These attractive creatures have a characteristic warning squeak or whistle, which is very difficult to pinpoint. During late summer, pikas begin to lay up a winter food store of leaves and plant stems, which they dry and store as miniature 'hayricks' or hide in cracks in rocks.

Many species of voles live in the mountains. Some, like that endemic to the Pamir, are extremely rare. Little is known of the biology of the high-mountain species. Four genera of voles are found in the high-mountain ranges: *Clethrionomys*, *Alticola* and *Microtus*. The *Alticola* voles are typical mountain species, living on the bare summits of eastern Siberia or on the subalpine or alpine belts of the Altai of the Central Asian mountains. Numerous species of

The map shows the Soviet Union's many mountain nature reserves. The Caucasus region is particularly generously endowed, with a chain of large reserves.

field voles (*Microtus*) live in or beyond the Caucasus.

Three species of birch mice (*Sicista*), relatives of the jerboas, live only in the mountains. One species lives in the Altai, the other in the Tien Shan and the Caucasus. They are very secretive and little is known of their biology.

The mountain nature reserves of the Soviet Union

The general principles of the conservation of nature in the USSR have already been discussed. This section provides a short account of the mountain nature reserves, indicating their area, geography and wildlife. Nature reserves are valuable for conserving areas of mountain in their natural state and as we have seen, any economic activity is forbidden in them.

CAUCASUS

The wildlife of the Great Caucasus Range is well protected in the 286 sq miles (741 sq km) of the Kabardino-Balkar High-Mountain Nature Reserve. Part of this magnificent reserve, established as recently as 1976, rises above a height of 16,400 ft (5,000 m).

TOP *A view of the forested slopes of the Lagodekh Nature Reserve, in the Caucasus Mountains.*
ABOVE *A female Caucasian Black Grouse sits tight on her clutch of eggs at the Caucasus Biosphere Nature Reserve. Established as long ago as 1924, it protects almost 200 bird species and 60 mammals in more than 1,000 sq miles.*

Dating from 1924 is the 1,017 sq miles (2,635 sq km) Kavkaz (Caucasus) Biosphere Nature Reserve. The mountains here include the Glavny (main) and Peredovoi (forward) ridges of the Great Caucasus. The highest point is Smidovich Peak, at 11,023 ft (3,360 m). About 1,500 plant species are found here, including many endemic forms and relicts, as well as 192 bird and 59 mammal species.

In the Bokovoi (side) range of the Great Caucasus, the 100 sq mile (259 sq km) Severo-Osetin (North Osetia) Nature Reserve, established in 1967, extends from 4,330 to 15,250 ft (1,350 to 4,646 m) above sea level. There is a remarkable variety of plants, with about 1,550 species, as well as 157 bird and 36 mammal species.

On the northern slopes of the Great Caucasus, the 328 sq mile (850 sq km) Teberda Reserve, established in 1936, rises to a high point of 13,261 ft (4,042 m). Its territory safeguards 1,250 species of plant, 186 of which are endemic to the Caucasus. Animals include seven species of reptiles, 170 of birds and 43 of mammals.

The Georgian SSR contains many small and medium-sized nature reserves, including the Alget (23 sq miles/60 sq km), Batsaro-Babaneur (15 sq miles/39 sq km), Gumistin (52 sq miles/134 sq km), Kazbek (17 sq miles/43 sq km), Kintrish (28 sq miles/72 sq km), Liakhvi (26 sq miles/68 sq km), Mariamdzhvar (4 sq miles/10 sq km) and Saguramo (20 sq miles/52 sq km). Larger, more important, Georgian

A pair of Hume's Lesser Whitethroats; these mountain warblers were photographed in June at their nest in the Aksu-Dzhabagly Nature Reserve.

nature reserves include the Borzhomi (70 sq miles/180 sq km), Lagodekh (69 sq miles/178 sq km) and Psukh (97 sq miles/252 sq km).

The Azerbaidzhan mountains contain the 27 sq mile (71 sq km) reserve of Gekgel, the 11 sq mile (29 sq km) Talysh Reserve, the 97 sq mile (252 sq km) Zakatal Reserve and the three areas of the Turianchai Reserve.

There are two nature reserves in the Armenian mountains, the Dilizhan, 120 sq miles (312 sq km), and the 90 sq mile (234 sq km) Khosrov Reserve.

TIEN SHAN

There is a wide network of nature reserves in the Tien Shan. The Chatkal Range has the 138 sq mile (358 sq km) Chatkal Biosphere Reserve, established in 1947, which extends from 3,280 to 12,470 ft (1,000 to 3,800 m). The plants are unusual, differing from those in adjoining areas. There is an impressive total of 1,100 species of flowering plants, of which 72 species are rare and endemic, and 109 bird and 31 mammal species.

The oldest nature reserve of Kazakhstan, also in the western Tien Shan Range, is the 'Aksu-Dzhabagly', created in 1927, which extends over the north-western slopes of the Talass Alatau range, on the adjoining Ugam ridge, and covers 290 sq miles (744 sq km). Its two main rivers are the Aksu and the Dzhabagly. Here is the famous Aksu Canyon, 1,640 ft (500 m) deep and 1,970 to 2,300 ft (600 to 700 m) wide. The reserve is between 3,600 and 13,450 ft (1100 and 4,100 m) above sea-level. The plant life is exceptionally varied, with 1,300 species, including many rare and endemic ones. The animals include nine species of reptiles, 238 of birds and 42 of mammals.

The wildlife of the Zailiiskii Alatau Range, in the northern Tien Shan, is safeguarded in the nature reserve of Alma-Ata. Established in 1931, it occupies 354 sq miles (916 sq km). The highest point in the reserve, the summit of Mount Talgar, is 16,455 ft (5,017 m). There are 934 species of plants, about 200 of birds and 64 of mammals.

In the Kirgiz territory of the Tien Shan there are three nature reserves: Besh-Aral (70 sq miles/182 sq km), Issyk-Kul (67 sq miles/173 sq km), and the Sary-Chelek Biosphere Reserve (92 sq miles/239 sq km) on the northeastern flank of the Chatkal ridge. These three reserves contain many rare plants, of which 52 species are endemic to the Tien Shan region, as well as 157 species of birds and 41 of mammals.

PAMIR-ALAI

In the Turkestan Range of Uzbekistan, the Zaamin Nature Reserve, created in 1959, occupies 41 sq miles (106 sq km) between 5,770 and 11,480 ft (1,760 and 3,500 m) above sea-level. About 694 species of plants, six of reptiles, 130 of birds and 38 of mammals are found there.

In the southwestern outliers of the Gissar Range of the Pamir-Alai, the Nature Reserve of Kyzylsui, established in 1975, covers 116 sq miles (301 sq km) between 5,900 and 13,120 ft (1,800 and 4,000 m) above sea-level.

Within the Nuratau Range lies the Nuratin Nature Reserve. Established in 1975, it covers 87 sq miles (225 sq km) and contains 629 species of flowering plants and several interesting species of mammals, including the Asiatic Mouflon (*Ovis orientalis severtsovi*), Severtzov's Jerboa (*Allactaga severtsovi*) and the Marbled Polecat (*Volmela peregusna*). About 160 bird species have been

A view of the superb panorama of mountain peaks making up the Bugultor and Ulken-Aksu Ranges of the western Tien Shan, in the Aksu-Dzhabagly Nature Reserve, in June.

recorded, including the magnificent and rare Lammergeier (*Gypaetus barbatus*), which nests in the reserve.

The nature reserve of 'Ramit', 62 sq miles (161 sq km) in area, is in Tadzhikstan, on the upper reaches of the Kafirnigan River, in the Gissar Range.

ALTAI AND SAYAN

The huge Altai Nature Reserve created in 1932, occupies 3,335 sq miles (8,637 sq km) and includes part of Lake Teletsk as well as a representative cross-section of habitats in this unique mountain region. The Altai Reserve lies in the catchment areas of the two largest Siberian Rivers, the Ob (River Bia) and the Yenisei (River Abakan). The mountains reach 11,482 ft (3,500 m), although Lake Teletsk, 78 km long (48.5 miles), is at 1,470 ft (450 m). The landscape is mountain taiga and mountain tundra. There are 1,270 plant species, many of them endemic. The animals include 310 species of birds, 73 of mammals and ten of amphibians, while 13 species of fish swim in the lake.

The 276 sq miles (714 sq km) of Lake Markakol Nature Reserve, established in 1976, are in the southern Altai Mountains, in eastern Kazakhstan.

The Sayano-Shushen Nature Reserve, created in 1976, covers 1504 sq miles (3,896 sq km) of the Sayan Mountains, to the northeast of the Altai. It contains many relict plants as well as endemic plants and animals from the Altai, Sayan and Mongolia.

8 STEPPES AND DESERTS

Steppes and deserts have two important features in common: they are both unwooded open areas, and both have a semi-arid or arid climate. The steppes once covered vast areas of the USSR and, although now much fragmented, they still stretch from the Ukraine to Manchuria. The steppe zone lies between the forest and desert zones. Transitional belts of wooded steppe and semi-desert protect it on its northern and southern boundaries. Neither of these belts is very specific, and neither has its own unique community of plants and animals. The transitional zones are usually colonized by a mixture of representatives from both zones.

The steppelands have been a source of food for many civilizations. This is one reason why the original steppe now survives mainly in the nature reserves. In the European part of the USSR almost all the steppes have been ploughed up to grow cereals, and only the nature reserves have preserved this unique community for later generations. More steppes have been saved in the Asian part of the USSR. In the east the steppe is interrupted by mountain ranges, and is restricted to the intervening valleys.

Grass-covered plains – steppe, prairie, savannah and pampas – total some 27 per cent of the earth's natural vegetation cover. The steppeland is a zone of little moisture, intermediate between the damp forest and the arid desert. The height of the grass depends on the amount of moisture: the wetter it is, the higher the grass can grow.

The natural steppe zone covers less than one-sixth of the total land area of the USSR. An interrupted belt of steppe extends as far as the Ob River. Not every area of grass counts as steppe. Steppe vegetation is markedly drought-resistant, with more or less close stands of grass, and the annual rainfall is from 12 to 20 in (300 to 500 mm).

Although there are many areas of steppe, two main types can be distinguished in the USSR: the damper, northern meadow and herbage type; and the drier, southern feather grass type. These two types are very different in many ways, but also have many attributes in common.

Both types of steppe are very rich in plant life, with a large number of species growing in a small area. In some northern steppes it is possible to find as many as 73 species in a square yard (80 species in a square metre), a larger variety than any other plant community in the USSR.

LEFT *One of the many reptiles of Soviet deserts, this little nocturnal gecko avoids the daytime heat by staying in its burrow, plugging the entrance with moist sand.*

The steppe plants have various adaptations for resisting drought. These include downy layers of hairs, grey coloured leaves with a waxy bloom, yellow leaves, narrow leaves, leaves reduced to mere spines, leaves arranged in riblike fashion up the stems, succulent leaves, and very deep roots.

Turf-forming grasses are very characteristic of steppes; they include the feather grasses (*Stipa*) and fescues (*Festuca*). There is a whole series of feather grasses, which dominate the vegetation in the southern steppes. These beautiful, elegant plants transform the steppe in spring as their long, feathery flower plumes sway in the wind, glistening in the sunlight.

The Saiga Antelope has a large proboscis-like nose which may filter out the dust that it kicks up in its steppeland home. Virtually extinct by 1917, it was protected after the Revolution and now herds number over a million animals.

Typical plants of meadow steppes include the Cord-rooted Sedge (*Carex humilis*), the Coastal Sedge (*Zernia riparia*) and the feather grasses *Stipa pennata* and *S. tirsa*. Herbage steppes have both Hairy Feather Grass (*S. capillata*) and Lessing's Feather Grass (*S. lessingiana*) and a fescue, *Festuca valisiaca*. Ukrainian Feather Grass (*S. ucrainica*) is typical of dry steppes. In eastern Kazakhstan, there are two common species of wormwood, or sagebrush, *Artemisia graciliscens* and *A. sublessingiana*. Typical species of the steppes of Trans-Baikal and Mongolia are the Baikal Feather Grass (*Stipa baicalensis*), Altai Oat Grass (*Helictotrichon altaicum*) and Chinese Wild Rye (*Aneurolepidium chinense*).

During spring and summer, a succession of flowers – of a great variety of plants, including crocuses, tulips, irises, valerians, and hyacinths – appears as if by magic, transforming the landscape with their exquisite colours. Their time is not long, however, for they will soon be bleached, like the grasses, by the hot summer sun.

The animal life of the steppes

The steppe faunas are not rich in species, but contain some distinctive creatures. Most of the typical steppe animals are found today in the Asian part of the zone. The European-Kazakhstan steppes contain a variety of insects, including many species of grasshoppers, ants, flies, bugs and beetles, including weevils, tiger beetles and ground beetles. There are very few amphibians in this dry terrain, but numerous reptiles, including Orsini's Viper (*Vipera ursinii*), the European Whip Snake (*Coluber jugularis*) and the Sand Lizard (*Lacerta agilis*).

The bird life of the steppes is especially interesting. The landscape may appear monotonous, but it provides a home for a variety of different species, although some have become rarer with agricultural development.

CRANES, BUSTARDS, PLOVERS AND PRATINCOLES
One of the most beautiful of all the birds that breed in the USSR is the Demoiselle Crane (*Anthropoides virgo*), which occurs throughout the steppe and semi-desert zones. Because of its increasing rarity, it is included in the Red Book of the USSR. Fortunately, this crane seems to be adapting to man-made landscapes; it is beginning to settle on cultivated land, particularly in the south Ukraine, where it has bred successfully.

In April, the cranes return to their nesting sites on the steppes from their wintering quarters in Africa and southern Asia. Immediately after their arrival, they perform elaborate courtship dances. The nest is a simple shallow pit in the ground, sometimes lined with a few dried grass stalks. There are usually two eggs, very rarely three. The cranes feed mainly on seeds and other vegetable matter; they also eat a few insects.

Bustards (family Otidae) are typical inhabitants of open spaces. There are three species in the USSR, two of which breed on the steppes; the third, the Houbara Bustard (*Chlamydotis undulata*) prefers the deserts.

The Great Bustard (*Otis tarda*) is one of the world's largest birds, varying in weight from 9 to 24 lb (4 to 11 kg), depending on the sex of the bird and the time of year; exceptionally large males can weigh 35 lb (16 kg). This

ABOVE *A view of the steppe on Chooryook Island, in Lake Sivash, near the Sea of Azov, containing many wild onion plants* Allium rotundum, *whose globe-shaped flowers are a common feature of the southern steppeland.*

ABOVE *The genus of grasses called* Koelera *is found exclusively in steppelands; this species, with its stems waving gracefully in the wind, is* Koelera gracilis, *one of four that are found in the European part of the USSR. Its delicate cream-coloured flowers beautify the flat landscape when they appear in springtime.*

ABOVE *The most characteristic plants of the southern steppes are the aptly named feather grasses, whose stately, feathery plumes of flowers appear in spring, swaying gracefully in the winds that blow across the great open landscapes. Found only on steppeland, the feather grasses include a number of scarce and endangered species.*

largely silent, cautious bird senses approaching danger from a long way off and takes off with a running start, ponderously flapping its heavy wings, but once in the air it flies fast and strongly. In March or April, as the snow starts to thaw, the bustards return from their wintering quarters further south, and gather at their steppeland nesting sites.

ABOVE *One of the most beautiful of all the birds of the USSR is the Demoiselle Crane. This one is at its nest on the steppe near Saratov, in the Volga Region.*

ABOVE *A Sociable Lapwing, or Sociable Plover, on the steppe in northern Kazakhstan. This boldly marked wader, found only in the USSR, is now much scarcer than it was.*

The males choose a flat area of steppe with a good view all round to perform their courtship displays, either alone or in small groups, usually before sunrise.

The nest is a shallow pit dug out by the female, who usually lays two or three olive-green eggs, which she alone incubates, remaining constantly alert. If danger threatens, she presses her head and body flat on the ground, her superb camouflage merging with the surroundings. After drying out, the fluffy mottled black and fawn chicks leave the nest, but stay nearby for several days, under the watchful eye of their mother, until they have grown stronger. At 35 to 40 days old, when their weight is half that of an adult female, they start to fly. By the end of July or the beginning of August, the young form flocks, leave the breeding grounds, and wander widely over the steppes. Adult Great Bustards are omnivorous: in winter, they eat mainly leaves, young shoots, flowers and seeds, and in summer they feed chiefly on insects, which are also the main diet of the young.

In the past, the Great Bustard was common but, with the agricultural development of the steppes, its numbers have fallen catastrophically and it is included in the Red Book of the USSR. Various measures have been taken to restore its population, including captive breeding.

The Little Bustard (*Tetrax tetrax*) resembles its larger relative, but is a great deal smaller, weighing only 21 to 34 oz (600 to 950 g). It prefers virgin steppe and fallow land, avoiding cultivated areas. Its life history is similar to that of the Great Bustard, except that the males display singly, and the females lay from 3 to 5 eggs. It is also included in the Red Book.

The Sociable Lapwing, or Sociable Plover (*Chettusia gregaria*) is endemic to the USSR, where it occurs on the dry steppes and semi-deserts. Formerly occupying a large area of the steppes of the Ukraine and Kazakhstan, this attractive wader is now found only in an area of dry wormwood (sagebrush) or feather-grass steppe between Kuibyshev and Barnaul. It nests in small groups, sometimes as many as 20 or 30 pairs. The nest is a small pit in the ground, and contains 4 or occasionally 5 eggs. This species is also listed in the Red Book of the USSR.

The family of coursers and pratincoles (Glareolidae) is a specialized group of Old World waders which live mainly in steppes and semi-deserts. The Cream-coloured Courser (*Cursorius cursor*) is a rare breeder in the deserts of south Central Asia. Three species of pratincoles occur in the USSR: the Black-winged Pratincole (*Glareola nordmanni*) and the Collared, or European, Pratincole (*G. pratincola*) are both fairly common in suitable areas, but the Oriental

Pratincole (*G. maldivarum*) is a very rare visitor to parts of the Transbaikal region only. Pratincoles are restless, sociable, noisy birds with long wings, fairly long, forked tails and an elegant flight, and superficially resemble overgrown swallows. Like swallows, and unlike other waders, they catch their insect prey, including beetles, grasshoppers and locusts, on the wing.

The Black-winged Pratincole lives between the Ukrainian steppes and the foothills of the Altai Mountains. It arrives on its breeding grounds in late April or early May, nesting in colonies containing anything from a few to several dozen pairs. The nest is a small pit in the ground. Both male and female incubate the eggs; usually there are 4, although there may be 3 or 5. Five to six weeks after hatching, the birds form flocks, sometimes large ones. The Collared Pratincole, which breeds further south, has a similar life history to that of its relative.

BIRDS OF PREY

Typical steppeland birds of prey include the Steppe Eagle (*Aquila rapax*) and the Long-legged Buzzard (*Buteo rufinus*). The Steppe Eagle is found on the dry plains of the European and Asian parts of the USSR. It builds its nest on the ground, rarely among rocks or in low trees, and lays two eggs in April or May. Incubation lasts 40 to 45 days and the young fledge after about two months in the nest. In the USSR the Steppe Eagle eats medium-sized rodents, mainly sousliks, but it will also take the chicks of other

The Long-legged Buzzard, seen here at its nest in May, is a typical predator of steppes and semi-deserts, especially in the desert foothills of Central Asia.

birds and carrion. It is becoming increasingly rare and is included in the Red Book of the USSR.

The Long-legged Buzzard breeds on the steppes and semi-deserts of the Trans-Caucasus, the Lower Volga, Kazakhstan and Central Asia. Its nest is built on rocks, on sandy or clayey cliffs, in river valleys and on the plains. From 2 to 4 eggs are laid in April. It feeds mainly on rodents such as voles and marmots.

LARKS

The most important group of perching birds (Order Passeriformes) in the steppes and deserts are the larks (family Alaudidae). Most of them have variegated plumage above but are pale with dark spots below. In most species the sexes are the same. Larks prefer open spaces — ploughed fields, steppes, semi-desert or desert — and only a few, such as the Woodlark (*Lullula arborea*), are found in forest edges or felled woodland. The boundless deserts and semi-deserts of north and central Africa are usually taken as the origin of this family.

Many larks are marvellous singers, with a long, resounding, tuneful song, especially in summer, during their courtship flights. They build their nests on the ground in small natural depressions or little pits they excavate

themselves. They lay from 4 to 6 eggs, which they incubate for 12 to 16 days. Newly-hatched chicks are naked and helpless. After 10 or 11 days they leave the nest, although they cannot yet fly. After another 8 or 10 days of being fed by their parents, they begin to fly and lead an independent life. Their parents then start to raise a second family.

Larks are ground feeders, eating a variety of weed seeds and insects, as well as cultivated plants. In suitable areas, there may be large populations of some species. The familiar Northern Skylark (*Alauda arvensis*) and the more southerly Crested Lark (*Galerida cristata*) are widespread in the USSR, including the steppes. More exotic steppeland larks include the Black Lark (*Melanocorypha yeltonensis*), and the White-winged Lark (*M. leucoptera*), both of which are endemic to the USSR.

The Black Lark is a large species, weighing as much as 2 oz (60 g), and the male's summer plumage is almost coal black. It nests on the wormwood (sagebrush) steppes, in semi-deserts and on areas of *solonchak* soils (pale salty soils) along the lower Volga and in Kazakhstan. Although not strictly migratory, it does form flocks in autumn and moves southwards and south-westwards. These winter wanderings soon cease, and as early as March the male Black Lark's song can once again be heard on the breeding grounds. He usually sings perched on a hillock, lifting his tail and lowering his wings. Soon after the birds start singing, several males can be seen chasing one female. There are noticeably more male Black Larks than females, in contrast to other larks.

The nest is a fragile structure made from the previous year's plant stalks, built directly on the ground, either in a

There are many species of larks in the Russian steppes and semi-deserts; this Calandra Lark was photographed at its nest near the delta of the River Atrek, in south Turkmenia.

natural hollow or in one excavated by the bird. Five or six greyish-brown eggs are laid in the second half of April, and the female incubates them for 15 or 16 days. By early June, the young birds are fledged, and the parents then begin their second family. In the spring and summer, Black Larks eat only insects – grasshoppers, locusts and beetles – but in winter their diet consists entirely of plant food. The White-winged Lark has a similar distribution and life history to the Black Lark.

There are three other *Melanocorypha* larks in the USSR: the Calandra Lark (*M. calandra*), the Bimaculated Lark (*M. bimaculata*) and the Mongolian Lark (*M. mongolica*). All three are large, distinctive birds with powerful bills, and an impressive courtship flight. The Calandra Lark prefers the steppes and semi-deserts of the Ukraine, Lower Volga, Kazakhstan and Central Asia. The Bimaculated Lark is more numerous in Kazakhstan and Central Asia, while the Mongolian Lark prefers the areas of Trans-Baikal and the Mongolian border. All these species are numerous in suitable habitats.

Four small larks of the genus *Calandrella* breed in the USSR. The Short-toed Lark (*C. cinerea*) and Lesser Short-toed Lark (*C. rufescens*) are widespread in steppes and deserts; Hume's Short-toed Lark (*C. acutirostris*) lives in semi-deserts of the Pamir Mountains only; and the Eastern Short-toed Lark (*C. cheleënsis*) is restricted to the *solonchak* soils of Central Asia. The Shore, or Horned, Lark (*Eremophila alpestris*) lives in the tundra and mountains.

MAMMALS

Most typical steppe mammals are rodents. They include the Bobak, or Steppe, Marmot (*Marmota bobac*), which is the size of a small cat. A marmot colony in the steppe stands out as a dark green patch of luxuriant vegetation in the dry yellow grass of the steppe between spring and late autumn. Marmots eat a total of over 100 species of grass, and show marked preferences for particular parts of the plants at different seasons. In early spring, they eat rhizomes and bulbs, in summer young shoots of grasses and a variety of other steppe plants. Every day, a marmot eats up to 2 or 3 lb (1 to 1.5 kg) of vegetation, normally obtaining all its water from its food. As well as plants, marmots eat locusts, grasshoppers, caterpillars, ant pupae and molluscs. In captivity, they eat meat with relish. These social creatures warn each other of danger by means of loud, piercing cries, audible almost $\frac{1}{3}$ mile (500 m) away. They have few enemies, the main ones being wolves (*Canis lupus*) and stray dogs. Mammal predators and birds of prey usually attack only sick and young marmots.

In September, marmots move to their permanent winter burrows, where they hibernate, after blocking the entrance with earth and stones. Marmots mate in April or May. After a pregnancy of 30 to 35 days, the female gives birth to a litter of between 1 and 11 young, usually between 4 and 6. They are weaned after about 50 days.

Sousliks, or ground squirrels (*Citellus*) are medium-sized rodents, with naked cheek pouches and, in most species, a tail less than half as long as the body. Most species have a similar lifestyle and live in open country, usually steppes or semi-desert, but some prefer mountains or even tundra. Sousliks are active by day, eating large quantities of succulent grasses, seeds and bulbs. Some species cause serious damage to farm crops and spread harmful diseases.

One of the smallest sousliks is the Little Souslik (*Citellus pygmaeus*), with an adult body length ranging from $7\frac{1}{2}$ to 8 in (19 to 21 cm). It lives in the steppes and semi-deserts of the Ukraine and Kazakhstan. The densest colonies of Little Sousliks are found in semi-deserts with a mosaic surface. Here, there may be as many as 20 sousliks per acre (50 per hectare), and in summer, after the young are born, three times as many. Other sousliks do not form such dense colonies. A new wintering burrow of a Little Souslik has a simple, uniform structure, a sloping entrance, and a nesting chamber at a depth of 5 to $6\frac{1}{2}$ ft (1.5 to 2 m). Old souslik colonies give the ground surface a hummocky relief. Little Sousliks eat the most succulent parts of plants, including large amounts of soft, unripe seeds and young, juicy stems and leaves.

ABOVE *An adult Bobak Marmot keeps a sharp lookout on the steppe in northern Kazakhstan; it will warn the two young behind it of any danger by means of loud piercing cries.*

ABOVE *This attractive little rodent is the Steppe Lemming, seen here in southern Kazakhstan. A close relative, the Sagebrush Vole, lives in the western United States.*

In spring, after their long hibernation, the first to awaken and reach the surface are the males. The females soon follow and the breeding season begins soon afterwards. After a pregnancy of 22 to 26 days, the female produces 5 to 9 young, each weighing about $\frac{1}{10}$ oz (3.5. to 4 g). After 20 to 25 days, the young begin to venture out and gradually become independent. When the young settle densely in empty burrows, parasites quickly spread among them. The Little Souslik is considered one of the most serious agricultural pests in the USSR. It spoils pasture by bringing the salty subsoil to the surface when burrowing, and eats crops, including oats. It also harbours ticks which transmit the disease brucellosis to livestock.

Another typical steppe rodent is the Common Hamster (*Cricetus cricetus*), a larger relative of the Golden Hamster (*Mesocricetus auratus*) from Syria, familiar as a pet to most readers. The Common Hamster is about 10 to 12 in (25 to 30 cm) long, with a beautiful black, rich brown and white coat. It is widespread on the steppes and wooded steppes of the European part of the USSR, Siberia and northern Kazakhstan. Unlike the marmots and sousliks, it is a solitary, nocturnal creature. This comical little animal digs complicated and durable burrows with several food-storage chambers, a maze of separate tunnels and escape routes, sometimes as deep as 8 ft (2.5 m). As autumn approaches, it busily fills its storage chambers with as much as 22 to 44 lb (10 to 20 kg) of potatoes, carrots, maize and other plant food. The hamster feeds on these provisions in winter when it occasionally wakes up from its deep sleep. From April to October, the female has two or three litters, each containing as many as 10 young, or even more.

The tables on pages 215–16 list most of the bird and mammal species of the steppes of the USSR. Some species found in the steppes that have a wider overall distribution, such as the Skylark (*Alauda arvensis*) and the Wolf (*Canis lupus*), are not included.

Nature reserves in the steppes

In the European part of the USSR, the opening up of the steppes for agriculture has left only a very few areas of virgin steppe, all of which are protected in nature reserves. Larger areas remain intact in the Asian part of the country, in Trans-Baikal.

In the wooded steppe zone of the Kursk and Belgorod regions is the 19 sq mile (48 sq km) Tsentralno-Chernozomny (Central Black Earth) Reserve. One of the most important steppe reserves is the Askania-Nova Reserve, near Kherson, on the mouth of the River Dniepr

TOP *Life sometimes appears as if by magic in the desert; here, an arrow snake suddenly emerges from the dead flowerhead of a broomrape plant at the Repetek Nature Reserve in the Kara-Kum sand desert, in Central Asia.*
ABOVE LEFT *A Caucasian Scorpion adopts a threat posture in the semi-desert of the Kopet-Dag foothills.*
ABOVE RIGHT *This grasshopper* Saxetania cultricollis, *also from Kopet-Dag, is a rare insect.*

on the north coast of the Black Sea. It comprises 43 sq miles (111 sq km) of sheep's fescue and feather-grass steppe, of which only 6 sq miles (15 sq km) have never been ploughed. This was the first private reserve in Russia, established in 1874, and has existed as a state nature reserve since 1921. It is famous for the variety of exotic animals, including llamas and emus, that are bred there, and the captive breeding programme to help the survival of such rare native species as the Great Bustard (*Otis tarda*) and the Asian Wild Ass, or Kulan (*Equus hemionus*). The reserve contains about 417 species of higher plants, of which 66 are included in the Red Book of the USSR, as well as a number of typical steppe birds and mammals.

The Lugan Reserve protects three separate areas, totalling 6 sq miles (15.8 sq km), near Voroshilovgrad in the Ukraine: the Streltsov steppe and the Stanichno-Lugan area, both 2 sq miles (4.9 sq km) in area, and the 2 sq mile (5.9 sq km) Proval steppe.

The 6 sq mile (16 sq km) Ukrainsky Reserve was created in 1961 from several areas, the largest being the 4 sq mile (10.3 sq km) Khomutovo steppe. The Khomutovo area has 528 plant species, and the Kamenny Mogili ('Stone Graves') region 464. Animal life is sparse.

Deserts

For many, the desert is a symbol of lifelessness, with sands stretching endlessly under a burning sun. But only the driest of the world's deserts are poor in animals and plants. The others are often full of life. Deserts cover about 15 per cent of the earth's surface, and occupy large areas of the USSR. About one-ninth of the USSR's land surface is occupied by a continuous desert, stretching from the lower reaches of the Ural River and the Trans-Caspian region to the foot of the Tien Shan Mountains; through the Dzhungarian Gate, it joins the great desert of western China.

Deserts are very varied, but their climates have several features in common. The annual rainfall is no more than 8 in (200 mm); mean summer temperatures are very high, around 104°F (40°C); winter temperatures are low, about 32°F (0°C); and evaporation is high, reaching 35 to 60 in (900 to 1500 mm) annually over open water. In summer the temperature is so high and the amount of rainfall so low that there is a shortage of water, both in the air and the soil.

There are three main sub-zones of desert in the USSR. The sub-zone of northern deserts includes the desert of Mangyshlak, on the Mangyshlak Peninsula, projecting into the Caspian Sea. Many of its animals and plants share a common origin with those in the North Caucasus. The largest northern desert is the Aral-Caspian Desert, stretching from the Lower Volga to Dzhungaria.

In the semi-desert sub-zone, steppe vegetation typically alternates with desert vegetation. The East European semi-desert occupies the north-western part of this sub-zone, and contains elements of the plant communities of the south Russian steppe. The area of semi-desert north of the Caucasus has vegetation resembling that of the Black Sea

steppes and the Mangyshlak Desert. The largest area of semi-desert, in Kazakhstan, stretching from the Lower Volga to the Altai foothills, contains European flora at its western end and Altai flora at the eastern end. The Zaisan semi-desert occupies the Lake Zaisan depression, and is cut off by the Altai mountains from the main semi-deserts of the USSR, although it is linked to the semi-desert regions of Central Asia.

The sub-zone of southern deserts includes the deserts of the southern part of the Trans-Caspian area and Central Asia, influenced climatically by both the Aral-Caspian Desert to the north and by the deserts of Iran and the Middle East to the south. In contrast to the northern deserts, there is no permanent snow cover and the plants and animals are distinctly southern. The daytime relative humidity varies from 10 to 20 per cent. At night, it rises to 40 per cent, compared with 80 to 90 per cent in the forest zone. The daytime shade temperature reaches 122°F (50°C), and the sand heats up to as much as 176°F (80°C).

The different soils of deserts contribute to their varied appearance. Within the USSR, there are four main types of deserts, based on their soil: clay, *solonchak* (pale salty soils), sand and stone.

The clay deserts are both more northerly and more southerly than the vast sandy deserts of Central Asia, the Kara-Kum (Black Sands) and Kyzyl-Kum (Red Sands). In the clay deserts of northern Central Asia, various species of wormwood, or sagebrush (*Artemisia*) form the main vegetation. The southern clay deserts are quite different; they occupy a fairly narrow strip, flanked on the south by sandy deserts, but extend south to the foothills of the Kopet-Dag, Tien Shan and Pamir-Alai Mountains. They contain many ephemeral plants, which have a brief burst of growth and complete their life-cycles in spring before being dried by the searing sun. The soil is fine-grained, with no harmful mineral salts. In places, they may be completely carpeted with thick grass in spring, when the soil is saturated with moisture and there is heavy rain at least once a week.

Solonchak deserts, typically with outcrops of salts and distinctive salt-tolerant plants, occupy a relatively small area. They have developed on the terraces of the Syr-Darya and Amu-Darya rivers, and in the south on those of the Tedzhen and Murgab rivers. They result from a lowering of the ground and a subsequent accumulation of salt-rich water. *Solonchak* deserts may contain areas called *takyrs*, seasonal salt lakes completely devoid of vegetation, and permanent salt lakes.

The largest deserts are the sandy deserts, which cover

Clay desert

Salt desert

Stone desert

ABOVE *There are four main types of deserts in the USSR. The clay desert is in the foothills of the Kopet-Dag Mountains. Stone deserts include the one in the Chu-Ili Mountains of Kazakhstan shown above. The salt desert shown here lies between the Chu and Ili rivers, and the sand desert is the Tau-Kum, south of the Ili.*

Sand desert

large areas of Kazakhstan and Central Asia. These include the Muyun-Kum, to the west of Lake Balkhash; the Kyzyl-Kum (Red Sands) to the south-west of the Muyun-Kum, and the vast Kara-Kum (Black Sands), which lies much further to the south-west, mainly in Turkmenistan.

Stony deserts, with stones covering up to 50 per cent of their area, are fairly widespread, and include the large desert tableland of the Ustyurt Plateau, lying between the Caspian and Aral Seas, and the Betpak-Dala semi-desert, to the west of Lake Balkhash.

Desert vegetation

Sandy deserts may contain a surprising wealth of plant species, from annual ephemeral flowers and perennial grasses to shrubs and even trees. The ephemerals are not drought resistant, relying instead for survival on a rapid life cycle. Ephemeral plants can cover as much as half the surface of some stable sandy deserts. They are succeeded by the perennial grasses, and then the shrubs burst into bloom. Many plants continue to grow until late autumn.

All these plants depend on the moisture trapped in the sandy subsoil. The highly permeable sand allows atmospheric water to percolate down quickly, especially in wet years. Sandy soils can condense water vapour to water. The sand also has little capillary action, so the lower subsoil — and the plant roots — remain damp. There is generally a damp layer in sandy deserts, between 40 and 55 in (100 to 140 cm) deep, all year round. Of course, the plants do have to cope with various adverse conditions. These include the extremely hot, dry air and the merciless sun, which leads to high levels of evaporation, and the shifting nature of the sand, which makes it difficult for the plants to anchor themselves.

Desert plants have evolved a multitude of adaptations to their dry environment. The leaves of most of the shrubs and trees, including the abundant saxaul trees (*Arthrophytum*) are so narrow that it is fruitless to use them to provide shade from the burning sun. Their narrowness greatly reduces the amount of water they lose. Some desert plants have very stiff leaves with thickened cell walls. Other plants, such as the salt bush *Atriplex dimorphostegia* bear bubbles on the underside of their leaves. At night these bubbles fill with water, which the plants can use during the heat of the following day.

There are very few bulb- or tuber-forming plants in sandy deserts, probably because of the shifting subsoil. The plants that do live there have to cope with this problem, and some do so by developing accessory shoots or roots to avoid being buried alive.

There are distinct communities of plants on the different areas of desert dunes. On their summits, pioneer species, such as Three-Awn Grass (*Aristida pennata*), which bind the shifting sand by developing an extensive network of roots, like the familiar Marram Grass (*Ammophila arenaria*) of coastal dunes. The upper slopes of the dunes are colonized by shrubs and a few perennial grasses. The lower slopes are the home of succulent plants, such as giant fennels (*Ferula*) and the wild rhubarb *Rheum turkestanicum*. In the hollows between the dunes, where the soil is more compacted, ephemeral sedges flourish. Sand Sedge (*Carex physodes*) stabilize the sand with their much-branched root systems. Some desert plants have root systems that occupy from two to six times the volume of their above-ground parts, and some individual roots as much as 250 ft (75 m) long.

ABOVE *These broomrape plants, typical of the southern deserts of Kazakhstan and Central Asia, lack chlorophyll and obtain their food by parasitizing other desert plants.*

ABOVE *Calligonum plants are common in the Central Asian deserts; this one is* Calligonum setosum. *Despite the harsh conditions, the desert blooms with delicate flowers.*

Desert animals

The deserts of the USSR contain a wealth of highly specialized animals, including many endemic species, as well as endemic genera of insects with only one species, indicating their antiquity. In Central Asia there are many endemic species of beetles, including weevils, ground beetles and dung beetles. There are also many species of two-winged flies, termites and butterflies.

More reptiles live in the deserts than in any other geographical zone of the USSR. Being 'cold-blooded', their body temperature depends chiefly on that of their surroundings. During the cold desert winter, they become torpid, but in the hot summer days, they are very active. The many small species of desert lizards feed chiefly on insects, but the larger lizards and poisonous snakes eat their smaller relatives, small mammals and the eggs and chicks of birds.

The struggle for existence in the sand deserts of Central Asia, which teem with animal life, is very fierce. In order to survive, many animals have adopted remarkable adaptations. Some reptiles are camouflaged to look like flowers; some can bury themselves in the sand with lightning speed; others are exceptionally agile on the surface. Mammals, especially small rodents, adapt well to desert conditions. While it is difficult to single out a group of birds which live and breed only in deserts, two groups of mammals are restricted almost entirely to the desert zone: the gerbils and jerboas.

A Long-eared Hedgehog takes a walk in the Chimkent region of Kazakhstan; this little mammal, widespread in the deserts of the USSR, ranges from North Africa to Mongolia.

Desert birds may have drab yellowish or pale grey plumage, providing superb camouflage, and hide their nests in the densest, most prickly shrubs. But this is generally the extent of their adaptability; unlike reptiles, they are 'warm-blooded' and are exhausted rather than galvanized into action by the intense heat, losing water easily by evaporation; a loss they cannot easily reduce by burrowing into the sand like the reptiles or mammals. If we compare the numbers of bird species nesting in deserts with those in similarly sized areas of forest or mountain, the deserts are clearly the losers; with reptiles, the opposite is decidedly true.

REPTILES

A typical and common reptile of the Central Asian deserts is Horsfield's Tortoise (*Testudo horsfieldi*), which is only 20 cm (8 in) long. In suitable habitats, there may be as many as 4 individuals per acre (10 per hectare). They feed on various ephemeral plants and on the tender young shoots of shrubs and cultivated plants, and do not need to drink, as they can obtain enough water in their succulent food. However, if there is water nearby they will gladly drink it. The tortoises emerge from their underground hibernation chambers in early spring and soon start mating. In May or June the female lays from 2 to 5 eggs, and she may have two further successful broods in the same season. The eggs take several months to hatch. After mating, the adults begin to hibernate as early as June because the ephemeral plants have by then dried up. They dig out their own burrow or widen that of a jerboa or a gerbil. The tortoises grow very slowly, and do not become sexually mature until they are 10 years old; they are not fully grown until they have reached some 20 to 30 years old.

Turning to the lizards, I shall begin with the gecko family (Gekkonidae). In 1977, zoologists were excited to learn of a newly described species in the sub-family Eublepharinae, *Eublepharis turkmenica*, found in the stony desert foothills of the Kopet-Dag Range in south Turkmenia. This rare lizard is illustrated for the first time in colour in the photograph on the next page. To date, no more than 20 individuals have been seen. We still know little of this lizard's life. From its morphology and close similarities to some other *Eublepharis* geckos (there are 16 species worldwide), it seems to be nocturnal, feeding on a huge variety of insects.

The great majority of geckos belong to the sub-family of true geckos, the Gekkoninae, which includes many species that are most active during the twilight hours. Five extremely similar species of skink-like geckos live in the

ABOVE *A Horsfield's Tortoise labours patiently across a dune in the great Tau-Kum sand desert, in southeastern Kazakhstan during the cooler morning. Desert tortoises avoid the fierce heat of the desert sun by burying themselves deeply in the sand.*

LEFT *A pair of Horsfield's Tortoises mating in April in the Kalkan Mountain region of the middle reaches of the River Ili in southeastern Kazakhstan.*

This rare little lizard, the gecko Eublepharis turkmenica, *was not discovered by scientists until 1977. It lives in the foothills of the Kopet-Dag Range, south Turkmenia.*

deserts of Central Asia, one of which, *Teratoscincus scincus*, is found in the USSR, in Kazakhstan as well as Central Asia. This attractive reptile lives in areas of shifting sand and dunes, but is also found in clay deserts. It digs its burrow in soft sand, tunnelling as far as the layer of moist sand, and blocks the entrance with a plug of moist sand. The gecko stays in its burrow all day, emerging at dusk to hunt for large insects and their larvae. In June, the female begins to lay her eggs. She places them in small, shallow chambers dug out of the hot sand so that they incubate properly and are out of sight of predators. There are no more than 2 eggs in each brood, but there may be from 2 to 4 broods in a single season. Geckos moult their skins no less than three times in a season.

The large family of agama lizards (Agamidae) contains more than 300 species worldwide, including many desert-dwellers. One of the most typical inhabitants of the Russian steppes and deserts is the Steppe Agama (*Agama sanguinolenta*), which may grow to 1 ft (30 cm) long. Widespread in the arid plains of Kazakhstan and Central Asia, it occurs in sand, clay or stone deserts and semi-deserts with well-developed shrubs and low trees, and is also found in riverside forests. It shelters in rodents' burrows, rarely digging its own. It eats a huge variety of insects and spiders, as well as the succulent parts of plants, and can climb trees and shrubs with great agility. Each adult lizard occupies its own small territory, which it rarely leaves. In the breeding season, the males climb up to the topmost branches of shrubs, from which they can command a good view of the neighbourhood. If a rival male

appears, the lizard slips down to the ground to meet him and force him to leave. One female, rarely two, lives in each male's territory. In late April or early May she digs a small pit in the soft desert soil, in which she lays from 5 to 10 eggs. The first brood is usually followed by two more. The eggs hatch after 50 to 60 days in the hot sun.

The genus of toad-headed agamids (*Phrynocephalus*) differs from other agama lizards in having a short head, rounded in front; a wide, flattened body; and a tail that curves over onto the back. Their colour usually camouflages them superbly against their surroundings. Most species live in sand, clay or stone deserts or semi-deserts. They eat a great range of insects and other invertebrates.

One of the most characteristic lizards of sandy deserts in Central Asia and Kazakhstan is the toad-headed agamid *P. mystaceus*. It is larger than other species, reaching 10 in (24 cm) in length, and lives among sand dunes, digging itself one or two horizontal burrows 3 ft (1 m) long at the bottom of a dune, usually ending in a widened chamber at the level of damp sand. Toad-heads defend their refuge energetically against intruders, whether of their own or other species. In summer, they rarely use their burrows, digging themselves into the sand at night and remaining down there until dawn. A toad-head can bury itself almost instantly. Flattening itself on the ground, it pushes the sand out from beneath it with quick sideways movements of its body. The sand soon covers the lizard, which gradually disappears from view, head last. It always waits for a while before reappearing. At first, it protrudes only its head, then

This Steppe Agama lizard, photographed in the Repetek Nature Reserve, in the vast Kara-Kum sand desert, is one of the most widespread of the USSR's desert lizards.

One of the toad-headed agamid lizards, Phrynocephalus mystaceus, *adopts an aggressive pose, coiling its tail like a watchspring and revealing bright red mouth flanges.*

gradually the rest of its body. Toad-heads have a varied diet, including insects, spiders, flowers, fruits and leaves.

They are solitary animals, apart from the breeding season. The males patrol their territories, frequently climbing the the crest of the nearest dune and surveying the area for rivals. They allow a human intruder to come no nearer than 30 ft (10 m) before disappearing behind the dune, but reappear after a few seconds to see whether the danger is past. In late May or early June the females starts to lay their first clutch of 2 to 6 eggs in the damp sand zone, deep in the burrow. They lay a second clutch later. In early to mid-October, the toad-heads hide in their burrows for winter, where they remain until they emerge in late February or early March.

Another toad-head of the deserts of Kazakhstan and Central Asia, *Phrynocephalus interscapularis*, lives not only on sand dunes with some plant cover, but also in desert areas virtually devoid of vegetation. Its burrow is a simple tunnel about 6 in (15 cm) long which it re-opens every time it goes to sleep for the night. It eats ants, beetles and caterpillars, and sometimes catches butterflies on the wing, leaping nimbly into the air. Egg laying begins in the second half of April, and takes place three or four times per season. The large eggs, 4 to 6 in (10 to 15 cm) in diameter, mature alternately in the right and left ovaries.

The skink family (Scincidae) is not well represented in the USSR. Schneider's Skink (*Eumeces schneideri*), up to 17 in (43 cm) long, lives in the deserts of Central Asia. It lives on dry stony slopes with grassy or semi-shrub vegetation in silt or clay deserts, occasionally in sandy deserts. Its

refuge is beneath a stone or in a rodent's burrow, but it may also dig its own burrow, 6½ ft (2 m) or more long. It appears with the first hot weather in late April or early May. By the end of August the adult lizards are rarely seen, and soon they disappear completely until the following spring. Schneider's Skinks feed on insects and other invertebrates, and lay 5 to 9 eggs in July.

The largest existing lizards are the monitors (family Varanidae). They have a well-proportioned muscular body, and powerful limbs with five fingers ending in large curved claws. In the USSR there is one species, the Desert Monitor (*Varanus griseus*), which is fairly widespread in Central Asian deserts. The largest lizard in the USSR, it may reach 5 ft (1.6 m) long and weigh 5½ lb (2.5 kg). Its movements are extremely fast, and it can run at a speed of 320 to 390 ft (100 to 120 m) per minute. It feeds on various animals, insects, snakes (including poisonous species), birds and rodents. The monitor covers a large area in search of food each day, ranging as far as ⅓ mile (500 m) from its home, generally following the same route, which takes in all the nearest gerbil colonies, birds' nests and other potential food sites.

The monitors are not sexually mature until they are three years old, by which time they are 2 to 2½ ft (60 to 80 cm) long. They mate in May, and in the first half of June the female lays from 8 to 23 eggs, burying them deep in the sand. The young do not emerge until September. Monitors spend the winter sleeping in deep burrows, after blocking the entrances with sand.

There is also a variety of snakes in the deserts of the USSR. Widespread in Central Asia and the desert north of the Caucasus is one of the sand boas, *Eryx miliaris*, a member of the family Boidae. This snake is only 2½ ft (80 cm) long; its head is flattened and its eyes look almost vertically upwards. It can live in both stabilized and shifting sand, and first appears on the surface in April or May. Its diet includes lizards, rodents and birds. It keeps a close watch on the rodent burrows in its territory, crawling into them one by one, and from time to time buries itself in the sand and glides along beneath it. It is able to catch prey seemingly out of reach with a lightning-quick movement of its head, armed with powerful jaws, then coils its muscular body around the animal, crushing the life from it. Such sudden attacks make a striking contrast to its relatively sluggish behaviour at other times. In July or August the female gives birth to as many as ten live young. The snakes become sexually mature when four years old.

Also found in Central Asian deserts is the Arrow Snake (*Psammophis lineolatus*), which may reach 3 ft (90 cm) in

length and lives on sandy, stony or clay slopes. Its name refers to its extremely swift movements. It is adept at climbing trees, and its shape and colour help to camouflage it against the branches. Its diet consists entirely of lizards.

A number of snakes live in the USSR that are potentially dangerous to man. Of the world's six species of cobra, one, *Naja oxyana*, lives on the borders of the USSR in the Central Asian deserts and foothills. It likes hilly areas with sparse grass, abundant shelter and many rodent burrows, and is quite rare, being included in the Red Book of the USSR. It is most active in spring, when it hunts by day. In the hot desert summer, it emerges only in the cooler early morning and late evening. The snakes mate in spring, and in July the females lay 8 to 12 eggs, from which the young hatch in September. The cobra eats amphibians,

TOP *The Desert Monitor is the largest lizard in the Soviet Union, growing as much as 5 ft (1.6 m) long. It is quite widely distributed in the Central Asian deserts.*
RIGHT *The most impressive-looking of the USSR's snakes is the Central Asian Cobra, seen here giving its dramatic threat display. This one was photographed in the Kopet-Dag foothills, south Turkmenia.*

reptiles, birds and small rodents. Its poison is very powerful, but authenticated instances of bites to humans, or even farm animals, are extremely rare. Fortunately, the snakes gives plenty of warning of an attack, adopting a distinctive defensive posture when threatened, holding the front of its body erect and hissing loudly. Even if the intruder ignores this display, the cobra is still reluctant to use its fangs, striking with closed jaws.

Another very poisonous snake in the USSR is the Blunt-nosed Viper (*Vipera lebetina*), which can reach more than 5

ABOVE *The Saw-scaled Viper, although growing only up to 31 in (80 cm) long, is one of the most aggressive and most poisonous of the USSR's snakes.*

ft (1.6 m) long. Although still plentiful in some areas, it is generally becoming scarcer. It prefers dry foothills, canyons and slopes with sparse shrubs, where it finds shelter in rodent burrows or rock crevices, spending the winter communally. When the snakes emerge in March, they warm themselves by day, and do not hunt immediately. With the onset of the summer heat, they may hide in crevices where some water is trapped, hunting during the cooler twilight and night-time hours. Their diet includes lizards and young hares, but they feed mainly on small rodents such as gerbils. The vipers mate in April or May, and the young appear in early autumn. It is interesting that over most of the snake's range, the females give birth to live young, but in Central Asia they lay from 15 to 20 eggs, occasionally more, which are incubated by the sun's heat for about 40 days.

The Blunt-nosed Viper is potentially very dangerous. Like other wild animals, it first attempts to hide when confronted by humans. But if its way is barred, it hisses

loudly and threateningly and moves alarmingly fast towards the intruders. Zoologists regard the catching of this snake as particularly hazardous work. On several occasions, a captured viper, apparently rendered harmless by a firm grip on its jaws, has managed to bite its captor's hand after first penetrating its own lower jaw. Although weaker than that of a cobra, the viper's venom acts very quickly. It injects up to 50 milligrams, which breaks up the red corpuscles, damages the walls of blood vessels and clots the blood. If victims do not receive skilled help, they may soon lose consciousness and die. On the credit side, the venom is widely used in medicine.

The tables on pages 216–17 list the most typical reptiles of the deserts and semi-deserts of the USSR.

DESERT BIRDS

These include both genuine desert species that have evolved various adaptations for coping with the harsh environment and species like the Common Whitethroat (*Sylvia communis*) that also occur in other habitats, from mountains to forests. Since most of the USSR's deserts have hard winters, with lasting snow absent only from those in the far south, most desert birds are forced to migrate south during winter.

Two specialized plovers live in the clay deserts of the Trans-Caucasus and Central Asia. The Greater Sand Plover (*Charadrius leschenaultii*) breeds in clay and salt deserts with wormwood (*Artemisia*) and Russian thistles, or saltworts (*Salsola*) and also on flat gravelly deserts with sparse vegetation. Sometimes the conditions are so harsh that the plovers are the only birds that can survive. They can make do without water, but after the 3 or 4 chicks hatch, they move to river or lake banks where there is ample food. The Caspian Plover (*C. asiaticus*) is found further north than the Greater Sand Plover, in similar habitats, and has similar habits to those of its slightly larger relative.

In the clay deserts of Central Asia lives the Egyptian Nightjar (*Caprimulgus aegyptius*). Like the other members of the nightjar family (Caprimulgidae), this species is active during the twilight, catching moths and other flying insects. Its broad bill is fringed with bristles that help to funnel the prey into it. The nightjar's nest is a small pit in the ground. Here it lays 2 greyish eggs, which are superbly camouflaged against the grey desert soil, as is the sitting bird. To reduce further the chance of being spotted, it almost shuts its large black eyes, leaving only narrow slits through which it can sense any danger.

The Eurasian Roller (*Coracias garrulus*) is common in the desert foothills of Central Asia but cannot be counted among the true desert birds, as it is also widespread in the forest zone. Nevertheless, it is most abundant in the deserts, and nests in holes in the soft clay or loess cliffs that

ABOVE *The Greater Sand Plover, seen here in the Betpak-Dala semi-desert west of Lake Balkhash, is one of the few waders to have adapted to the desert, coping with the harsh environment of the clay and stone deserts.*

ABOVE *The Blue-cheeked Bee-eater is widespread in the semi-deserts and deserts of the USSR; this lovely bird does indeed catch and eat bees, as its name suggests.*

occur in the river valleys of the foothills. Rollers feed chiefly on large insects such as grasshoppers, locusts and beetles which they catch mainly on the ground.

Two species of bee-eater occur in the USSR: like the roller, they are not exclusively desert birds, although the Blue-cheeked Bee-eater (*Merops superciliosus*) is most often found in desert areas. It likes hilly places with soft cliffs in which it can dig out its nest holes, but also occurs in flat areas, where it excavates its holes in the ground. It usually nests in noisy colonies, but is sometimes a solitary breeder. The European Bee-eater (*Merops apiaster*) is a common bird in many types of open country, with similar breeding habits. Both species catch large insects, mainly bees and wasps, on the wing.

Among the woodpeckers (family Picidae) there is only one species typical of Soviet deserts: the White-winged Spotted Woodpecker (*Dendrocopos leucopterus*), which occurs in Kazakhstan and Central Asia, preferring areas of sandy desert with saxauls and other trees. The birds start to chisel out their nesting holes in the trees in April, and lay 4 to 7 white eggs inside. They feed on insects and their larvae.

Among the many species in the great order of Passeriformes (perching birds), the thrushes and their relatives (Turdidae) and the warblers (Sylviidae) are fairly well represented in deserts. Among the thrush family, various species of wheatear (*Oenanthe*) prefer deserts. Rocky, stony or sandy desert plains are the home of the Desert Wheatear (*O. deserti*). It builds its nest in rock crevices, and lays 4 to 5 eggs. It eats insects.

The Rufous Bush Chat (*Cercotrichas galactotes*) is another typical desert member of the thrush family. It prefers flat deserts with shrubs. It is not evenly distributed, but may be plentiful in suitable habitats, with nests only 260 to 330 ft (80 to 100 m) apart. It is most numerous in thick saxaul woods with many fallen trees. Bush chats arrive on their breeding grounds at the end of April and courtship and pair-formation start soon afterwards, during which the males perform vigorous song-flights. The nest is usually built in the fork of a tree trunk or side branch, although it may be sited on the ground at the foot of the shrub. The 4 to 6 eggs are laid in the first half of May. The bush chats feed mainly on insects which they catch in the trees and on the ground.

Among the warblers, one of the most typical desert species is the Streaked Scrub Warbler (*Scotocerca inquieta*). It prefers areas of desert with scattered shrubs, and its range may extend up the mountain foothills. It is unevenly distributed and rare on the edges of its range. This lively

TOP *A Rufous Bush Chat at the Repetek Reserve; this restless little bird constantly moves its tail, spreading it like a fan and even stretching it along its back.*

ABOVE *Ménétries' Warbler breeds in the Turkmen deserts.*

LEFT *Nest and eggs of Pander's Ground Jay at Repetek.*

little bird is confiding and inquisitive, but many of the details of its life history remain unknown. Its diet consists mainly of insects in summer and seeds in winter. It lays from 6 to 9 eggs in a nest built by both parents, usually low down in a thick shrub. Two other warblers are found in

The Marbled Polecat, one of the most attractive members of the weasel family, is a rare inhabitant of the deserts and steppes of the USSR. It feeds on birds and small mammals.

Strict protection, scientific study and a programme of captive breeding have helped the rare and elegant Goitred Gazelle of the Soviet deserts.

similar habitats: the Desert Warbler (*Sylvia nana*) and Ménétries' Warbler (*S. mystacea*).

Pander's Ground Jay (*Podoces panderi*) is a fairly rare and unusual member of the crow family (Corvidae). It is endemic to the desert zone, and lives in several widely separated areas of the USSR, including the great sandy deserts of the Kara-Kum and Kyzyl-Kum (page 176) and those lying to the south of Lake Balkhash. This interesting bird is very vulnerable to human disturbance and has been driven out of some of its former haunts. It spends most of its time on the ground, walking or running ceaselessly across the sand. It will fly when disturbed, but soon lands and continues running. Its call, a pleasant, tremulous whistle, carries for great distances. Ground jays are solitary breeders, pairs remaining together throughout the year. They feed mainly on insects and the seeds of desert bushes.

In favourable areas, the nests, which are probably used year after year, may be as little as 1600 to 3300 ft (0.5 to 1 km) apart. The birds arrive on their breeding grounds in late February or early March. The nest is a spherical structure, similar to that of a Magpie (*Pica pica*), and is skillfully camouflaged by a layer of interwoven twigs. The 3 to 6 pale blue-green eggs are laid in April. The female alone incubates, for 17 to 19 days. The male feeds her while she is sitting, and may attempt to drive off predators. On the approach of a human intruder, the female slips stealthily from the nest and runs off across the sand. The chicks grow fast; two weeks after hatching, they are feathered and can run fast, although they cannot fly properly. Many details of the ground jays' behaviour remain unknown, although it has been discovered that family groups may wander widely over the desert in autumn.

The most typical desert-dwelling member of the finch family (Fringillidae) is the Black-billed Desert Finch (*Rhodospiza obsoleta*). The sole member of the genus *Rhodospiza*, it has much in common with two other desert finches, the Trumpeter Finch (*Bucanetes githagineus*) and the Mongolian Trumpeter Finch (*B. mongolica*). In the USSR, the Black-billed Desert Finch is most abundant in the deserts of Kazakhstan, although it has been recorded from all the Asian deserts. It is chiefly a bird of the desert plains, where it is a solitary nester in desert trees and shrubs, preferring saxaul trees (*Arthrophytum*). In the wild, it is extremely wary, but in towns or villages, where it often nests, it is surprisingly confiding. It feeds only on seeds throughout the year, taking its food from the ground and from various plants. Black-billed Desert Finches arrive early on their breeding grounds, in March. Soon after arrival, they pair

These two magnificent Cheetahs, standing proudly over their prey on the Ustyurt Plateau, Kazakhstan, are kept in semi-captivity for re-introduction into the wild.

off and establish their territories. The 3 to 7 eggs are incubated by the female alone for 13 to 15 days while the male feeds her. The chicks, which are fed on an all-seed diet, have evolved particularly wide gullets to cope with their dry food. They fledge after 12 to 13 days in the nest and are tended by the male until able to fly, while the female prepares for her second brood. After the young have fledged, they stay together for a while, but soon form nomadic flocks.

Desert mammals

Several species of cats (family Felidae) live in the deserts of the USSR, but they are all rare. One reason is that the Soviet deserts lie on the edges of the range of most of these species; another is that changes in their habitats have driven them out. Various species of small cats lead a secretive and mainly nocturnal existence in the desert zone of the USSR. In many of the clay and sand deserts of Central Asia, the African Wild Cat (*Felis libyca*) lives in shrub thickets and forested foothills, eating rodents, hares and the occasional bird. Small numbers of Caracal Lynx (*F. caracal*) still live in the sandy deserts and foothills of Turkmenia and Uzbekistan. Virtually nothing is known of its life-style in the USSR. Pallas's Cat (*F. manul*) lives in a greater variety of habitats, not only in the deserts but also in steppes and mountains. Its diet consists almost entirely of rodents. There is practically no information about its

breeding behaviour in natural conditions. In the sandy deserts of Central Asia, the small Sand Cat (*F. margarita*) is restricted to areas of dunes with saxaul trees (*Arthrophytum*), 'Sandy Acacia' (*Ammodendron connolyi*) and other shrubs, where it feeds on rodents. It digs its own shallow burrow or uses a fox's earth. Here, in early April, from 2 to 5 kittens are born, but, again, further details of its breeding are very scanty.

The largest cat of the clay and sandy deserts is the magnificent Asiatic race of the Cheetah (*Acinonyx jubatus venaticus*), which is now so rare that there is considerable doubt as to its continued existence in the USSR. Its distribution is generally considered to include southern Turkmenia and the desert tableland of Ustyurt, where a nature reserve of more than 850 sq miles (2200 sq km) was recently created. The Cheetah's biology has been well studied in Africa but, because of its rarity, hardly at all in the Asian deserts. It is proposed to reintroduce this splendid animal to the Ustyurt Reserve in the near future.

Among the hoofed mammals, two species are typical of the Soviet deserts. One is the Asian Wild Ass, Kulan, or Dzhigetai (*Equus hemionus*), the other the Goitred Gazelle (*Gazella subgutturosa*). The Asian Wild Ass is elegant, slim and long-legged, with a handsome fawn and white coat, set off by a black mane and a black stripe down the back, and it lives in the deserts and semi-deserts of Central Asia. Its range has contracted and its population has fallen steeply, and it is included in the Red Books of both the USSR and the IUCN. Fortunately, the species has recently recovered from its 'endangered' status and is gradually re-establishing its numbers in several parts of its former range in the Soviet Union.

The Wild Ass eats a wide variety of plants, especially grasses, wormwoods (*Artemisia*) and Russian thistles (*Salsola*). It can alter its diet considerably to suit the season, but it always needs watering places. In the hot summer, when it has to eat dry plant food, the ass must drink regularly, so its distribution is determined largely by that of suitable water-holes. The asses travel slowly to the water, setting off shortly before sunset, so that they drink in darkness. In autumn and winter, the asses form herds of up to 100 individuals. Each herd has a complex social structure. The herd leader is a stallion, but there is also a senior mare who shares some of the functions of leadership. One or two other mares act as intermediaries; the rest are submissive.

Although they can be inquisitive, the asses are cautious animals, with superb vision, hearing and sense of smell. It is almost impossible to approach closer than about $\frac{3}{4}$ mile (1.2 km) without being noticed. The asses rely on their ability to run far and fast to escape danger. They can sustain a speed of 40 mph (64 km/hr) for many miles, and can gallop faster over short distances.

The mares are sexually mature at 2 or 3 years old, giving birth to their first colts at three or four years of age. The male is sexually mature at 3 years, but cannot mate until he has displaced the dominant male from a herd. The herd leaders are between 4 and 10 years old, and reign for about 5 or 6 years, after which they are chased from the herd by younger males. The exiled leaders often join unmated colts. During the mating period, these small herds of males split up in search of mares, and bitter fights break out between the bachelors and the new herd leaders. Baring their teeth, with ears laid back and eyes blazing, the asses rush at each other, trying to seize an ankle joint. It one succeeds, it twists its opponent's leg until the animal crashes to the ground. Immediately, the victor rushes in to bite the neck of its rival. If the loser manages to stagger to his feet and gallop away, the dominant male usually chases him and grabs his tail in his mouth to prevent his escape. He then tries to trip up the unfortunate male again and inflict further injuries. The males bear evidence of these battles in the form of numerous, often large, scars, but

deaths have never been recorded and are probably very rare indeed.

The mares are pregnant for 345 days. During the last few days before birth, a mare grazes away from the herd and allows no other ass, not even her famished previous year's foal, to approach her. As soon as the new foal is born, she licks it, and a few hours later, it is standing unsteadily, grazing with its mother. The mare and foal rejoin the herd two or three days after the birth. The other asses all sniff the foal; some may try to bite it, but the mare protects her offspring fiercely, as does the herd leader. However, if a foal is ill, it is attacked and chased out by the entire herd, including its mother, and is not welcomed back until it is well again.

There are now large numbers of Asian Wild Asses in the Badkhyz Nature Reserve in south Turkmenia, and on the island of Barsakelmes in the Aral Sea. Fortunately, they breed well in captivity, providing stocks of animals for release into the wild.

The Goitred Gazelle is an elegant, long-legged, medium-sized gazelle, weighing from 40 to 73 lb (18 to 33 kg). The females are smaller than the males, and usually lack horns. In the USSR, it occurs in the deserts of Azerbaidzhan, Kazakhstan, Uzbekistan, Kirgizia, Tadzhikistan and Turkmenia, living on plains or hills, and preferring firm gound. Its range also includes the deserts of Arabia, Iran, Afghanistan, West Pakistan and eastern China. It eats various grasses and shrubs. It can run at almost 40 mph (62 km/hr). In spring and summer it lives singly or in small groups, but in autumn it forms herds, each containing several dozen individuals. The mating period is in October and November, and pregnancy lasts about $5\frac{1}{2}$ months. Before giving birth, a female leaves the herd and chooses a flat area hidden by low shrubs. There she gives birth to twins, or, rarely, a single calf. At about two months old, the calves start to graze away from their mother, and start to become independent. Wolves are the gazelles' chief enemy, and in a snowy winter, many are killed. Because of its rarity and diminishing numbers, the Goitred Gazelle is being specially protected in a number of reserves. In addition, special nurseries have been created for captive breeding.

The most highly adapted of the desert mammals are the remarkable little rodents known as jerboas (family Dipodidae). More than 20 species live in the Old World semi-deserts and deserts, from the Sahara to the Gobi. Few members of the vast order of rodents can run on two legs, and the jerboas are among the fastest. Some species can run as fast as 33 ft (10 m) per second, or 22 mph (36 km/hr), and

As wild as the remote Kazakhstan desert landscape in which it lives, this Asian Wild Ass, or Kulan, is ready to run, at 40 mph (60 km per hour) or more, at the first sign of danger.

leap 10 ft (3 m) or more. Their high speed is combined with exceptional manoeuvrability, enabling them to change direction abruptly and unexpectedly, an important method of escaping predators. Many of their potential enemies can run faster, but none can change direction abruptly and unexpectedly at high speed, and many give up the chase.

Surprisingly, the jerboas' superb running ability on their long back legs is combined with great proficiency in digging burrows with their tiny front legs. These underground refuges, where the little animals hide during the day, may contain several chambers joined by tunnels. Exits from the burrow are closed from within by a plug of soil, which not only camouflages the openings but also helps to keep the burrow at a constant temperature. Some of the side tunnels end just below the surface, and the jerboas can use these as escape routes, digging their way to the surface almost instantly in case of danger.

Jerboas have remarkably keen senses of hearing and sight. Some species have very long, mobile ears. The field of view of the large protruding eyes can cover almost 360 degrees in both the horizontal and vertical planes. Sitting motionless, a jerboa detects the slightest movement from any direction.

In deserts, where the temperature may drop below freezing point in winter, the jerboas hibernate for 6 to 7 months. With the first frosts, they dig their deep winter burrows, which are remarkably complex in plan. Here they hibernate, rolled into a ball, until spring.

The Pygmy Jerboa (*Salpingotus crassicauda*) has a disproportionately large head. It lives in the deserts to the northwest of Lake Balkhash, in the Kara-Kum Desert, in the Zaisan depression in southern Kazakhstan, and also in the Gobi Desert. Until recently, the details of this animal's life were unknown, but some features have now been recorded. Pygmy Jerboas live on the edges of sparsely wooded, sandy hillocks, and on clay plains with small patches of sand and little vegetation. Their permanent burrows are very large relative to the small size of the animal, and reach a depth of $6\frac{1}{2}$ to 10 ft (2 to 3 m). They are provided with various exits and nesting chambers. The little animals dig so fast that it is impossible to see the ends of their paws as they flash up and down. So far, information about breeding

Pygmy Jerboa (Salpingota crassicauda)

Small Five-toed Jerboa (Allactaga elater)

Comb-toed Jerboa (Paradipus ctenodactylus)

Great Gerbil (Rhombomys opimus)

ABOVE *The Soviet deserts contain a great variety of small burrowing rodents, notably the jerboas and gerbils. These little mammals can run extremely fast on their hind legs.*

is sparse. There are from 2 to 5 young in each litter, most often 3. At 6 days old, the young can already make small frog-like jumps, landing on all four legs. This behaviour has not been seen in other jerboas. Hibernation starts with the first frosts and lasts until late spring.

Best represented in the deserts of the USSR are the five-toed jerboas *Allactaga*, of which there are about 10 species. The Northern Five-toed, or Great, Jerboa (*A. major*) is the largest jerboa in the USSR, reaching some 10 in (26 cm) in length. In the deserts of Central Asia lives the Lesser Fat-tailed Jerboa (*Pygeretmus platyurus*) and the Lesser Five-toed Jerboa (*Alactagulus acontion*), the only member of its

genus, which can dig burrows in very dense clay soil. The main tunnel may be as much as 16 or even 20 ft (5 or 6 m) long.

The three-toed jerboas include the Comb-toed Jerboa (*Paradipus ctenodactylus*), the only member of its genus. This little animal lives in the sandy Kara-Kum and Kyzyl-Kum deserts, and is endemic to the USSR.

The gerbils and jirds (sub-family Gerbillinae) are another group of rodents with many desert representatives. Of the 102 species in the world, 9 live in the USSR. These little animals resemble rats or mice, except that the tail is furry and often bears a tassel at the end. The commonest, the Great Gerbil (*Rhombomys opimus*), can grow to 8 in (20 cm) long. It is found in deserts and semi-deserts, especially sandy ones, from the Caspian Sea to Central Asia. It is a prodigious digger, and its complex, deep burrows may have hundreds of exits. It lives in colonies and is active by day. It eats mainly the green parts of grasses and the twigs of shrubs, and stores food for the winter. Between March and June, the female produces 2 or 3 litters, each containing from 2 to 12 young, usually 4 to 6. Unfortunately, the Great Gerbil carries diseases such as plague.

The tables of typical birds and mammals of deserts, on pages 217–18, do not contain animals such as the Red Fox (*Vulpes vulpes*) that are common in other zones, too, but they still contain many species, including 50 of mammals. This high figure is due largely to the rodents, especially the jerboas.

BELOW *There is an impressive number of nature reserves in the steppes and deserts of the Soviet Union; some, like the Repetek reserve, have existed for over 50 years. Others have only been established recently, like the large reserve of 860 sq miles (2230 sq km), created in 1985 in the Ustyurt Plateau.*

Desert nature reserves

The landscapes, flora and fauna of a typical ephemeral-plant desert are conserved in the Arnasai Reserve, with an area of 245 sq miles (634 sq km), created in 1977 in the Dzhizak area of Uzbekistan. In 1971 the Karakul Reserve, with an area of 55 sq miles (143 sq km), was created near Bukhara, Uzbekistan. Another nature reserve, the Kyzyl-Kum, with an area of 15 sq miles (40 sq km), lies on the boundary between Uzbekistan and Turkmenistan, on the middle reaches of the Amu-Darya River. It contains 255 species of birds and 37 of mammals. The island of Barsakelmes in the Aral Sea, with an area of 71 sq miles (183 sq km), was converted into a nature reserve in 1939 and has a typical northern desert landscape. It contains large herds of Goitred Gazelles (*Gazella subgutturosa*) and Asian Wild Asses (*Equus hemionus*). There is a total of 257 species of higher plants, 8 of mammals and 202 of birds, mostly introduced from the mainland.

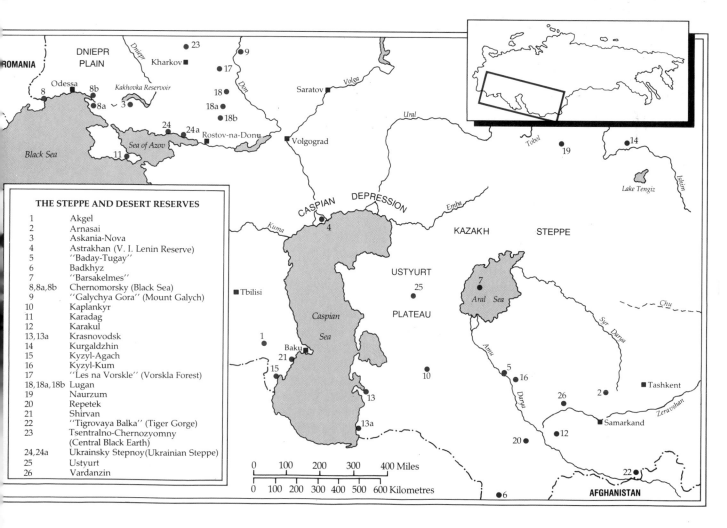

THE STEPPE AND DESERT RESERVES

1 Akgel
2 Arnasai
3 Askania-Nova
4 Astrakhan (V. I. Lenin Reserve)
5 "Baday-Tugay"
6 Badkhyz
7 "Barsakelmes"
8,8a,8b Chernomorsky (Black Sea)
9 "Galychya Gora" (Mount Galych)
10 Kaplankyr
11 Karadag
12 Karakul
13,13a Krasnovodsk
14 Kurgaldzhin
15 Kyzyl-Agach
16 Kyzyl-Kum
17 "Les na Vorskle" (Vorskla Forest)
18,18a,18b Lugan
19 Naurzum
20 Repetek
21 Shirvan
22 "Tigrovaya Balka" (Tiger Gorge)
23 Tsentralno-Chernozyomny (Central Black Earth)
24,24a Ukrainsky Stepnoy (Ukrainian Steppe)
25 Ustyurt
26 Vardanzin

TOP *A Giant Fennel towers above the sand at the Badkhyz Nature Reserve, in the extreme south of the Soviet Union; these imposing plants may grow more than 6 ft (2 m) high, and provide a home for a great variety of beetles and other insects.*
ABOVE Placoderus scapularis, *one of the many species of beetles that live on the Giant Fennel plants, photographed at the Badkhyz Nature Reserve.*

ABOVE *The Repetek Biosphere Nature Reserve was established way back in 1928 to protect a corner of the southeastern part of the great Kara-Kum sand desert.*
LEFT *A view along the Kyzyl–Dzhar Ravine at Badkhyz.*

One of the most interesting desert reserves is Badkhyz, in the extreme south of the USSR, which was created in 1941 with an area of 340 sq miles (880 sq km). It includes the Er-Oilan-Duz depression and its salt lake. There are 430 species of higher plants, of which about 10 per cent are endemic to the region. There are no fewer than 37 species of reptiles, 255 of birds, and 40 of mammals.

The vast Kaplankyr Reserve in Turkmenia, with an area of 2200 sq miles (5700 sq km), was established in 1979 to protect an area of gravelly, stony and clay deserts. The Krasnovodsk Reserve, with two areas on the shore of the Caspian Sea covering a total of 1012 sq miles (2620 sq km), was created in 1932.

The 134 sq miles (346 sq km) Repetek Biosphere Nature Reserve conserves the unique natural history of the southeast Kara-Kum sandy desert. It was created in 1928 from a previous station set up in 1912. It contains 211 species of higher plants, 23 of reptiles, 196 of birds and 29 of mammals including a number of rare species.

9 WETLANDS

In this chapter, I shall give a brief survey of the USSR's rivers and lakes, but will concentrate mainly on the vast marshy areas that form wetlands of international importance, and their rich birdlife.

Wetlands have a variety of distinctive plants and animals, especially birds. They may occur in any of the geographical zones, from the cold northern tundra to the hot southern deserts. Large numbers of waterbirds, from herons to gulls and waders, breed on lake shores and islands, marshes and reedbeds. Their colonies may contain several hundred thousand individuals. The great southern lakes and inland seas, such as the Caspian Sea, are also internationally important wintering sites for waterbirds migrating south from the vast taiga and tundra regions.

The Caspian Sea is the largest inland sea in the world. The world's deepest inland sea, Lake Baikal, also lies in the USSR. Mighty rivers flow through the country, fed by masses of springs and larger tributaries which drain vast areas of land. There are about 3 million rivers in the USSR. More than 80 per cent of their water flows northwards and eastwards, into the Arctic and Pacific Oceans. Most of them are less than 600 miles (1000 km) long, but the longest – the Yenisei, Lena, Ob and Irtysh – are more than 2485 miles (4000 km) long. The longest river system, the Ob-Irtysh, is 3362 miles (5410 km) long; in the European part of the USSR, the Volga is 2194 miles (3530 km) long, but in volume of water transported, the Yenisei, the fifth largest river in the world, is the largest, with an average annual flow of 685,100 cu ft (19,400 cu m) of water per second. Other large rivers include the Amur, Pechora, Kolyma, Severnaya Dvina, Amu-darya, Indigirka and Dniepr. Most of the rivers freeze over for 2 to 7 months of the year.

The USSR has 2.8 million lakes, with a total area of about 189,200 sq miles (490,000 sq km), excluding the Caspian Sea and Aral Sea. Fourteen lakes, with a water area larger than 386 sq miles (1000 sq km), are among the largest lakes in the world. These 14 lakes contain 6530 sq miles (27,200 cu km) of water, of which 85 per cent is in Lake Baikal. Most of the lakes lie in the northwestern European part of the USSR; the tundra, especially, has many lakes. The largest mountain lakes, including Issyk-Kul, Teletsk and Karakul, are mostly in the Central Asian mountains. The amount of salts dissolved in the lake waters varies a great deal. Most of the lakes contain fresh water, but in the dry steppe and semi-deserts, there are many salt-lakes, formed as a result of evaporation in the hot sun.

LEFT *The 'Žuvintas' Nature Reserve in Lithuania.*
RIGHT *The stately Khanka Lotus grows in the vast Khanka marshes in Ussuriland, in the extreme south of the Soviet Far East.*

Types of marshes

These occupy about 772, 260 sq miles (2 million sq km), or some 10 per cent of the USSR's land area. Because of climatic and other conditions, most of them are in the forest zone. The marshiest areas are in Polese, along the Pripyat River in Belorussia, as well as in the north European part of the USSR, the West Siberian Plain and the Taimyr Plain. Although there are marshes in every zone, the largest areas are in the forest zone.

ABOVE *The Long-toed Stint, photographed here in June on Sakhalin Island, is an attractive little wader which breeds only in the Soviet Far East.*

There are two main types of marsh, the low marsh and raised marsh, or bog. Low marshes are generally on low ground where the groundwater is near the surface, and contain a great variety of dominant plants, including sedges, birch and alder trees. Raised marshes, dominated by sphagnum mosses, may evolve from low marshes, or result when lakes are overgrown with water plants. They are most common in the forest zone, and contain a great variety of unique plants, including a number of drought-resistant types. Despite the wet environment, they suffer from physiological drought in the cold, acid subsoil. There are no raised marshes in the southern part of the USSR, as the hot climate prevents the growth of sphagnum moss.

Marsh birds

Different species are characteristic of low and raised marshes. In the raised marshes of the middle forest zone, live many tundra birds, including the Willow Ptarmigan (*Lagopus lagopus*) and the Golden Plover (*Pluvialis apricaria*) as well as tundra insects, including relict species. Low marshes provide a refuge for more southerly species. The great majority of these are from the wooded steppe or mixed forest zones, occasionally the taiga zone.

TOP *A Hooded Crane at its nest in the River Bikin valley, Ussuriland, in May. The first nest was found in 1974.*
ABOVE *A close-up view of the nest and eggs.*

A Far Eastern Curlew on a raised marsh in the middle reaches of the River Bikin, in June.

Among the birds, almost all the USSR's cranes live in the marshes; only the Demoiselle Crane (*Anthropoides virgo*) nests in the steppe and semi-desert. The Great White, or Siberian Crane (*Grus leucogeranus*) and the Sandhill Crane (*G. canadensis*) live in the tundra marshes, the rest in the marshes of temperate latitudes. The most common and widespread species is the Common Crane (*G. grus*), which prefers to nest on raised marshes in the forest zone. The Ussuri area, with its vast marshes and the great Khanka Lowland, is a real paradise for the exotic species of cranes. Three species of crane live there. The Manchurian Crane (*G. japonensis*) and the White-naped Crane (*G. vipio*) both nest in great marshes overgrown with reeds and other plants, while the Hooded Crane (*G. monachus*) prefers the dense raised marshes of the taiga, along the upper reaches of the larger rivers of the Sikhote-Alin Mountains. Until recently, nothing was known of the biology of the Hooded Crane. Then, in 1974, the nest and eggs were described, together with other aspects of its biology. In the valley of the Bikin River in the middle of the Ussuri region, where the first Hooded Crane's nest was found, it appears in early April. Immediately after their arrival, a pair begin their courtship dances, which are solitary affairs, in contrast to the group performances of other cranes.

The habitat of this bird is mountain-taiga raised marsh, often hummocky, with sphagnum moss and scattered larch trees, lying in the valleys between the conical Ussuri hills. The nesting area, on the same site as the courtship grounds, is usually limited by the area of the chosen marsh, some $1\frac{1}{2}$ to $2\frac{1}{3}$ sq miles (4 to 6 sq km). Egg-laying begins in the second half of April. The nest is a heap of vegetation about 330 ft (100 m) out in the marsh, among stunted woody shrubs. There are only 2 eggs in a clutch. From the middle of August, the cranes fly south to winter in Japan.

Most of the Manchurian Cranes nest on Lake Khanka. Surveys at Lake Khanka in summer have shown that more than 100 birds live there; about half the adults breed and only 18 chicks a year survive to maturity. Nevertheless, the Khanka population of Japanese cranes is thought to be the largest in the USSR – an indication of just how rare these beautiful birds are.

Another marsh bird of the Ussuri, the Far Eastern Curlew (*Numenius madagascariensis*), breeds among raised marshes and hummocky meadows in the Soviet Far East and in eastern Siberia, wintering mainly in Australia. This little-known wader does not adapt easily to changes in land-use, and its population is now high only where there are no people. The birds settle in comparatively dry but partly flooded marshes, especially those with abundant mosses and lichens. The nest is in a little pit on the ground, and the full clutch is 4 eggs.

In the marshes of Sakhalin Island lives an extremely rare, unique wader, the Spotted Greenshank (*Tringa guttifer*), an endemic of the USSR with a restricted range. It is included in both the Red Book of the USSR and the Red Data Book of the IUCN. Until recently nothing was known of its nesting and distribution. It has now been established that it nests in Sakhalin Island near muddy pools and lagoon shores, preferably marshy inlets close to larch woods. Such sites are flooded by the sea during windy weather, and so, unlike most waders, the Spotted Greenshank builds a nest in trees at about 8 to 15 ft (2.5 to 4.5 m) above the ground, in small colonies. Little is known of this bird's life-history, but it is certain that the population is small. During migration the birds fly south in pairs, alone or with other waders, to Taiwan, the Philippines, or Borneo. The colour photographs on this page of the adult bird and its fluffy day-old chick, which my friend Yuri Shibnev photographed in Sakhalin, are unique.

Wetlands of international importance

Those wetlands in the USSR which are most important for nesting, migrating, or wintering birds have been assigned to the MAR International Wetlands Programme. The share of this land which is in nature reserves is considerable. For example, the Gulf of Kandalaksha on the White Sea has the Kandalaksha Reserve and the Volga Delta has the Astrakhan Reserve. One of the main purposes of the

TOP *The Spotted Greenshank is a rare wader that breeds only on Sakhalin Island in the Soviet Far East. Although a few relatives lay their eggs in abandoned songbird nests above ground, this species is unique in building its own nest in a tree; other waders nest on the ground.*
ABOVE *A one-day-old Spotted Greenshank chick; this is the first photograph ever taken in the wild.*

MAR programme is the conservation of migratory birds which may nest in one country, winter in another and, during migration, rest in several others. The wetlands are especially important for maintaining the migration routes of birds, and this was taken account of in the USSR's 1980 law on conservation and the uses of animal species, which ensures the protection of the major migratory sites, including the banning or controlling of hunting.

On the west Estonian coast is the Gulf of Matsalu, known to naturalists for more than a century as a stronghold of breeding birds. The State nature reserve created here in 1957 with an area of 153 sq miles (397 sq km) now forms part of a larger area of 188 sq miles (486 sq km), which forms an internationally important wetland reserve. More than half of the nature reserve – 102 sq miles (263 sq km) is water. Matsalu was declared a wetland of international importance in 1975.

The most distinctive feature of Matsalu is its huge area of reedbeds, covering over $11\frac{1}{2}$ sq miles (30 sq km). On the land side the reeds are sparse and mixed with grasses; nearer the gulf the reeds become taller and more luxuriant, but only near the deep water do the rich water plants and invertebrates of the spring floods appear.

The reedbeds are a fine feeding ground for the birds. The most interesting birds of the nature reserve nest there, including the Greylag Goose (*Anser anser*, 220 nesting pairs), the Mute Swan (*Cygnus olor*, about 35 pairs), the Eurasian Bittern, (*Botaurus stellaris*, about 15 pairs), the fairly numerous Marsh Harrier (*Circus aeruginosus*), large colonies of Black-headed Gulls (*Larus ridibundus*, 10,000 pairs), and huge numbers of Common Coots (*Fulica atra*), as well as large populations of various species of duck. Matsalu is also an important stop-over for thousands of Common Cranes (*Grus grus*) on their autumn migration.

Matsalu is one of the few Soviet nature reserves where a limited amount of human activity is allowed. This is done to conserve many habitats of the nature reserve, such as flood plains, or coastal pastures, which serve as nesting sites for waders and other birds. If the grass is not cut in time, shrubs grow in the water meadows, reducing their

The Paddyfield Warbler nests among large reedbeds in the southern USSR. This one was photographed in June near Azov, on the north-east shore of the Sea of Azov.

value as a habitat for birds. The birds which breed in these areas are mainly waders, including the colourful Ruff (*Philomachus pugnax*), which conducts its communal spring courtship tournaments on small hillocks, the Northern Lapwing (*Vanellus vanellus*), Common Greenshank (*Tringa totanus*), and Black-tailed Godwit (*Limosa limosa*).

The unusual stony islands, overgrown with juniper, contain many nesting birds, including the Common Eider (*Somateria mollissima*), the Velvet, or White-winged, Scoter

A Eurasian Bittern sits motionless at its nest hidden deep in a dense reedbed at Zhuvintas Reserve, Lithuania, its vertical markings camouflaging it superbly.

An Arctic Tern at the Gulf of Matsalu Nature Reserve on the west coast of Estonia. This graceful bird migrates to Antarctica each year, further than any other species.

A clutch of Eider Duck eggs in the process of hatching in their down-lined nest in the Gulf of Kandalaksha Nature Reserve, a major wetland reserve on the White Sea.

(*Melanitta fusca*) and Caspian Tern (*Hydroprogne caspia*). Three species of gull breed there: the Great Black-backed Gull (*Larus marinus*), the Common, or Mew, Gull (*Larus canus*), and the Herring Gull (*Larus argentatus*). There is a constant struggle for existence as gulls rob the nests of the other birds and seize their chicks.

On the island of Papilaid in 1983 my colleagues and I found a nest of the Barnacle Goose (*Branta leucopsis*), an extraordinary find in these latitudes, considering that the main breeding area is on Novaya Zemlya and Spitsbergen. Local ornithologists told us that this was their third nesting year. They have also nested elsewhere in the Baltic, on the Swedish island of Gotland.

THE GULF OF KANDALAKSHA

This internationally important wetland in the White Sea, with a total area of 800 sq miles (2080 sq km), is based on the 224 sq miles (581 sq km) Kandalaksha Reserve, of which 157 sq miles (406 sq km) is water and 43 sq miles (112 sq km) forest and meadow. The wetland was established in 1975, but the nature reserve dates from as long ago as 1939.

The nature reserve lies in the wooded tundra and tundra sub-zones of the northern European taiga. Its vegetation is

characteristic of these sub-zones, apart from the fact that Kandalaksha has no permafrost. The larger islands of the Gulf of Kandalaksha are covered with pine-spruce woods. The shrub layer consists of Bilberry (*Vaccinium myrtilus*), Northern Bilberry (*V. uliginosum*) and Cowberry (*V. vitis-idiae*). The lower levels of the beaches teem with marine invertebrates, including worms, sandhoppers, molluscs, and crustaceans. Birdlife is particularly rich, especially the Kandalaksha population of Eider Ducks (*Somateria mollissima*) which is 20 times as large as it was when the reserve was created, thanks to the removal of hunting and other human pressures. Apart from the Eiders, waterbirds which regularly nest here include the Mallard (*Anas platyrhynchos*), Common Goldeneye (*Bucephala clangula*), Common Scoter (*Melanitta nigra*), Velvet Scoter (*M. fusca*), Red-breasted Merganser (*Mergus serrator*) and many species of waders. In addition, there are 550 species of plants, 23 of land mammals, and 10 of marine mammals, chiefly seals, as well as about 210 nesting and migratory bird species.

Apart from the Kandalaksha Gulf, the conservation area includes the 'Seven Islands' Reserve protecting part of the Barents Sea and the Ainov Islands; these islands have large bird colonies.

ABOVE *Papilaid Island, part of the Matsalu Nature Reserve.*
LEFT *A Barnacle Goose at its nest on Papilaid, far to the south of its normal breeding range in the high Arctic.*

THE V.I. LENIN NATURE RESERVE AT ASTRAKHAN

One of the oldest nature reserves in the USSR, this was created in 1919 by a decree of Lenin to conserve the unique natural complex of the Volga Delta, notably the huge breeding colonies of birds, the moulting grounds for waterfowl and the vast spawning grounds of commercially useful fish. The area of the nature reserve includes three areas of the Volga Delta covering 245 sq miles (634 sq km). Since 1975 it has formed part of the internationally important 'Volga Delta' Wetland, 2500 sq miles (6500 sq km) in area. The reserve is in the Caspian lowland, 90 ft (27 m) below sea-level. It is a fine example of a large river delta with a variety of different landscapes, especially near the sea. The coastline of the delta stretches for 124 miles (200 km). The Volga flows into the Caspian Sea through nearly 800 channels. There are nine natural zones in the delta, the most important of which are the middle, lower, and cultivated zones of the delta, the island zone of the fore-delta, and the fore-delta itself. The climate is moderately continental with a hot summer and a cold winter. There are many oxbows and delta lakes; the nature reserve contains only fresh water. The land of the delta is constantly growing at the expense of the sea, thanks to the huge volume of sediment borne and deposited by the Volga.

The nature reserve lies in the Caspian desert zone, but the vegetation is clearly intrazonal, typical of a delta, with mainly riverside plants. There are 290 plant species, including many endemic and relict forms. About 500 species of freshwater invertebrates have been recorded in the waters of the nature reserve, including an extremely rich variety of crustaceans. There are 1,250 insect species. An unpleasant aspect of the insect fauna is the large number of bloodsucking insects. The vast spawning grounds of the Volga Delta, together with the rich feeding grounds for adult as well as immature fish, have resulted in the most varied fish population in the reserve. There are some 50 fish species, the most valuable being the Sturgeon (*Acipenser sturio*). There are 2 species of amphibians and 6 of reptiles. Various mammals, including the Wild Boar (*Sus scrofa*) live there, too. The Volga Delta is a veritable bird paradise. In the nature reserve more than 250 species have been recorded, of which 100 nest there. Thanks to the high productivity of the waters and the dense vegetation, both carnivorous and vegetarian birds can find plenty of food and shelter. The huge populations of delta birds form an island of life in the desert around the delta. The overwhelming majority are water and marsh birds.

In the fore-delta, common birds include the Mute Swan (*Cygnus olor*), Mallard (*Anas platyrhynchos*), greylag goose (*Anser anser*), and Red-crested Pochard (*Netta rufina*); masses of Common Coots (*Fulica atra*) and Great-crested Grebes (*Podiceps cristatus*) also nest there. Some of the most interesting species are the Eastern White Pelican (*Pelecanus onocrotalus*) and the Dalmatian Pelican (*P. crispus*). The Eastern White Pelican is a large bird weighing up to 24 lb (11 kg). The males appear identical to the females, but the young do not have the adults' pink-tinted feathers. This pelican is now rare, and in many places endangered. In the USSR it is found on large lakes and river deltas on the Black and Caspian Seas, and in the salt lakes of Kazakhstan.

In the Volga Delta, pelicans are seen as early as the first days of March. In mid-April they collect in groups at the nesting site, in pairs, and indulge in courtship displays, in which they make strange 'mooing' calls, lift their wings, jump up or fly in a circle, land again and rub each others' bills. The female then sits tightly on the site of her future nest. Colonies of pelicans may have 700 or more nests. Unfortunately the colonies in the Volga Delta have recently contained only a few dozen. Pelican colonies are in shallow standing water and, if there are many nests, a large raft-like structure is created. In the Volga Delta artificial rafts are also now being built for these birds. The male helps his mate to build the huge nest very quickly, in

A party of Eastern White Pelicans on the shore of Lake Manych-Gudilo, in the Kalmyk Republic in the north Caucasus region. Sadly, these are now rare birds.

A Caspian Turtle on the delta of the River Atrek, which flows into the south-eastern part of the Caspian Sea. This area contains many interesting animals.

A male Black-crowned Night Heron stands guard at its nest in the Danube Delta Reserve. This bird, largely nocturnal as its name suggests, is common in suitable areas.

Another member of the heron family, also photographed at the Danube Delta Reserve, is this Squacco Heron. Like the others, it feeds on frogs, fish and insects.

two or three days. The birds may steal material from their neighbours, especially from related species such as the Dalmatian Pelican. The normal clutch is 2 eggs, which the female incubates for 33 days. At first, when the chicks are still weak, the parents feed them with half-digested food. Later they bring them small fish, which the chicks take from their gullets. Migration from the nesting area is late, after the first light frosts. Pelicans feed largely on fish. The birds cannot dive but they can plunge the neck and upper body into the water. Usually they fish in well co-ordinated groups, driving the fish to the bank so that they are easier to catch. The slightly more widespread Dalmatian Pelican is very similar in its life-style to the Eastern White Pelican, but it lays more eggs — up to four.

In reedbeds and shrub thickets of the Volga Delta there are colonies of various species of herons and related birds, including the Great White Egret and Little Egret (*Egretta alba, E. garzetta*), Great Cormorant (*Phalacrocorax carbo*), Grey Heron (*Ardea cinerea*), Cattle Egret (*Bubulcus ibis*), Squacco Heron (*Ardeola ralloides*), Black-crowned Night-heron (*Nycticorax nycticorax*), Glossy Ibis (*Plegadis falcinellus*), and small numbers of Eurasian Spoonbills (*Platalea leucorodia*).

A handsome Little Egret at the Volga Delta; in addition to this and the other two herons shown on this page, a number of other herons are found in the Soviet wetlands.

LEFT *This beautiful Glossy Ibis was photographed at the Danube Delta Reserve in June. It nests in colonies, often in the company of Spoonbills, herons and cormorants, and also breeds in a few other wetland areas of southern USSR, although it is generally rather scarce.*

The Great White Egret is a large snow-white bird, weighing, on average, 3.3 lb (1.5 kg). It is a very widespread migratory species, preferring to breed in steppe or desert wetlands with vast reed or bulrush beds. Its nesting site is the least accessible part of a reed or bulrush bed, but in search of food it may visit cultivated land, where it is extremely wary. The birds pair for life. Rarely a nest is built in a tree. The nest has 3 to 5 eggs and incubation lasts 25 or 26 days. The egret's diet consists of fish, water insects and their larvae, grasshoppers, locusts, and small mammals. The Little Egret often breeds in the same sites as its much larger relative. Apart from the size difference, the two species are similar, though the Little Egret is the less wary. Its nest is often built in a tree, and contains 4 to 6 eggs. It eats small fish, insects and their larvae and other water invertebrates.

The Black-crowned Night-heron is almost cosmopolitan in its distribution. Unlike daytime herons, it has a fairly stumpy body structure and a short neck. It likes marshes overgrown with woody plants and it nests in trees, rarely in reedbeds. Night-heron colonies can be very large – as many as several thousand pairs, usually mixed with other species of herons. As its name suggests, this heron is nocturnal, usually spending the day standing motionless in small flocks in trees or bulrushes, hiding from the sunlight.

Like other herons it prefers animal food. In the Volga Delta its main food is water animals, insects, frogs, lizards, and small rodents.

The Eurasian Penduline Tit (*Remiz pendulinus*) is a typical perching-bird of the Volga Delta. Its nest, skilfully woven of poplar catkins and other vegetable material, can sometimes be seen on the drooping ends of willow branches. This bird, widespread in the USSR, prefers thickets or woods on river banks that flood occasionally. It is common in the mountain foothills. In the Tien Shan Mountains, for example, the black-headed subspecies (*R. p. coronatus*) occurs in the willow thickets of the mountain river valleys. Pair formation takes place in the second half of April and the birds soon start nest-building. The walls of the nest are so strong that it hangs from the tree without breaking for several years. It is usually built at the end of a drooping branch over the water, no more than 10 ft (3 m) above it. The birds take no less than three weeks to build a nest. They sometimes start laying their eggs before the nest is completed, but more often do so two or three days after it is completed. There are 6 to 9 white eggs in a typical clutch. The female incubates for 13 or 14 days and the young fledge after 16 to 18 days in the nest. After the young have flown, the adults continue feeding them for several days, after which the family flock moves to the

thickets beside the water. The diet of the Penduline Tit consists mainly of small insects and their larvae.

The Volga Delta in the summer months is a moulting retreat for many of the river ducks from much of the USSR, especially the Mallard (*Anas platyrhynchos*), Northern Pintail (*A. acuta*), Teal (*A. crecca*), Garganey (*A. querquedula*), Gadwall (*A. strepera*), and Northern Shoveler (*A. clypeata*). The Greylag Goose (*Anser anser*) is also common.

The delta also forms an important 'crossroads' for the migration routes of many waterfowl. The birds that rest in the fore-delta each spring include the species of duck mentioned above, as well as Tufted Ducks (*Aythya fuligula*). In autumn the relative numbers of the different species change somewhat, the most numerous species being the Teal, Garganey, Mallard, Gadwall, Mute Swan (*Cygnus olor*) and Whooper Swan (*Cygnus cygnus*).

A flock of Sandwich Terns takes a rest at the Black Sea Nature Reserve. This is one of ten species of terns that breed in the USSR. Graceful in flight, these slender relatives of gulls have been aptly called 'sea swallows'.

The 17 mammals of the Volga Delta include large numbers of the impressive Wild Boar (*Sus scrofa*). It has ample food in the form of water chestnuts, seedlings, and roots of water plants. The nature reserve undertakes scientific investigations into changes in the natural communities of the Lower Volga as a result of a generally falling water level in the Caspian Sea. In recent years, however, the sea level has risen by 43 in (108 cm). The Caspian ornithological station in the nature reserve coordinates investigations into the Caspian area, and rings (or bands) birds to study their movements.

THE BLACK SEA WETLANDS

The Black Sea nature reserve, in the Kherson area of the Ukraine, was created in 1927 and covers 278 sq miles (719 sq km), of which 76 sq miles (197 sq km) are dry land, mostly coastal. It comprises five separate areas. In 1973 it was enlarged because new land was exposed by the falling sea level in the eastern Gulf of Tendrov and part of the Gulf of Yagorlits. In 1981, a subsidiary area of the nature reserve, created in the Danube Delta, was reorganized to form a separate nature reserve. Since 1975 the whole territory of the nature reserve has formed part of an internationally important wetland, occupying 400 sq miles (1038 sq km). The various areas of the reserve have different relief and landscapes; but the land is generally alluvial, of marine origin. The climate is moderately continental, with sultry summers and relatively mild winters. The snow lies for 20 to 40 days in an average winter.

This nature reserve is in the zone of dry south European steppes. There are 595 species of plants, including typical plant communities from steppe, wooded steppe, *solonchak* soil (pale soil rich in soluble salts), salt-resistant plants growing on sand, and plants that grow on the shoreline or submerged in the water.

The steppe and wooded steppe are very rich in insects. The sea contains a rich population of fishes, including Anchovy (*Engraulis encrasicolus*), Sardine (*Sardina pilchardus*), Mackerel (*Scomber scombrus*) and Bonito (*Katsuwonus pelamis*). The reserve has 6 amphibian species and 9 species of reptile.

Most valuable from the viewpoint of conservation are the birds, and it was for them that this unique nature reserve was created. It includes 280 species of nesting, migratory, and wintering birds. There are 153 nesting species, of which 17 do not migrate. Most valuable are the colonies of gulls and terns, particularly those of the Mediterranean Gull (*Larus melanocephalus*), Slender-billed Gull (*L. genei*) and Sandwich Tern (*Sterna sandvicensis*).

ABOVE *A Black-winged Stilt at its nest on the shores of the Sea of Azov; this delicately built, long-legged wader nests in noisy colonies.*

ABOVE *The nature reserves created in the Black Sea and Sea of Azov region protect major wetlands; this is Chooryook Island in the Gulf of Sivash, in the Sea of Azov.*

ABOVE *A mixed breeding colony of Slender-billed Gulls and Mediterranean Gulls (the latter with the black heads) at the Black Sea Nature Reserve, photographed in June.*

Many species of waterfowl nest here, including the Red-breasted Merganser (*Mergus serrator*) Shelduck (*Tadorna tadorna*), Mallard (*Anas platyrhynchos*) Gadwall (*A. strepera*) and Mute Swan (*Cygnus olor*). This reserve also contains many nesting colonies of waders, including the Avocet (*Recurvirostra avosetta*), Black-winged stilt (*Himantopus himantopus*), European Pratincole (*Glareola pratincola*) and Black-winged Pratincole (*Glareola nordmanni*). There are also large breeding colonies of herons and egrets.

Caspian Terns are the world's largest terns. Here a colony shares its breeding site with Sandwich Terns near Azov.

The Gulf of Yagorlits is an important moulting ground for the Mute Swan (*Cygnus olor*). Some 48 species of migratory birds visit the reserve, mainly ducks, waders and perching birds, and there are 47 species of winter visitors. The most southerly nesting colony of Eider Ducks (*Somateria mollissima*) occurs here.

Gulls and terns

The Mediterranean Gull has a restricted range, including only the eastern Mediterranean and Black Sea coasts, although some move to the western Mediterranean, and very small numbers wander to north-west Europe, where a handful have stayed to breed, as in Britain. Its wintering sites are almost identical to its nesting areas. The nature reserves established in the Black Sea protect major colonies of this beautiful gull. The Slender-billed Gull (*Larus genei*) is a particularly elegant bird, with a delicate pink bloom to its underparts, a graceful flight, thin bill, and long wings. It is more widespread than the Mediterranean Gull, and occurs in Asia Minor, the Sea of Azov, the Caspian Sea, and some of the larger lakes in Kazakhstan. Part migratory and part resident, it winters in the Mediterranean and south Caspian areas. It nests in large colonies on the coast and islands, often forming mixed colonies with other gulls, including the Mediterranean Gull. The nests are densely packed in the colony, almost touching one another. The birds lay 2 or 3 eggs. At nesting time they fly far from the breeding colonies to areas of steppe and cultivated land where they gather large quantities of locusts and other insects for their chicks. By the light of the rising sun, a continuous line of gulls can be seen stretching inland on their way to the feeding grounds. As the sun sets over the sea, the flock silently returns to the colony.

The world's largest tern is the Caspian Tern (*Hydroprogne caspia*), which weighs up to 25 oz (700 g). It is a cosmopolitan species. In the USSR it is typical of southern waters, especially the large salt lakes and inland seas. Its preferred nesting site is a sandy or pebbly sea beach or island, usually in a colony of some dozens of pairs, rarely more. The Caspian Tern arrives in the USSR in April, already paired, but the 1 to 3 eggs are not laid until the end of May. Both parents incubate for 22 to 25 days, beginning with the laying of the first egg. The young do not fledge until they are 5 weeks old; September, they embark on their long southward migrations.

The largest gull of the USSR's southern waters is the Great Black-headed Gull (*Larus ichthyaetus*). One of the most powerful of all gulls, it is the size of a Greylag Goose (*Anser anser*) and weighs as much as $4\frac{1}{2}$ lb (2 kg). Its main nesting sites are in the USSR, including dense colonies of several hundred nests, sometimes more. This impressive bird starts nesting in April, usually laying three eggs. The chicks are covered with pale grey down, unlike all other gulls except the rare Relict Gull (*Larus relictus*), described below. Its population fluctuates greatly from year to year.

ABOVE   *Great Black-headed Gulls are among the largest and most impressive of all the world's gulls. This colony was photographed at Lake Sivash, near Azov, in May.*

ABOVE   *This photograph of the very rare Relict Gulls was taken by the author when he had the great fortune to visit a breeding colony at Lake Alakol, Kazakhstan, in May 1978.*

Because this gull is scarce, and its main nesting sites lie in the Soviet Union, it has been included in the Red Book of the USSR. Its population in the USSR has been estimated at about 20,000 nesting pairs, but may be slightly less. Its preferred diet is fish, but it also eats small rodents, such as sousliks, and large insects. For various reasons, including the reduced number of fish and increasing salinity of the water, the areas suitable for this gull are becoming smaller.

The Relict Gull (*Larus relictus*) is much rarer, and nests only in the USSR. There are two widely separated colonies, one in Lake Barun-Torei in the southeast of the Transbaikal, and the other in Lake Alakol in eastern Kazakhstan, near the Chinese border. A single nest discovered in 1984 in Lake Balkhash in a colony of Caspian Terns (*Hydroprogne caspia*) may be that of a pair of gulls wandering away from the Lake Alakol population. The discovery of this gull makes an interesting story. It was first described in 1931 as a subspecies of the Mediterranean Gull. Other ornithologists considered it a hybrid of the Mediterranean Gull and the Great Black-headed Gull. Its true identity was not discovered until 1963, because until then, no-one even knew where these enigmatic birds lived and nested. Then, the first colony was found on Lake Barun-Torei, and the Relict Gull was accepted as a full species. None of the arguments that it was merely a subspecies of the Mediterranean Gull could be sustained; a major piece of evidence was the fact that the Relict Gull's chicks are covered with light grey down, while those of the Mediterranean Gull have grey-brown down with black spots. In modern schemes of zoological classification, the Relict Gull is placed between the Mediterranean and Great Black-headed Gulls.

The Relict Gull is a very rare bird. Ornithologists had hoped that it would be found in other places, in Mongolia and China, and that its total population would be larger than the small numbers that survive in the two remote Russian lakes. To date, however, all searches have been completely in vain.

Several years ago, the author was lucky enough to visit Lake Alakol to see, and photograph, this lovely bird, one of the rarest of the world's gulls. Both nest-sites experience very strong winds for much of the year. Even in summer, there are gales and severe rain storms which can flood or even wash away the small nesting islands. At Alakol, this is because of the position of the lake; about 60 miles (100 km) long, it lies at the very entrance to the Dzhungarian Gate. This relatively low pass lies east of the Dzhungar Alatau Range of the Tien Shan Mountains and the low range of Tarbagatai on the southern flanks of the Altai Mountains,

and has for centuries provided a route from China across Mongolia to Kazakhstan and beyond. The great mountain ranges funnel winds that blow strongly across the Dzhungarian Gate in various directions.

The gulls nest on several islands in the lake, but mainly on Srednii (Middle) Island, about 19 miles (30 km) from the shore. Many other birds breed at Lake Alakol, including large colonies of Great Black-headed Gulls (*Larus ichthyaetus*), Caspian Terns (*Hydroprogne caspia*), Gull-billed Terns (*Gelochelidon nilotica*), and Great Cormorants (*Phalacrocorax carbo*).

In late May 1978, the time of our visit, we found to our delight that the Relict Gulls were starting to nest on a sandy islet only $\frac{1}{2}$ mile (1 km) from the shore. This was a great stroke of luck, because attempting to reach the main colony on Srednii without a powerful boat would have been foolhardy at this time of year, with the chance of a sudden storm. As well as the Relict Gulls, there were other gulls, ducks, geese, and a pair of Mute Swans (*Cygnus olor*) on the islet. I shall never forget the almost black sand of the lake shore and the islet, or my first sight of the rare gulls. We had to photograph them with utmost caution, to avoid the slightest chance of disturbance. They are particularly nervous birds and, if disturbed, may break their eggs with their bills and abandon the colony. Luckily, unauthorized human visits are almost impossible, thanks both to the remoteness of their breeding sites and the stringent conservation laws. Fortunately, the birds were not alarmed, and did not even leave their nests as we approached them stealthily.

Sadly, we learned later from our friends in Kazakhstan that the islet had been washed away during a storm and that the colony had perished – the same sad fate that has befallen many other colonies of this vulnerable bird. The total world population of Relict Gulls is now estimated at a maximum of 1500 to 1800 nesting pairs, although the various colonies experience sharp fluctuations in numbers from year to year. At Alakol, for example, the population fluctuates widely, between a minimum of 30 and a maximum of 1200 nesting pairs. As well as the great losses of eggs and chicks caused by storms and cold, wet weather, the birds suffer from periodic shortages of food. At nesting time, the birds feed almost entirely on chironomid midges. The population of these insects is directly related to the water level. As the level falls, so does the supply of midges, and the gulls and their chicks may starve.

Hopefully, despite the great problems it faces, the Relict Gull will continue to delight naturalists fortunate enough to venture into its remote breeding grounds.

Appendices

The following tables list the most typical animals of each major natural region of the USSR. Latin names given in parentheses are those preferred by many biologists in the West.

TYPICAL BIRDS OF THE ARCTIC COASTS AND ISLANDS

Common name	Latin name	Northern Europe	Western Siberia	Eastern Siberia
Northern Fulmar	Fulmarus glacialis	●		●
Pelagic Cormorant	Phalacrocorax pelagicus			●
Barnacle Goose	Branta leucopsis	●		
Snow Goose	Chen caerulescens (Anser caerulescens)			●
Great Black-backed Gull	Larus marinus	●		
Black-legged Kittiwake	Rissa tridactyla	●	●	●
Ivory Gull	Pagophila eburnea	●		
Little Auk (US: Dovekie)	Alle alle	●		
Razorbill	Alca torda	●		
Guillemot (US: Common Murre)	Uria aalge	●		●
Brünnich's Guillemot (US: Thick-billed Murre)	U. lomvia	●	●	●
Black Guillemot	Cepphus grylle	●	●	●
Pigeon Guillemot	C. columba			●
Crested Auklet	Aethia cristatella			●
Least Auklet	A. pusilla			●
Parakeet Auklet	Cyclorrhynchus psittacula			●
Atlantic Puffin	Fratercula arctica	●		
Horned Puffin	F. corniculata			●
Tufted Puffin	Lunda cirrhata			●

TYPICAL BIRDS OF THE TUNDRA

Common name	Latin name	Northern Europe	Western Siberia	Eastern Siberia
Red-throated Diver (US: Red-throated Loon)	Gavia stellata	●	●	●
Black-throated Diver (US: Arctic Loon)	G. arctica	●	●	
Pacific Diver	G. pacifica			●
White-billed Diver (US: Yellow-billed Loon)	G. adamsii	●	●	●
Bewick's Swan (US: Whistling Swan, Tundra Swan)	Cygnus bewickii (C. columbianus bewickii)	●	●	●
White-fronted Goose (US: Greater White-fronted Goose)	Anser albifrons	●	●	●
Lesser White-fronted Goose	A. erythropus	●	●	●
Bean Goose	A. fabalis	●	●	●
Emperor Goose	Philacta canagica (Anser canagicus)			●
Russian or Dark-bellied Brent Goose (US: Brant)	Branta bernicla (B. b. bernicla)	●	●	
Pacific Brent Goose (US: Black Brant)	B. nigricans (B. b. nigricans)			●
Red-breasted Goose	Rufibrenta ruficollis (Branta ruficollis)		●	
Scaup (US: Greater Scaup)	Aythya marila	●	●	●
Eider (US: Common Eider)	Somateria mollissima	●	●	●
King Eider	S. spectabilis	●	●	●
Spectacled Eider	S. fischeri			●
Steller's Eider	Polysticta stelleri			●
Long-tailed Duck (US: Oldsquaw)	Clangula hyemalis	●	●	●
Common Scoter	Melanitta nigra (M. n. nigra)	●	●	
American Black Scoter (US: Black Scoter)	Melanitta americana (M. n. americana)			●
American White-winged Scoter	Melanitta deglandi (M. fusca deglandi)		●	●
Velvet Scoter (US: European White-winged Scoter)	Melanitta fusca (M. f. fusca)	●	●	
Rough-legged Buzzard	Buteo lagopus	●	●	●
Gyrfalcon	Falco rusticolus	●	●	●
Peregrine	F. peregrinus	●	●	●
Willow Grouse (US: Willow Ptarmigan)	Lagopus lagopus	●	●	●
Rock Ptarmigan	L. mutus	●	●	●
Sandhill Crane	Grus canadensis			●
Siberian White Crane	G. leucogeranus		●	●
Grey Plover (US: Black-bellied Plover)	Squatarola squatarola (Pluvialis squatarola)	●	●	●
Lesser Golden Plover	P. dominica		●	●
Golden Plover (US: Greater Golden Plover)	P. apricaria	●	●	
Ringed Plover (US: Common Ringed Plover)	Charadrius hiaticula	●	●	●
Dotterel (US: Eurasian Dotterel)	Eudromias morinellus (Charadrius morinellus)	●	●	●
Turnstone (US: Ruddy Turnstone)	Arenaria interpres	●	●	●
Wood Sandpiper	Tringa glareola	●	●	●
Spotted Redshank	T. erythropus	●	●	●
Grey Phalarope (US: Red Phalarope)	Phalaropus fulicarius	●	●	●
Red-necked Phalarope (US: Northern Phalarope)	P. lobatus	●	●	●
Spoon-billed Sandpiper	Eurynorhynchus pygmeus			●
Little Stint	Calidris minuta	●	●	●
Red-necked Stint (US: Rufous-necked Stint)	C. ruficollis		●	●
Temminck's Stint	C. temminckii	●	●	●
Baird's Sandpiper	C. bairdii			●
Curlew Sandpiper	C. ferruginea		●	●
Dunlin	C. alpina	●	●	●
Rock Sandpiper	C. ptilocnemis			●
Sharp-tailed Sandpiper	C. acuminata			●
Pectoral Sandpiper	C. melanotos			●

Common name	Latin name	Northern Europe	Western Siberia	Eastern Siberia
Knot (US: Red Knot)	C. canutus		•	•
Western Sandpiper	C. mauri			•
Sanderling	C. alba		•	•
Broad-billed Sandpiper	Limicola falcinellus	•	•	•
Bar-tailed Godwit	Limosa lapponica	•	•	•
Pomarine Skua (US: Pomarine Jaeger)	Stercorarius pomarinus	•	•	•
Arctic Skua (US: Parasitic Jaeger)	S. parasiticus	•	•	•
Long-tailed Skua (US: Long-tailed Jaeger)	S. longicaudus	•	•	•
Glaucous Gull	Larus hyperboreus	•	•	•
Sabine's Gull	Xema sabini (L. sabini)		•	•
Ross's Gull	Rhodostethia rosea			•
Arctic Tern	Sterna paradisaea	•	•	•
Snowy Owl	Nyctea scandiaca	•	•	•
Pechora Pipit	Anthus gustavi	•	•	•
Red-throated Pipit	A. cervinus	•	•	•
Common Redpoll	Acanthis flammea	•	•	•
Arctic Redpoll (US: Hoary Redpoll)	A. hornemanni	•	•	•
Little Bunting	Emberiza pusilla	•	•	•
Lapland Bunting (US: Lapland Longspur)	Calcarius lapponicus	•	•	•
Snow Bunting	Plectrophenax nivalis	•	•	•

TYPICAL LAND MAMMALS OF THE ARCTIC COASTS, ISLANDS AND TUNDRA

Common name	Latin name	Northern Europe	Western Siberia	Eastern Siberia
Arctic Fox	Alopex lagopus	•	•	•
Polar Bear	Thalarctos maritimus (Ursus maritimus)	•	•	•
Stoat (Ermine)	Mustela erminea	•	•	•
Common Weasel (US: Least Weasel)	M. nivalis	•	•	•
Reindeer (US: Caribou)	Rangifer tarandus	•	•	•
Arctic Hare	Lepus timidus	•	•	•
Arctic Ground Squirrel (Long-tailed Siberian Souslik)	Citellus undulatus (Spermophilus undulatus)			•
Norway Lemming	Lemmus lemmus	•		
Siberian Lemming (Brown Lemming)	L. obensis (L. sibiricus)	•		•
Arctic Collared Lemming (Hoofed Lemming)	Dicrostonyx torquatus	•		•
Grey-sided Vole	Clethrionomys rufocanus	•	•	•
'Lemming-type Vole'	Alticola lemminus (Eothenomys lemminus)			•
'Sub-Arctic Vole'	Microtus hyperboreus		•	•
Middendorff's Vole	M. middendorffi	•	•	
Narrow-skulled Vole	M. gregalis	•	•	•

TYPICAL BIRDS OF THE TAIGA FORESTS

Common name	Latin name	Northern Europe	Western Siberia	Eastern Siberia
Goshawk	Accipiter gentilis	•	•	•
Merlin	Falco columbarius	•	•	•
Black Grouse	Lyrurus tetrix (Tetrao tetrix)	•	•	•
(Western Capercaillie)	T. urogallus	•	•	•
Black-billed Capercaillie	T. parvirostris			•
Siberian Spruce Grouse	Falcipennis falcipennis (Dendragapus falcipennis)			•
Hazel Grouse (Hazel Hen)	Tetrastes (Bonasia) bonasia	•	•	•
Green Sandpiper	Tringa ochropus	•	•	•
Grey-rumped Sandpiper (US: Grey-tailed Tattler)	Heteroscelus brevipes		•	•
Oriental Cuckoo	Cuculus saturatus		•	•
Rufous Turtle Dove	Streptopelia orientalis		•	•
Eagle Owl	Bubo bubo	•	•	•
Tengmalm's Owl (US: Boreal Owl)	Aegolius funereus	•	•	•
Eurasian Pygmy Owl	Glaucidium passerinum	•	•	•
Hawk Owl	Surnia ulula	•	•	•
Ural Owl	Strix uralensis	•	•	•
Great Grey Owl	S. nebulosa	•	•	•
Black Woodpecker	Dryocopus martius	•	•	•
Northern Three-toed Woodpecker	Picoides tridactylus	•	•	•
Siberian Jay	Perisoreus infaustus	•	•	•
Nutcracker	Nucifraga caryocatactes	•	•	•
Waxwing (US: Bohemian Waxwing)	Bombycilla garrulus	•	•	•
Siberian Accentor	Prunella montanella		•	•
Willow Warbler	Phylloscopus trochilus	•	•	•
Arctic Warbler	P. borealis	•	•	•
Greenish Warbler	P. trochiloides		•	•
Yellow-browed Warbler	P. inornatus	•	•	•
Pallas's Warbler	P. proregulus		•	•
Dusky Warbler	P. fuscatus		•	•
Goldcrest	Regulus regulus	•	•	•
Mugimaki Flycatcher	Ficedula mugimaki			•
Sooty Flycatcher	Muscicapa sibirica			•
Grey-spotted Flycatcher	M. griseisticta			•
European Robin (Robin)	Erithacus rubecula	•	•	•
Siberian Rubythroat	Calliope (Luscinia) calliope	•	•	•
Whistling Nightingale	L. sibilans		•	•
Red-flanked Bluetail	Tarsiger cyanurus	•	•	•
Pale Thrush	Turdus pallidus		•	•
Eye-browed Thrush	T. obscurus			•
Red-throated Thrush (Dark-throated Thrush)	T. ruficollis (T. r. ruficollis)		•	•
Black-throated Thrush (Dark-throated Thrush)	T. atrogularis (T. r. atrogularis)	•	•	•

Common name	Latin name	Northern Europe	Western Siberia	Eastern Siberia
Naumann's Thrush	T. naumanni (T. n. naumanni)		•	•
Dusky Thrush	T. eunomus (T. n. eunomus)		•	•
Redwing	T. iliacus	•	•	•
Song Thrush	T. philomelos	•	•	•
Siberian Thrush	T. sibiricus (Zoothera sibirica)		•	•
White's Thrush	Z. dauma		•	•
Marsh Tit	Parus palustris	•	•	•
Willow Tit	P. montanus	•	•	•
Siberian Tit	P. cinctus	•	•	•
Crested Tit	P. cristatus	•		
Coal Tit	P. ater	•	•	•
Great Tit	P. major	•	•	•
Eurasian Nuthatch	Sitta europaea	•	•	•
Common Treecreeper	Certhia familiaris	•	•	•
Brambling	Fringilla montifringilla	•	•	•
Siskin	Spinus spinus (Carduelis spinus)	•	•	•
Pine Grosbeak	Pinicola enucleator	•	•	•
Parrot Crossbill	Loxia pytyopsittacus	•	•	
Red Crossbill	L. curvirostra	•	•	•
White-winged Crossbill (Two-barred Crossbill)	L. leucoptera	•	•	•
Bullfinch (US: Eurasian Bullfinch)	Pyrrhula pyrrhula	•	•	•
Japanese Bullfinch	P. griseiventris (P. p. griseiventris)			•
'Altai Bullfinch'	P. cineracea (P. p. cineracea)			•
Pine Bunting	Emberiza leucocephalos		•	•
Yellow-browed Bunting	E. chrysophrys			•
Black-faced Bunting	E. spodocephala		•	•
Chestnut Bunting	E. rutila			•

TYPICAL MAMMALS OF THE TAIGA FORESTS

Common name	Latin name	Northern Europe	Western Siberia	Eastern Siberia
Large-toothed Siberian Shrew	Sorex daphaenodon	•	•	•
Laxmann's Shrew	S. cacutiensis (S. cacutiens)	•	•	•
Eurasian Common Shrew	S. araneus	•	•	•
Northern Bat	Vespertilio nilssoni (Eptesicus nilssoni)	•	•	•
Wolf (Grey Wolf)	Canis lupus	•	•	•
Red Fox	Vulpes vulpes	•	•	•

Common name	Latin name	Northern Europe	Western Siberia	Eastern Siberia
Brown Bear (Grizzly Bear)	Ursus arctos	•	•	•
Siberian Weasel (Kolinsky)	Mustela sibirica	•	•	•
Sable	Martes zibellina	•	•	•
Pine Marten	M. martes	•	•	•
Wolverine (Glutton)	Gulo gulo	•	•	•
Lynx (Northern Lynx)	Lynx lynx (Felis lynx)	•	•	•
Musk Deer	Moschus moschiferus	•	•	•
Elk (US: Moose)	Alces alces	•	•	•
Arctic Hare	Lepus timidus	•	•	•
Siberian Flying Squirrel	Pteromys volans	•	•	•
Red Squirrel	Sciurus vulgaris	•	•	•
Siberian Chipmunk	Eutamias sibiricus (Tamias sibiricus)	•	•	•
Large Japanese Field Mouse	Apodemus speciosus			•
Wood Mouse	A. sylvaticus	•	•	•
Wood Lemming	Myopus schisticolor	•	•	•
Bank Vole	Clethrionomys glareolus	•	•	
Northern Red-backed Vole	C. rutilus	•	•	•
Grey-sided Vole	C. rufocanus	•	•	•
Field Vole	Microtus agrestis	•	•	

The following two tables list only those species that are most characteristic of the Ussuri forests. Widespread animals of the USSR, like the Coal Tit (*Parus ater*), Nuthatch (*Sitta europaea*), Elk (*Alces alces*), Wolf (*Canis lupus*), Red Fox (*Vulpes vulpes*) and many rodents, are not included.

TYPICAL BIRDS OF THE USSURI FORESTS

Common name	Latin name	Deciduous valley forest	Mixed conifer/deciduous forest	Dark-conifer and larch forest
Striated Heron (Green Heron)	Butorides striatus	•		
Mandarin (Mandarin Duck)	Aix galericulata	•	•	
Chinese Merganser	Mergus squamatus		•	
Osprey	Pandion haliaetus		•	
Crested Honey Buzzard	Pernis ptilorhynchus	•	•	
Horsfield's or Chinese Sparrowhawk	Accipiter soloensis	•		
Besra Sparrowhawk	A. virgatus	•		
Grey-faced Buzzard Eagle	Butastur indicus	•	•	
Greater Spotted Eagle	Aquila clanga		•	
Steller's Sea Eagle	Haliaeetus pelagicus		•	
Manchurian Red-footed Falcon (Amur Red-footed Falcon)	Falco amurensis		•	
Siberian Spruce Grouse	Falcipennis falcipennis (Dendragapus falcipennis)			•
Black-billed Capercaillie	Tetrao parvirostris			•
Rufous Turtle Dove	Streptopelia orientalis	•	•	
Fugitive Hawk Cuckoo	Hierococcyx fugax		•	•
Indian Cuckoo	Cuculus micropterus		•	
Oriental Cuckoo	C. saturatus	•	•	•

Common name	Latin name	Deciduous valley (oak) forest	Mixed conifer/deciduous forest	Dark-conifer and larch forest
Little Cuckoo	C. poliocephalus	●		
Blakiston's Fish Owl	Ketupa blakistoni		●	
Indian Scops Owl	Otus sunia	●	●	
Collared Scops Owl	O. bakkamoena		●	
Brown Hawk Owl	Ninox scutulata	●		
Ural Owl	Strix uralensis	●	●	●
Great Grey Owl	S. nebulosa			●
Jungle Nightjar	Caprimulgus indicus		●	
Needle-tailed Swift	Hirundapus caudacutus		●	
Eastern Broad-billed Roller	Eurystomus orientalis	●	●	
Grey-headed Pied Woodpecker	Yungipicus caniacapillus (Dendrocopos caniacapillus)		●	
Japanese Pygmy Woodpecker	Y. kizuki (D. kizuki)	●		
Forest Wagtail	Dendronanthus indicus	●		
Bull-headed Shrike	Lanius bucephalus	●		
Thick-billed Shrike	L. tigrinus	●		
Chinese Great Grey Shrike	L. sphenocercus	●	●	
Brown Shrike	L. cristatus	●		
Black-naped Oriole	Oriolus chinensis	●		
Grey Starling	Sturnus cineraceus	●		
Daurian Starling	Sturnia sturnina	●		
Purple-backed Starling	(Sturnus sturninus)			
Azure-winged Magpie	Cyanopica cyana	●		
Large-billed Crow	Corvus macrorhynchos	●	●	
Ashy Minivet	Pericrocotus divaricatus	●		
Short-tailed Bush Warbler	Urosphena squameiceps (Cettia squameiceps)	●	●	
Gray's Grasshopper Warbler	Locustella fasciolata	●		
Thick-billed Reed Warbler	Phragmaticola aedon (Acrocephalus aedon)	●		
Pale-legged Leaf Warbler	Phylloscopus tenellipes	●	●	
Eastern Crowned Leaf Warbler	P. coronatus	●	●	
Pallas's Warbler	P. proregulus			●
Radde's Warbler	P. schwarzi	●		
Asian Paradise Flycatcher	Terpsiphone paradisi	●		
Yellow-rumped Flycatcher	Ficedula zanthopygia	●	●	
Mugimaki Flycatcher	F. mugimaki		●	
Blue-and-white Flycatcher	Cyanoptila cyanomelana (Muscicapa cyanomelana)	●	●	
Sooty Flycatcher	M. sibirica		●	
Grey-spotted Flycatcher	M. griseisticta			●
Brown Flycatcher	M. latirostris	●	●	
White-throated Rock Thrush	Petrophila gularis (Monticola gularis)		●	
Daurian Redstart	Phoenicurus auroreus	●		
Siberian Rubythroat	Luscinia calliope	●		
Siberian Blue Robin	L. cyane	●	●	
Whistling Nightingale	L. sibilans			●
Red-flanked Bluetail	Tarsiger cyanurus			●
Pale Thrush	Turdus pallidus		●	●
Eye-browed Thrush	T. obscurus		●	●
Grey-backed Thrush	T. hortulorum	●		
Siberian Thrush	T. sibiricus (Zoothera sibirica)		●	
White's Thrush	Z. dauma	●	●	●
Chestnut-flanked White-eye	Zosterops erythropleura	●		
Oriental Greenfinch	Chloris sinica (Carduelis sinica)	●		
Long-tailed Rosefinch	Uragus sibiricus	●		
Japanese Bullfinch	Pyrrhula griseiventris (P. p. griseiventris)			●
Yellow-billed Grosbeak	Eophona migratoria	●		
Japanese Grosbeak	E. personata		●	
Siberian Meadow Bunting	Emberiza cioides	●		
Yellow-throated Bunting	E. elegans	●		
Tristram's Bunting	E. tristrami	●	●	●
Black-faced Bunting	E. spodocephala	●		
Chestnut Bunting	E. rutila		●	●

TYPICAL MAMMALS OF THE USSURI FORESTS

Common name	Latin name	Deciduous valley (oak) forest	Mixed conifer/deciduous forest	Dark-conifer and larch forest
Western Hedgehog	Erinaceus europaeus	●		
Large Japanese Mole	Mogera rubusta (Talpa robusta)	●		
Least Shrew	Sorex minutissimus	●	●	
Large-toothed Shrew	S. daphaenodon	●	●	●
Long-clawed Shrew	S. unguiculatus	●	●	
Pacific Shrew	S. pacificus	●	●	
Ussuri White-toothed Shrew	Crocidura lasiura	●		
Natterer's Bat	Myotis nattereri	●	●	
(a bat)	M. ikonnikovi		●	
(a tube-nosed bat)	Murina ussuriensis		●	●
(a tube-nosed bat)	M. hilgendorfi		●	●
Racoon Dog	Nyctereutes procyonoides	●	●	
Dhole (Asian Wild Dog)	Cuon alpinus		●	
Asian Black Bear (Himalayan Black Bear)	Ursus tibetanus (Selenarctos thibetanus)		●	
Altai Weasel	Mustela altaica		●	
Yellow-throated Marten	Martes flavigula		●	●
Far-Eastern Wild Cat (Amur Forest Cat)	Felis euptylura (F. bengalensis)	●	●	●
Siberian Tiger	Panthera tigris altaica		●	●
Amur Leopard	P. pardus orientalis		●	
Sika Deer (Japanese Deer)	Cervus nippon	●	●	
Manchurian Hare	Lepus mandshuricus	●	●	
Chinese Birch Mouse	Sicista caudata			●
(a vole)	Microtus maximoviczii	●		

The following two tables list only true mountain species. Those which occur also in other habitats are omitted; examples are the Rock Ptarmigan (*Lagopus mutus*), also found in the tundra, the Eagle Owl (*Bubo bubo*), which lives also in the lowland forests, steppe and deserts; and the Wolf (*Canis lupus*), found in all habitats.

TYPICAL BIRDS OF THE MOUNTAINS

Common name	Latin name	Caucasus	Tien-Shan	Pamir-Alai	Altai
Bar-headed Goose	*Anser indicus*			•	
Golden Eagle	*Aquila chrysaetos*	•	•	•	•
Lammergeier (Bearded Vulture)	*Gypaetus barbatus*	•	•	•	•
Egyptian Vulture	*Neophron percnopterus*	•	•	•	
Black or Cinereous Vulture	*Aegypius monachus*	•	•	•	•
Griffon Vulture	*Gyps fulvus*	•	•	•	
Himalayan Griffon	*G. himalayensis*		•	•	
Caucasian Black Grouse	*Lyrurus mlokosiewiczi* (*Tetrao mlokosiewiczi*)	•			
Caucasian Snowcock	*Tetraogallus caucasicus*	•			
Caspian Snowcock	*T. caspius*	•			
Himalayan Snowcock	*T. himalayensis*		•	•	
Tibetan Snowcock	*T. tibetanus*			•	
Altai Snowcock	*T. altaicus*				•
Chukar (Chukar Partridge)	*Alectoris chukar*	•	•	•	•
Ibisbill	*Ibidorhyncha struthersii*		•	•	
Solitary Snipe	*Gallinago solitaria*		•	•	•
Brown-headed Gull	*Larus brunnicephalus*			•	
Tibetan Sandgrouse	*Syrrhaptes tibetanus*			•	
Eastern Rock Dove	*Columba rupestris*		•	•	•
Snow Pigeon	*C. leuconota*			•?	
Alpine Swift	*Apus melba*	•	•	•	
Crag Martin	*Ptyonoprogne rupestris*	•	•	•	•
Water Pipit	*Anthus spinoletta*	•	•	•	•
Grey Wagtail	*Motacilla cinerea*	•	•	•	•
Red-billed Chough	*Pyrrhocorax pyrrhocorax*	•	•	•	•
Alpine Chough	*P. graculus*	•	•	•	•
Eurasian Dipper	*Cinclus cinclus*	•	•	•	•
Brown Dipper	*C. pallasii*		•	•	•
Alpine Accentor	*Prunella collaris*	•	•	•	•
Himalayan Accentor	*P. himalayana*		•	•	•
Brown Accentor	*P. fulvescens*		•	•	•
Radde's Accentor	*P. ocularis*	•			
Black-throated Accentor	*P. atrogularis*		•	•	•
Hume's Lesser Whitethroat	*Sylvia althaea* (*S. curruca althaea*)	•	•	•	
Caucasian Chiffchaff (Mountain Chiffchaff)	*Phylloscopus lorenzii* (*P. sindianus*) (*P. collybita lorenzii*)	•			
Green Warbler	*P. nitidus*	•			
Sulphur-bellied Warbler	*P. griseolus*		•	•	•
White-browed Tit Warbler	*Leptopoecile sophiae*		•	•	
Rufous-tailed Flycatcher	*Muscicapa ruficauda*		?	•	
Eastern Pied Wheatear	*Oenanthe picata*		•	•	
Red-tailed Wheatear	*O. xanthoprymna*	•	•	•	
Rock Thrush	*Monticola saxatilis*	•	•	•	•
Blue Rock Thrush	*M. solitarius*	•	•	•	
Blue-headed Redstart	*Phoenicurus caeruleocephalus*		•	•	
Black Redstart	*P. ochruros*	•	•	•	•
Eversmann's Redstart	*P. erythronotus*		•	•	•
Güldenstädt's Redstart	*P. erythrogaster*	•	•	•	•
White-capped Redstart (Water Redstart; River Chat)	*Chaimarrornis leucocephalus*			•	
Himalayan Rubythroat	*Calliope pectoralis* (*Luscinia pectoralis*)		•	•	
White-throated Robin (Persian Robin)	*Irania gutturalis*	•	•	•	
Blue Whistling Thrush	*Myiophoneus caeruleus*			•	
Little Forktail	*Microcichla scouleri* (*Enicurus scouleri*)			•	
Streaked Laughing Thrush	*Garrulax lineatus*			•	
Central Asian Willow Tit	*Parus songarus* (*P. montanus songarus*)		•		
Iranian Sombre Tit	*P. hyrcanus* (*P. lugubris hyrcanus*)	•			
Simla Tit (Rufous-naped Tit)	*P. rufonuchalis*		•	•	
Yellow-breasted Azure Tit	*P. flavipectus* (*P. cyanus flavipectus*)		•	•	
Rock Nuthatch	*Sitta neumayer*	•			
Eastern Rock Nuthatch	*S. tephronota*	•	•	•	
Himalayan Treecreeper	*Certhia himalayana*		•	•	
Wallcreeper	*Tichodroma muraria*	•	•	•	
Rock Sparrow	*Petronia petronia*	•	•	•	•
Snow Finch	*Montifringilla nivalis*	•	•	•	•
Red-fronted Serin	*Serinus pusillus*	•	•	•	
Twite	*Acanthis flavirostris* (*Carduelis flavirostris*)	•	•	•	•
Grey-headed Goldfinch	*C. caniceps* (*C. carduelis caniceps*)		•	•	
Hodgson's Mountain Finch	*Leucosticte nemoricola*		•	•	•
Brandt's Rosy Finch	*L. brandti*		•	•	•
Japanese Rosy Finch	*L. arctoa*				•
Crimson-winged Finch	*Rhodopechys sanguinea*	•	•	•	
Red-mantled Rosefinch	*Carpodacus rhodochlamys*		•	•	•
Himalayan (or Thin-billed) Red-mantled Rosefinch	*C. grandis* (*C. rhodochlamysgrandis*)		•	•	
Great Rosefinch	*C. rubicilla*	•	•	•	•
Red-breasted Rosefinch	*Pyrrhospiza punicea* (*Carpodacus puniceus*)		•	•	
White-winged Grosbeak	*Mycerobas carnipes*		•	•	
White-capped Bunting	*Emberiza stewarti*		•	•	
Rock Bunting	*E. cia*	•	•	•	•
Grey-necked Bunting	*E. buchanani*	•	•	•	•

TYPICAL MAMMALS OF THE MOUNTAINS

Common name	Latin name	Caucasus	Tien-Shan	Pamir-Alai	Altai
Pamir Shrew	Sorex buchariensis			•	
Pygmy White-toothed Shrew (Etruscan Shrew)	Suncus etruscus			•	
Dhole (Asian Wild Dog)	Cuon alpinus		•?	•?	•?
Syrian Brown Bear	Ursus arctos syriacus	•			
Tien Shan Brown Bear	U. a. isabellinus		•	•	
Mountain Weasel	Mustela altaica		•	•	
Beech Marten	Martes foina	•	•	•	•
Snow Leopard (Ounce)	Panthera uncia		•	•	•
Chamois	Rupicapra rupicapra	•			
Wild Goat (Bezoar)	Capra aegagrus	•			
Siberian Mountain Goat (Siberian Ibex)	C. sibirica (C. ibex sibirica)		•	•	•
West Caucasian Tur	C. caucasica	•			
East Caucasian Tur (Dagestan Tur)	C. cylindricornis	•			
Markhor	C. falconeri		•	•	
Argalis (Argali)	Ovis ammon	•	•	•	
Daurian Pika	Ochotona daurica				•
Pallas's Pika	O. pallasi		•		•
Red Pika	O. rutila		•	•	
Royle's Pika	O. roylei		•	•	
Altai Pika	O. alpina				•
Persian Squirrel	Sciurus anomalus	•			
Grey Marmot	Marmota baibacina		•		•
Long-tailed Marmot	M. caudata		•	•	
Menzbier's Marmot	M. menzbieri		•		
Tien-Shan Souslik	Citellus relictus		•	•	
Forest or Tree Dormouse (Tree Dormouse)	Dryomys nitedula	•	•	•	•
Altai Birch Mouse	Sicista napaea				•
Chinese Birch Mouse	S. concolor	•	•		
Broad-toothed Mouse	Apodemus mystacinus	•			
Large-eared Vole	Alticola macrotis				•
Royle's Mountain Vole	A. roylei		•	•	•
Flat-headed Vole	A. strelzowi				•
Juniper Vole	Pitymys juldaschi			•	
Major's Pine Vole	P. majori	•	•	•	
(a meadow vole)	Microtus gud	•			
Snow Vole	M. nivalis	•			
Robert's Vole	M. roberti	•			
Long-clawed Mole-vole	Prometheomys schaposchnikowi	•			
Southern Mole-vole	Ellobius fuscocapillus	•			
Northern Mole-vole	E. talpinus		•		•
West Siberian Zokor	Myospalax myospalax				•

The following table includes some species that are found also in steppelike areas of forests, deserts or mountains, although most are restricted to the true steppeland.

TYPICAL BIRDS OF THE STEPPES

Common name	Latin name	European USSR	Kazakhstan & West Siberia	East of Lake Baikal
Pallid Harrier	Circus macrourus	•	•	?
Steppe Eagle	Aquila rapax	•	•	•
Imperial Eagle	A. heliaca	•	•	
Long-legged Buzzard	Buteo rufinus	•	•	
Lesser Kestrel	Falco naumanni	•	•	
Red-footed Falcon	F. vespertinus	•	•	
Daurian Partridge	Perdix dauuricae		•	•
Common Quail	Coturnix coturnix	•	•	
Japanese Quail	C. japonica			•
Demoiselle Crane	Anthropoides virgo	•	•	•
Great Bustard	Otis tarda	•	•	•
Little Bustard	O. tetrax (Tetrax tetrax)	•	•	
Sociable Lapwing (Sociable Plover)	Chettusia gregaria	•	•	
Bee-eater (European Bee-eater)	Merops apiaster	•	•	
Blue-cheeked Bee-eater	M. superciliosus	•	•	
Short-toed Lark (Greater Short-toed Lark)	Calandrella cinerea (C. brachydactyla)	•	•	
Lesser Short-toed Lark	C. rufescens	•	•	
Eastern Short-toed Lark	C. cheleensis (C. rufescens cheleensis)		•	
Calandra Lark	Melanocorypha calandra	•	•	
Bimaculated Lark	M. bimaculata		•	
Mongolian Lark	M. mongolica			•
White-winged Lark	M. leucoptera	•	•	
Black Lark	M. yeltoniensis	•	•	
Richard's Pipit	Anthus richardi (A. novaeseelandiae richardi)		•	•
Blyth's Pipit	A. godlewskii			•
Isabelline Wheatear	Oenanthe isabellina	•	•	
Père David's Snow Finch (Small Snow Finch)	Pyrgilauda davidiana (Montifringilla davidiana)			•
Corn Bunting	Emberiza calandra (Miliaria calandra)	•	•	

TYPICAL MAMMALS OF THE STEPPES

Common name	Latin name	European USSR	Kazakhstan & West Siberia	East of Lake Baikal
Steppe Polecat	*Mustela eversmanni*	●	●	●
Mongolian Gazelle	*Procapra gutturosa*			●?
Saiga Antelope (Saiga)	*Saiga tatarica*	●	●	
Daurian Pika	*Ochotona daurica*		●	●
Pallas's Pika	*O. pallasi*			●
Steppe Pika (Small Pika)	*O. pusilla*	●	●	
Steppe or Bobak Marmot	*Marmota bobac*	●	●	
Siberian Marmot	*M. sibirica*		●	●
Little Souslik	*Citellus pygmaeus* (*Spermophilus pygmaeus*)	●	●	
Red-cheeked Souslik	*C. major* (*S. major*)	●	●	
(a souslik)	*C. erythrogenys* (*S. erythrogenys*)		●	
Spotted Souslik	*C. suslicus* (*S. suslicus*)	●		
European Souslik	*C. citellus* (*S. citellus*)	●		
Daurian Ground Squirrel	*C. dauricus* (*S. dauricus*)			●
Southern Birch Mouse	*Sicista subtilis*	●	●	
Northern Five-toed Jerboa	*Allactaga jaculus*	●	●	
Common Russian Mole-rat	*Spalax microphthalmus*	●		
Common Hamster	*Cricetus cricetus*	●	●	
Radde's Hamster	*Mesocricetus raddei*	●		
Eversmann's Ratlike Hamster	*Allocricetulus eversmanni* (*Cricetulus eversmanni*)	●	●	
Short Ratlike Hamster	*A. curtatus* (*C. curtatus*)		●	
Chinese Striped Hamster	*C. barabensis*	●	●	
Striped Dwarf Hamster	*Phodopus sungorus*		●	●
Clawed Jird	*Meriones unguiculatus*		●	●
Steppe Lemming	*Lagurus lagurus*	●	●	
Mongolian Vole	*Microtus mongolicus*			●
Social Vole	*M. socialis*	●	●	
Brandt's Vole	*M. brandti*			●
Mandarin Vole	*M. mandarinus*			●
(a zokor)	*Myospalax dybowskyi*			●
Manchurian Zokor	*M. psilurus*			●

This table gives an idea of the great variety of reptiles found in the desert and semi-desert regions; well over half of all the USSR's reptiles occur in these habitats.

TYPICAL REPTILES OF THE DESERTS AND SEMI-DESERTS

Common name	Latin name	Caucasus & Trans-Caucasus, semi-desert	Caucasus & Trans-Caucasus, foothills	Kazakhstan & Central Asia, sandy desert	Kazakhstan & Central Asia, foothills	Kazakhstan & Central Asia, clay and salt deserts
Spur-thighed Tortoise	*Testudo graeca*	●	●			
Horsfield's Tortoise	*T. horsfieldi*			●	●	●
(a skink-like gecko)	*Teratoscincus scincus*			●		
(geckos)	*Crossobamon eversmanni*		●			
	Asophylax pipiens			●	●	
	A. laevis					●
	A. spinicauda			●		
	Gymnodactylus russowi			●		
	G. fedtschenkoi				●	
Panther Gecko	*Eublepharis macularius*				●	
'Kopet-Dag Gecko'	*Eublepharis turkmenica*				●	
Steppe Agama Lizard	*Agama sanguinolenta*	●		●	●	
(agamas)	*A. ruderata*		●			
	A erythrogastra				●	●
(toad-headed agamid lizards)	*Phrynocephalus helioscopus*	●	●		●	
	P. rossikowi			●		●
	P. raddei					
	P. reticulatus			●		
	P. guttatus	●		●		
	P. interscapularis			●		
	P. mystaceus	●		●		
Desert Monitor	*Varanus griseus*			●	●	●
Schneider's Skink	*Eumeces schneideri*		●		●	
(skinks)	*E. taeniolatus*				●	
	Mabuya aurata				●	
(a lidless skink)	*Ablepharus deserti*				●	
(racerunner lizards)	*Eremias guttulata*					●
	E. velox	●		●	●	
	E. strauchi	●				
	E. pleskei	●				
	E. lineolata			●		
	E. scripta			●		
	E. intermedia			●		
	E. grammica			●		
	E. nigrocellata					●
	E. arguta	●	●		●	●
(a sand lizard)	*Lacerta strigata*	●	●			
Three-lined Emerald Lizard	*L. trilineata*		●			
Snake-eyed Lizard	*Ophisops elegans*	●				
Blind Snake (Worm Snake)	*Typhlops vermicularis*		●		●	
Javelin Sand Boa	*Eryx jaculus*		●		●	
(sand boas)	*E. elegans*			●		
	E. miliaris	●			●	
	E. tataricus				●	
	Lycodon striatus			●		

Common name	Latin name	Sandy deserts	Stony clay & salt deserts	Desert foothills
Slender Racer (a whip snake)	Coluber najadum		●	●
(whip snakes)	C. rhodorhachis			
	C. karelini	●	●	●
	C. ravergieri		●	●
	Spalerosophis diadema		●	●
	Lythorhynchus ridgewayi	●	●	
Leopard Snake (a rat snake)	Elaphe situla	●		
(rat snakes)	E. hohenackeri	●		
	Rhynchocalamus melanocephalus	●		
(dwarf snakes)	Eirenis collaris	●		
	E. media		●	
	E. modestus	●		
	E. punctatolineatus	●		
Cat Snake (A tree snake)	Telescopus falax	●	●	
	Boiga trigonatum		●	●
Montpellier Snake	Malpolon monspessulanus	●	●	
Arrow Snake	Psammophis lineolatus	●		
Central Asian Cobra	Naja oxyana		●	
Nose-horned Viper	Vipera ammodytes	●		
Blunt-nosed Viper (Levantine Viper)	V. lebetina	●	●	
(a saw-scaled viper)	Echis carinatus		●	●

TYPICAL BIRDS OF SOVIET CENTRAL ASIAN DESERTS

Common name	Latin name	Sandy deserts	Stony clay & salt deserts	Desert foothills
See-see Partridge (See-See)	Ammoperdix griseogularis			●
Stone Curlew	Burhinus oedicnemus	●	●	
Houbara Bustard (Houbara)	Chlamydotis undulata	●	●	
Greater Sand Plover	Charadrius leschenaultii		●	
Caspian Plover	C. asiaticus		●	
Black-bellied Sandgrouse	Pterocles orientalis	●	●	
Pintailed Sandgrouse	P. alchata	●	●	
Pallas's Sandgrouse	Syrrhaptes paradoxus	●	●	
Striated Scops Owl	Otus brucei	●	●	●
Blue-cheeked Bee-eater	Merops superciliosus	●		
White-winged Spotted Woodpecker	Dendrocopos leucopterus	●		
Desert Lark	Ammomanes deserti		●	
Hume's Short-toed Lark	Calandrella acutirostris		●	
Pander's Ground Jay	Podoces panderi	●		
Brown-necked Raven	Corvus ruficollis	●		
Olivaceous Warbler	Hippolais pallida	●		
Upcher's Warbler	H. languida	●		
Ménétries's Warbler	Sylvia mystacea	●		
Desert Warbler	S. nana	●		
Streaked Scrub Warbler	Scotocerca inquieta	●		
Desert Wheatear	Oenanthe deserti	●	●	●
Rufous Bush Chat	Cercotrichas galactotes	●		
Turkestan Tit	Parus bokharensis (P. major bokharensis)	●		
Rock Nuthatch	Sitta neumayer			●
Eastern Rock Nuthatch	S. tephronota			●
Saxaul Sparrow	Passer ammodendri	●		
Desert Sparrow	P. simplex	●		
Rock Sparrow	Petronia petronia			●
Trumpeter Finch	Bucanetes githagineus		●	●
Black-billed Desert Finch	Rhodospiza obsoleta	●		

TYPICAL MAMMALS OF THE DESERTS OF SOVIET CENTRAL ASIA AND KAZAKHSTAN

Common name	Latin name	Sandy deserts	Stony, clay & salt deserts	Desert foothills
Long-eared Hedgehog	Hemiechinus auritus	●	●	
Brandt's Hedgehog	Paraechinus hypomelas	●	●	●
Piebald Shrew	Diplomesodon pulchellum	●		
Lesser Horseshoe Bat	Rhinolophus hipposideros		●	●
Bukhara Horseshoe Bat	R. bocharicus	●	●	●
Blasius's Horseshoe Bat	R. blasii		●	●
(a serotine bat)	Vespertilio bobrinski (Eptesicus bobrinski)	●		●
Hemprich's Long-eared Bat	Otonycteris hemprichi		●	●
Corsac Fox	Vulpes corsac	●	●	●
Striped Hyena	Hyaena hyaena		●	●
Marbled Polecat	Vormela peregusna	●	●	
Honey Badger (Ratel)	Mellivora indica (M. capensis)	●		
African Wild Cat	Felis libyca (F. sylvestris libyca)	●	●	
Caracal (Caracal Lynx)	F. caracal	●		●
Pallas's Cat (Manul)	F. manul	●		●
Sand Cat	F. margarita	●		
Asiatic Cheetah	Acinonyx jubatus venaticus	●?	●?	
Asian Wild Ass (Kulan, Dzhigetai)	Equus hemionus	●	●	
Goitred Gazelle	Gazella subgutturosa	●	●	
Tolai Hare	Lepus tolai	●		
Long-clawed Ground Squirrel	Spermophilopsis leptodactylus	●		
Large-toothed Souslik	Citellus fulvus (Spermophilus fulvus)	●	●	
White-tailed Porcupine	Hystrix leucura (H. indica leucura)			●
Mouse-like Dormouse	Myomimus personatus			●
Desert Dormouse	Selevinia betpakdalensis		●	
Five-toed Dwarf Jerboa	Cardiocranius paradoxus		●	
Thick-tailed Pygmy Jerboa	Salpingotus crassicuada			●

Common name	Latin name	Sandy deserts	Stony, clay & salt deserts	Desert foothills
Small Five-toed Jerboa	*Allactaga elater*		•	
Severtzov's Jerboa	*A. severtzovi*		•	
Bobrinski's Jerboa	*A. bobrinskii*		•	
(a jerboa)	*A. saltator*	•	•	
(a jerboa)	*Alactagulus acontion*		•	
Lesser Fat-tailed Jerboa	*Pygeretmus platyurus*		•	
Greater Fat-tailed Jerboa	*P. zhitkovi*		•	
(a fat-tailed jerboa)	*P. vinogradovi*	•	•	
Northern Three-toed Jerboa	*Dipus sagitta*	•		
Thick-tailed Three-toed Jerboa	*Scirtodops telum* (*Stylodipus telum*)	•	•	
Comb-toed Jerboa	*Paradipus ctenodactylus*	•		
Lichtenstein's Jerboa	*Eremodipus lichtensteini* (*Jaculus lichtensteini*)	•	•	
Turkmen Jerboa	*J. turkmenicus*	•	•	
Roborovsky's Dwarf Hamster	*Phodopus roborovskii*	•		
Great Gerbil	*Rhombomys opimus*	•	•	
(a jird)	*Meriones erythrourus*	•	•	
Midday Gerbil	*Meriones meridianus*	•		
Persian Jird	*M. persicus*			•
(a jird)	*M. zarudnyi*			•
Yellow Steppe Lemming	*Lagurus luteus*	•		
Afghan Vole	*Microtus afghanus* (*Pitymys afghanus*)			•
Northern Mole-vole	*Ellobius talpinus*	•	•	
Southern or Afghan Mole-vole	*E. fuscocapillus*			•

This table does not include many of the water or marsh birds which prefer woodland or tundra during the nesting season. These are listed under the appropriate habitats.

TYPICAL BIRDS OF THE WETLANDS OF THE USSR

Common name	Latin name	Lakes, rivers, and marshes of the forest, wooded steppe and mountain zones	Lakes, rivers, coasts and islands of the southern steppe, desert and semi-desert zones
Red-throated Diver (US: Red-throated Loon)	*Gavia stellata*	•	•
Black-throated Diver (US: Arctic Loon)	*G. arctica*	•	
Little Grebe (Dabchick)	*Podiceps ruficollis* (*Tachybaptus ruficollis*)	•	•
Black-necked Grebe (US: Eared Grebe)	*P. nigricollis*	•	•
Slavonian Grebe (US: Horned Grebe)	*P. auritus*	•	
Red-necked Grebe	*P. grisegena*	•	•
Great Crested Grebe	*P. cristatus*	•	•
Eastern White Pelican	*Pelecanus onocrotalus*		•
Dalmatian Pelican	*P. crispus*		•
Great Cormorant	*Phalacrocorax carbo*	•	•
Shag	*P. aristotelis*		•
Pygmy Cormorant	*P. pygmeus*		•
Bittern (Eurasian Bittern)	*Botaurus stellaris*	•	•
Little Bittern	*Ixobrychus minutus*	•	•
Schrenck's Little Bittern	*I. eurhythmus*	•	
Black-crowned Night Heron	*Nycticorax nycticorax*		•
Squacco Heron	*Ardeola ralloides*		•
Cattle Egret	*Bubulcus ibis*		•
Great White Egret	*Egretta alba*		•
Little Egret	*E. garzetta*		•
Grey Heron	*Ardea cinerea*	•	•
Purple Heron	*A. purpurea*		•
Spoonbill	*Platalea leucorodia*		•
Glossy Ibis	*Plegadis falcinellus*		•
Greater Flamingo	*Phoenicopterus roseus* (*P. ruber*)		•
Greylag Goose	*Anser anser*	•	•
Swan Goose	*Cygnopsis cygnoides* (*Anser cygnoides*)	•	
Mute Swan	*Cygnus olor*	•	•
Whooper Swan	*C. cygnus*	•	
Ruddy Shelduck	*Tadorna ferruginea*	•	•
Shelduck	*T. tadorna*	•	•
Mallard	*Anas platyrhynchos*	•	•
Spotbill Duck	*A. poecilorhyncha*	•	
Teal	*A. crecca*	•	•
Baikal Teal	*A. formosa*	•	
Falcated Teal	*A. falcata*	•	
Gadwall	*A. strepera*	•	•
European Wigeon	*A. penelope*	•	
Pintail	*A. acuta*	•	
Garganey	*A. querquedula*	•	•
Shoveler	*A. clypeata*	•	•
Marbled Teal	*A. angustirostris* (*Marmaronetta angustirostris*)		•
Red-crested Pochard	*Netta rufina*		•
Pochard	*Aythya ferina*	•	•
Ferruginous Duck	*A. nyroca*	•	•
Baer's Pochard	*A. baeri*	•	
Tufted Duck	*A. fuligula*	•	
Goldeneye	*Bucephala clangula*	•	
White-headed Duck	*Oxyura leucocephala*		•
Smew	*Mergus albellus*	•	
Red-breasted Merganser	*M. serrator*	•	•
Chinese Merganser	*M. squamatus*	•	
Goosander (US: Common Merganser)	*M. merganser*	•	•
Hen Harrier (US: Marsh Hawk)	*Circus cyaneus*	•	•

Common name	Scientific name		
Montagu's Harrier	C. pygargus	•	
Pied Harrier	C. melanoleucos	•	
Marsh Harrier	C. aeruginosus	•	
Black Grouse	Lyrurus tetrix (Tetrao tetrix)	•	
Manchurian Crane	Grus japonensis	•	
Common Crane	G. grus	•	
White-naped Crane	G. vipio	•	
Hooded Crane	G. monachus (G. monacha)	•	
Water Rail	Rallus aquaticus	•	•
Spotted Crake	Porzana porzana	•	•
Little Crake	P. parva	•	•
Baillon's Crake	P. pusilla	•	•
Siberian Ruddy Crake	P. paykullii	•	
Swinhoe's Yellow Rail	P. exquisita (Coturnicops exquisita)	•	
Moorhen (US: Common Gallinule)	Gallinula chloropus	•	•
Purple Gallinule (US: Purple Swamphen)	Porphyrio porphyrio		•
Coot	Fulica atra	•	•
Golden Plover (US: Greater Golden Plover)	Pluvialis apricaria	•	
Little Ringed Plover	Charadrius dubius	•	
Long-billed Plover	C. placidus	•	
Kentish Plover (US: Snowy Plover)	C. alexandrinus		
White-tailed Lapwing	Vanellochettusia leucura (Chettusia leucura)		
Black-winged Stilt	Himantopus himantopus		
Avocet	Recurvirostra avosetta		
Oystercatcher	Haematopus ostralegus	•	
Wood Sandpiper	Tringa glareola	•	
Greenshank	T. nebularia	•	
Spotted Greenshank	T. guttifer	•	
Common Redshank	T. totanus	•	
Marsh Sandpiper	T. stagnatilis	•	
Common Sandpiper	Actitis hypoleucos	•	
Terek Sandpiper	Xenus cinereus	•	
Ruff	Philomachus pugnax	•	
Long-toed Stint	Calidris subminuta	•	
Dunlin	C. alpina	•	
Jack Snipe	Lymnocryptes minimus	•	
Common Snipe	Gallinago gallinago	•	
Swinhoe's Snipe	G. megala	•	
Pintail Snipe	G. stenura	•	
Great Snipe	G. media	•	
Little Curlew	Numenius minutus	•	
Curlew	N. arquata	•	
Slender-billed Curlew	N. tenuirostris	•?	
Far Eastern Curlew	N. madagascariensis	•	
Whimbrel	N. phaeopus	•	
Black-tailed Godwit	Limosa limosa	•	•
Asiatic Dowitcher	Limnodromus semipalmatus	•	
Great-Black-headed Gull	Larus ichthyaetus		•

Common name	Scientific name		
Relict Gull	L. relictus	•	•
Mediterranean Gull	L. melanocephalus		•
Little Gull	L. minutus	•	•
Black-headed Gull	L. ridibundus	•	•
Slender-billed Gull	L. genei		•
Herring Gull	L. argentatus	•	•
Common Gull (US: Mew Gull)	L. canus	•	
Black Tern	Chlidonias niger	•	•
White-winged Black Tern (US: White-winged Tern)	C. leucopterus	•	•
Whiskered Tern	C. hybridus	•	•
Gull-billed Tern	Gelochelidon nilotica		•
Caspian Tern	Hydroprogne caspia (Sterna caspia)	•	•
Sandwich Tern	Sterna sandvicensis	•	•
Common Tern	S. hirundo	•	•
Little Tern	S. albifrons	•	•
Short-eared Owl	Asio flammeus		•
Kingfisher (US: Eurasian Kingfisher)	Alcedo atthis	•	•
Sand Martin (US: Bank Swallow)	Riparia riparia	•	•
Citrine Wagtail	Motacilla citreola	•	•
Savi's Warbler	Locustella luscinioides	•	•
Pallas's Grasshopper Warbler	L. certhiola	•	
Moustached Warbler	Lusciniola melanopogon (Acrocephalus melanopogon)		•
Aquatic Warbler	A. paludicola	•	•
Sedge Warbler	A. schoenobaenus	•	
Paddyfield Warbler	A. agricola		
Reed Warbler	A. scirpaceus	•	•
Marsh Warbler	A. palustris	•	
Clamorous Reed Warbler	A. stentoreus		•
Great Reed Warbler	A. arundinaceus	•	•
Bluethroat	Luscinia svecica	•	•
Reed (Yangtse) Parrotbill	Paradoxornis heudei	•	
Bearded Tit	Panurus biarmicus	•	•
Penduline Tit	Remiz pendulinus	•	•
Central Asian Penduline Tit	Remiz macronyx (R. p. macronyx)		•

Bibliography

BANNIKOV, A. G. (1969) *Nature Reserves of the USSR.* (In English.) Israel Program for Scientific Translations, Jerusalem. (Originally published in Russian, 1966, by Mysl', Moscow, who have also published, in 1974, a 2nd, revised, edition.)

BANNIKOV, A. G., DAREVSKIY, I. S. & RUSTAMOV, A. K. (1971) *Zemnovodnye i Presmykayushchiesya SSSR. Spravochnik-Opredelitel'.* (Amphibians & Reptiles of the USSR. Handbook & Identification Guide.) (In Russian.) Mysl', Moscow.

BORODIN, A. M. & SYROECHKOVSKIY, E. E. (eds.) (1983) *Zapovedniki SSSR Spravochnik.* (Nature Reserves of the USSR. A Guide.) (In Russian.) Lesnaya promyshlennost', Moscow.

BORODIN, A. M. (1984–5) *Krasnaya Kniga SSSR 1–2.* (Red Data Book of USSR Vols. 1–2.) (In Russian.) 2nd revised and enlarged edition. Lesnaya promyshlennost', Moscow.

CERNOV, YU. I. (1985) *The Living Tundra. Studies in Polar Research.* (In English.) Cambridge University Press, Cambridge.

DEMENTIEV, G. P. & GLADKOV, N. A. (1966–70) *The Birds of the Soviet Union.* In 6 vols. (In English.) Israel Program for Scientific Translations, Jerusalem. (Originally published in Russian, 1951–4, by Sovetskaya Nauka.)

DOLGUSHIN, I. A., KORELOV, M. N., KUZ'MINA, M. A. *et al* (1960–74) *Pitsy Kazakhstana* (The Birds of Kazakhstan). (In Russian.) In 5 vols. Nauka Kazakh SSr, Alma Ata, USSR.

DURRELL, G. & DURRELL, L. (1986) *Durrell in Russia.* (In English.) Macdonald, London.

FLINT, V. E., CHUGUNOV, Y. D. & SMIRIN, V. M. (1965) *Mlekopitayushchie SSSR. Spravochnik-Opredelitel'* (Mammals of the USSR. Handbook & Identification Guide). (In Russian.) Mysl', Moscow.

FLINT, V. E., BOEHME, R. L., KOSTIN, Y. V. & KUZNETSOV, A. A. (1984) *A Field Guide to Birds of the USSR.* (In English.) Princeton University Press, Princeton, N.J., USA. (Originally published in Russian, 1968, Mysl'.)

GEPTNER, V. G., *et al.* (1961–76) *Mlekopitayushchie Sovetskogo Soyuza* (Mammals of the Soviet Union). (In Russian.) In 4 vols. Vysshaya Shkola, Moscow.

GROMOV, I. M. & BARANOVA, G. I. (eds.) (1981) *Katalog Mlekopitayushchikh SSSR. Pliotsen-Sovremennost'* (A Catalogue of the Mammals of the USSR. From the Pliocene to the Present). (In Russian.) Nauka, Leningrad.

ILYCHEV, V. D. & FLINT, V. E. (eds.) (1982) *Plitsy SSSR 1* (The Birds of the USSR, Vol. 1); 12 vols. are planned; Vol. 2 was published in 1986. (In Russian.) Nauka, Moscow.

IL'ČEV V. D. & FLINT, V. E. (1985) *Handbuch der Vögel der Sowjetunion 1* (Vol. 1 of the above Russian title, translated into German; Vol. 2 will follow in 1987). A. Ziemsen Verlag, Wittenberg Lutherstadt, GDR.

KNYSTAUTAS, A. & LIUTKUS, A. (1982) *In the World of Birds.* (In Lithuanian, Russian & English.) Mokslas Publishers, Vilnius, Lithuanian SSR, USSR.

KNYSTAUTAS, A. & SHIBNEV, Yu. (1986) *Die Vogelwelt Ussuriens* (The Bird World of Ussuriland). (In German.) A. Ziemsen Verlag, Wittenberg Lutherstadt, GDR.

KOMAROV, V. L. (ed.) (1936–60) *Flora SSSR* (The Flora of the USSR). In 30 vols. (In Russian.) Nauka, Leningrad.

KUMARI, E., MÄEMETS, A. & RENNO, O. (1974) *Estonian Wetlands and their Life.* (In English.) Valgus, Tallinn, Estonian SSR, USSR.

KUMARI, E. (1981) *An Ornithological Journey through the Estonian SSR.* (In English.) Valgus, Tallinn, Estonian SSR, USSR.

OGNEV, S. I. (1960–4) *Animals of the USSR and Adjoining Countries.* In 7 vols. (First 3 vols. entitled 'Animals of Eastern Europe & Northern Asia'.) (In English, translated from original Russian edition, Moscow 1928–50.) Israel Program for Scientific Translations, Jerusalem.

PRIDE, P. R. (1972) *Conservation in the Soviet Union.* (In English.) Cambridge University Press, Cambridge.

PUKINSKI, J. (1983) *In der Ussuri-Taiga* (In the Ussuri Taiga.) (In German; a translation of the original 1975 Russian title Po Taezhnoy reke Bikin – Along the Bikin, River of the Taiga.) VEB F.A. Brockhaus Verlag, Leipzig, GDR and Progress Publishers, Moscow.

PUKINSKIY, YU. B. (1964) *Pitsy Ussuriyskoy Taygi* (The Birds of the Ussuri Taiga). (In Russian.) Khabarovsk Book Publishers, Khabarovsk.

PUKINSKIY, YU. B. (1985) *Bird Sounds of the Ussuri Taiga*: Melodiya 92 46559 009. (In Russian.) A 17 cm $33\frac{1}{3}$ r.p.m. mono disc, designed to accompany Pukinskiy's 1984 book (see above). Melodiya, Moscow.

ST. GEORGE, G. (1974) *Soviet Deserts & Mountains* (The World's Wild Places series). (In English.) Time-Life Books, Amsterdam.

STEPANYAN, L. S. (1975–8) *Sostav i Raspredelenie Ptits Fauny SSSR* (Composition and Distribution of the USSR's Bird Fauna). In 2 vols. (In Russian.) Nauka, Moscow.

VOROBIEV, K. A. (1963) *Ptitsy Yakutii* (The Birds of Yakutiya). (In Russian.) Nauka, Moscow.

Picture Credits

Index